[英汉对照]

西方学术经典文库

社会契约论

THE SOCIAL CONTRACT

[法] 让·雅克·卢梭 著

徐强 译

九州出版社
JIUZHOUPRESS

图书在版编目（CIP）数据

社会契约论／（法）卢梭（Rousseau,J.J.）著；徐强译．—北京：九州出版社，2006.10（2008.2重印）

（西方学术经典文库）

ISBN 978-7-80195-567-8

Ⅰ.社… Ⅱ.①卢…②徐… Ⅲ.政治哲学—法国—近代—汉、英 Ⅳ.D095.654

中国版本图书馆CIP数据核字（2006）第127622号

社会契约论

作　　者	[法]让·雅克·卢梭　著　　徐强　译
出　　版	九州出版社
出 版 人	徐尚定
地　　址	北京市西城区阜外大街甲35号（100037）
发行电话	（010）68992190/2/3/5/6
网　　址	www.jiuzhoupress.com
电子信箱	jiuzhou@jiuzhoupress.com
印　　刷	九洲财鑫印刷有限公司
开　　本	630×970毫米　1/16开
印　　张	22.75
字　　数	244千字
版　　次	2007年1月第1版
印　　次	2008年2月第2次印刷
书　　号	ISBN 978-7-80195-567-8/C·118
定　　价	48.00元

出版说明

在西方学术思想的发展流变中，出现过很多影响深远的经典著作，这些著作穿越时空，为人们长久研读，有的甚至影响了整个人类文明的发展进程。这套《西方学术经典文库》（英汉对照本），精选了其中最有代表性的一些名著，计划达到一百部，将陆续分批出版直至全部完成。

《西方学术经典文库》由多位专家学者指导分类选目，内容涵盖哲学、文学、宗教学、政治学、经济学、社会学、人类学、心理学、法学、历史学等类，注重权威性、学术性和影响性，收录了不同国家、不同时代、不同流派的诸多名著。

《西方学术经典文库》中译本译自英文原著或其他文种的英文译本，以英汉对照的形式出版，读者可以参照原文对作品有更加客观的理解，更好地把握西方学术思想的精髓。

为加以区别，原文中的英文注释，注释号用①、②……形式表示；中文译者注释则以〔1〕、〔2〕……形式表示。至于英译本中出现的原文页码和特殊索引等问题，中文译者在“译者后记”中将予以解释、说明。另外，在英文原著中，有一些表示着重意义的斜体或大写等字体，考虑到读者可以在对照英文阅读中看到，因此在中译文中，没有照样标出，还望读者理解。

九州出版社

The Social Contract
By *Jean-Jacques Rousseau*
English Translation By
Maurice Cranston

本书根据 Penguin Books Ltd. 1974 年版本译出

BOOK IV

第四卷

FOREWORD

This little treatise is part of a larger work which I undertook many years ago without thinking of the limitations of my powers, and have long since abandoned. Of the various fragments that might have been taken from what I wrote, this is the most considerable, and the one I think the least unworthy of being offered to the public. The rest no longer exists.

CONTENTS

目　录

BOOK I

第一卷

BOOK II

第二卷

BOOK III

第三卷

前　言

这篇小论文原是许多年前我没有充分考虑自己能力的限制就去写作的一部更大部头的著作的一部分,而这个更大部头的著作我已经放弃好多年了。在我已经写就的那些可以选取的各个片断中,这篇文章是最有意义的,也是我认为最值得公之于众的部分。而剩余的部分都已毁去。

BOOK I

My purpose is to consider if, in political society, there can be any legitimate and sure principle of government, taking men as they are and laws as they might be. In this inquiry I shall try always to bring together what right permits with what interest prescribes so that justice and utility are in no way divided.

I start without seeking to prove the importance of my subject. I may be asked whether I am a prince or a legislator that I should be writing about politics. I answer no: and indeed that that is my reason for doing so. If I were a prince or a legislator I should not waste my time saying what ought to be done; I should do it or keep silent.

Born as I was the citizen of a free state and a member of its sovereign body, the very right to vote imposes on me the duty to instruct myself in public affairs, however little influence my voice may have in them. And whenever I reflect upon governments, I am happy to find that my studies always give me fresh reasons for admiring that of my own country.

第一卷

我写本文的目的是考察：就人类的实际状况和法律的可能情形，在政治社会中能否有某种合法而确定的政权规则。在研究中，我会尽力把人们对权力的许可和对利益的要求这两者结合起来，这样，正义和功利就不会出现分歧。

这里，我在还没有证明问题的重要性之前，就开始研究它了。有人可能会问我，你写作有关政治的东西，是不是因为你是一个国王或者立法者？我会回答：不是。而且事实上，这恰恰是我论述政治的原因。因为如果我是一个国王或者立法者的话，我将不会浪费自己的时间去讨论什么事情应该做这种问题，我会切实去做那些事情或者干脆保持沉默。

生为一个自由国家的公民，并且作为这个政权的一个成员，不管我的声音对社会公共事务可能施加的影响是多么微弱，我享有的投票权就迫使我承担起对公共事务进行研究的义务。另外，每当我对政府进行反思的时候，我会很高兴地发现，我的研究总是给我新的理由，使我更热爱我们的政府。

CHAPTER I

The Subject Of Book I

Man was born free, and he is everywhere in chains. Those who think themselves the masters of others are indeed greater slaves than they. How did this transformation come about? I do not know. How can it be made legitimate? That question I believe I can answer.

If I were to consider only force and the effects of force, I should say: 'So long as a people is constrained to obey, and obeys, it does well; but as soon as it can shake off the yoke, and shakes it off, it does better; for since it regains its freedom by the same right as that which removed it, a people is either justified in taking back its freedom, or there is no justifying those who took it away.' But the social order is a sacred right which serves as a basis for all other rights. And as it is not a natural right, it must be one founded on covenants. The problem is to determine what those covenants are. But before we pass on to that question, I must substantiate what I have so far said.

第一章　第一卷的主题

人天生是自由的，但是，也无处不在枷锁当中。那些自认为是别人的主人的人，实际上是比其他人更加彻底的奴隶。这种转化是如何产生的呢？我不知道。而这种转化如何才能合法化呢？我相信我能回答这个问题。

假若我仅仅考虑到强力以及强力的影响，我要说："如果人民被强迫去服从，而且服从了，这么做很好；但是同样，一旦人民可以打破这种枷锁，而且也把这种枷锁打破了，这么做就更好。因为人民是根据当初别人剥夺他们的自由时所根据的权利来重新获得他们的自由的，那么他们重新获得自由是完全正当的。否则的话，当初别人剥夺他们的自由就是毫不正当的了。"但是，社会秩序是作为其他所有权利之基础的一种神圣的权利，而且社会秩序这种权利并不是一种自然的权利，它必须建立在约定的基础之上。我们面对的问题是必须弄清楚那些约定是什么。但是在我们转而论述这个问题之前，我必须首先证明以上我所提到的观点。

CHAPTER 2

The First Societies

The oldest of all societies, and the only natural one, is that of the family; yet children remain tied to their father by nature only so long as they need him for their preservation. As soon as this need ends, the natural bond is dissolved. Once the children are freed from the obedience they owe their father, and the father is freed from his responsibilities towards them, both parties equally regain their independence. If they continue to remain united, it is no longer nature, but their own choice, which unites them; and the family as such is kept in being only by agreement.

This common liberty is a consequence of man's nature. Man's first law is to watch over his own preservation; his first care he owes to himself; and as soon as he reaches the age of reason, he becomes the only judge of the best means to preserve himself; he becomes his own master.

The family may therefore perhaps be seen as the first model of political societies: the head of the state bears the image of the father, the people the image of his children, and all, being born free and equal, surrender their freedom only when they see advantage in doing so. The only difference is that in the family, a father's love for his children repays him for the care he bestows on them,

第二章　论第一社会

一切社会形态之中最古老而又唯一自然的社会就是家庭。然而孩子们也只有在需要父亲养育的时候才天然地与父亲保持依附关系。一旦这种养育的需要结束了，这种天然的关系也就解除了。一旦孩子们从对父亲的服从下解脱出来，而且父亲也从对孩子们应有的养育义务中解脱出来，父亲和孩子就平等地各自获得了他们的独立性。如果他们还是保持结合在一起的状态，那就不再是自然的了，除非是他们的自愿选择使他们结合在一起；而这样的家庭就只能依靠约定来维系。

这种极为普遍的自由是人类自然天性发展的结果。人类的第一条法则就是要维护自己的生存；人类的首要关怀就是要关注他自身；一旦人类达到有理性的年龄，他们就成为唯一的决策者，决定保护自己的最好方式，他们就成为自己的主人。

这样，家庭可能被看成是政治社会的第一形态：国家的首领就是对父亲形象的摹写，而人民就是孩子形象的摹写；而且，由于每个人生下来便是自由和平等的，所以他们只有在看到出让自由有利益时才会出让他们的自由。家庭和国家的唯一区别就是：在家庭中，父亲对孩子的爱足以偿还他们给予孩子们

while in the state, where the ruler can have no such feeling for his people, the pleasure of commanding must take the place of love.

Grotius denies that all human government is established for the benefit of the governed, and he cites the example of slavery. His characteristic method of reasoning is always to offer fact as a proof of right. ① It is possible to imagine a more logical method, but not one more favourable to tyrants.

According to Grotius, therefore, it is doubtful whether humanity belongs to a hundred men, or whether these hundred men belong to humanity, though he seems throughout his book to lean to the first of these views, which is also that of Hobbes. These authors show us the human race divided into herds of cattle, each with a master who preserves it only in order to devour its members.

Just as a shepherd possesses a nature superior to that of his flock, so do those shepherds of men, their rulers, have a nature superior to that of their people. Or so, we are told by Philo, the Emperor Caligula argued, concluding, reasonably enough on this same analogy, that kings were gods or alternatively that the people were animals.

The reasoning of Caligula coincides with that of Hobbes and Grotius. Indeed Aristotle, before any of them, said that men were not at all equal by nature, since some were born for slavery and others born to be masters.

---

① 'Learned researches on public law are often only the history of ancient abuses, and one is misled when one gives oneself the trouble of studying them too closely.' This is exactly what Grotius does.

的关怀；但是在国家中，由于统治者对于人民没有这种爱的感情，所以下达命令的乐趣就必然取代了父亲对孩子们的爱。

格劳秀斯否认所有的人类政府都是为了被统治者的利益而建立起来的，他举了奴隶制作为例子来说明。他在进行推理时所运用的具有代表性的方法，就是用既定事实来论证权利①。我们完全有可能设想一种更为合理的方法来论证，但是这种方法并非对暴君更加有利。

根据格劳秀斯的观点，究竟是全人类归属于某一百个人，还是这一百个人归属于全人类，是一个很值得怀疑的问题，虽然他的著作从头至尾看起来都倾向于前一种观点，而这也正是霍布斯的观点。根据这些作者的观点，人类便被当成一群一群的牲畜而被分开来，每一群都有它们的统领者，而这些统领者保护它们的目的只是为了要吞掉它们。

正像一个牧羊人会拥有比他的羊群更为优越的天生本性一样，这些人类的统领者，也就是人类的统治者，拥有比他所统治的人民更为优越的天生本性。根据斐洛的记载，我们大体可知，卡里古拉皇帝就是这样来推理的，并且根据这种类推方式得出结论：国王就是上帝，或者说人民都是牲畜。

卡里古拉皇帝的这种推理与霍布斯、格劳秀斯的推理完全一致。实际上，亚里士多德在他们之前就曾说过，人类根本就不是天生平等的，因为一些人生来就是要做奴隶的，而另外一些人生来就是要做主人的。

---

① “对公法的学术研究往往不过是古人们滥加妄用的历史罢了，而且当一个人不辞辛苦耗费精力从事这些研究的时候，他很容易会头脑发昏。”而这恰恰正是格劳秀斯所做的。

Aristotle was right; but he mistook the effect for the cause. Anyone born in slavery is born for slavery—nothing is more certain. Slaves, in their bondage, lose everything, even the desire to be free. They love their servitude even as the companions of Ulysses loved their life as brutes. ①But if there are slaves by nature, it is only because there has been slavery against nature. Force made the first slaves; and their cowardice perpetuates their slavery.

I have said nothing of the King Adam or of the Emperor Noah, father of the three great monarchs who shared out the universe among them, like the children of Saturn, with whom some authors have identified them. I hope my readers will be grateful for this moderation, for since I am directly descended from one of those princes, and perhaps in the eldest line, how do I know that if the deeds were checked, I might not find myself the legitimate king of the human race? However that may be, there is no gainsaying that Adam was the king of the world, as was Robinson Crusoe of his island, precisely because he was the sole inhabitant; and the great advantage of such an empire was that the monarch, secure upon his throne, had no occasion to fear rebellions, wars or conspirators.

---

① See a short treatise of Plutarch entitled: *That Animals use Reason.*

亚里士多德当然是对的，只是他错把结果当成了原因。出生于奴隶制度下的人天生就会是奴隶，这是当然的了。在枷锁束缚之下的奴隶丧失了一切，甚至丧失了摆脱枷锁获得自由的愿望。他们甚至喜欢他们的被奴役状态，就像优里塞斯的同伴们喜欢他们畜生一般的生活状态一样①。所以假若存在天生的奴隶的话，那只是因为首先存在着违反自然的奴隶制度。是强力制造出了最初的奴隶，而奴隶们的怯懦胆小使他们永远处于奴隶状态。

我一点都没有提到亚当国王或者挪亚大帝，也就是那共同划分了整个世界的三大君主的父亲，许多人把他们看得如同萨土林的儿子们一样。那么我希望我的读者们应为我的谦逊而感激不尽了，因为既然我本人作为这些君王中某一个君王的直系后裔，而且还极有可能是较长的那一支的后代，那么我怎么能知道：如果仔细考察我们的族谱，我就不可能发现我自己是整个人类的合法的国王呢？不管如何，我们都不能否认亚当曾是整个世界的国王，就像鲁滨逊·克鲁索曾经是他的小岛的国王一样，这完全是因为他是那个荒岛上唯一的居民。而且像这样一个帝国的极大的好处，就是这个帝国的国王可以安全地待在他的王位上，在任何情况下都不必害怕叛乱、战争或者阴谋篡权。

---

① 见普鲁塔克的一篇小论文，题目是《思考的动物》。

CHAPTER 3
The Right Of The Strongest

The strongest man is never strong enough to be master all the time, unless he transforms force into right and obedience into duty. Hence 'the right of the strongest'—a 'right' that sounds like something intended ironically, but is actually laid down as a principle. But shall we never have this phrase explained? Force is a physical power; I do not see how its effects could produce morality. To yield to force is an act of necessity, not of will; it is at best an act of prudence. In what sense can it be a moral duty?

Let us grant, for a moment, that this so-called right exists. I suggest it can only produce a tissue of bewildering nonsense; for once might is made to be right, cause and effect are reversed, and every force which overcomes another force inherits the right which belonged to the vanquished. As soon as man can disobey with impunity, his disobedience becomes legitimate; and as the strongest is always right, the only problem is how to become the strongest. But what can be the validity of a right which perishes with the force on which it rests? If force compels obedience, there is no need to invoke a duty to obey, and if force ceases to compel obedience, there is no longer any obligation.

第三章　论最强者的权利

即使是最强大的人也绝不足以强大到永远都做主人，除非他把力量转变成权利，把服从转变成别人的义务。因此“最强者的权利”—— 一种听起来很有讽刺意味的东西，实际上已经被确定为一种基础原则了。但是，难道我们不应当重新仔细解释一下这个名词吗？强力是一种物理性的力量，而对于这种力量，我根本看不出它的作用能产生道德。对强力的屈服，只是一种必要的行为，而不是一种意志的选择，它顶多也不过是一种聪明的行为。在哪种意义上，它可以成为一种道德性的义务呢？

让我们暂且假设这种所谓的权利是存在的。我觉得这样假设的结果只能是制造一系列令人困惑的胡说八道，因为一旦强力被转变成了权利，原因和结果就颠倒了，而且任何一种力量只要它强大到足以战胜另一种力量，它就可以承继原来属于被摧毁的那种力量的权利。只要人们不服从又可以不受处罚，他的不服从就是合法的了。既然最强者总是正确的，那么剩下的唯一问题就是如何成为最强者了。如果一种权利会随着它赖以为基础的强力瓦解而消失，那么这种权利的合法性何在呢？如果用强力去迫使人们服从，那么就根本不需要用义务要求人们服从；如果强迫人们服从的强力消失了，那么人们就将没有

Thus the word 'right' adds nothing to what is said by 'force'; it is meaningless.

'Obey those in power.' If this means 'yield to force' the precept is sound, but superfluous; it has never, I suggest, been violated. All power comes from God, I agree; but so does every disease, and no one forbids us to summon a physician. If I am held up by a robber at the edge of a wood, force compels me to hand over my purse. But if I could somehow contrive to keep the purse from him, would I still be obliged in conscience to surrender it? After all, the pistol in the robber's hand is undoubtedly a *power*.

Surely it must be admitted, then, that might does not make right, and that the duty of obedience is owed only to legitimate powers. Thus we are constantly led back to my original question.

任何义务和职责了。因此权利这个词根本不会给我们所说的“强力”增加任何内容，或者说它在这里是没有任何意义的。

“你当服从权力。”如果这意味着“向强力屈服”，那么可以说这是一条极好的律令，但却是完全多余的；我想这条原则是从来都不会被人们违反的。所有的权力都是来自于上帝的，这一点我赞同；但是任何疾病也都是来自上帝的，而没有任何人会阻止我们去看医生。假若我在森林的角落里被一个强盗劫持了，他用暴力强迫我把钱包交出来，这时如果我有办法把自己的钱包藏起来，使之不被强盗抢走，那么我的良心是不是也会要求我把钱包交给强盗呢？毕竟，强盗手中拿着的手枪是一种无可怀疑的权力啊。

所以，我们必须承认力量根本不能形成权利，人们只对合法的权力才有服从的义务。这样一来，我们最终要回到最原初的问题上。

CHAPTER 4
Slavery

Since no man has any natural authority over his fellows, and since force alone bestows no right, all legitimate authority among men must be based on covenants.

Grotius says: 'If an individual can alienate his freedom and become the slave of a master, why may not a whole people alienate its freedom and become the subject of a king?' In this remark there are several ambiguous words which call for explanation; but let us confine ourselves to one— to 'alienate'. To alienate is to give or sell. A man who becomes the slave of another does not give himself, he sells himself in return for at least a subsistence. But in return for what could a whole people be said to sell itself? A king, far from nourishing his subjects, draws his nourishment from them; and kings, according to Rabelais, need more than a little nourishment. Do subjects, then, give their persons to the king on condition that he will accept their property as well? If so, I fail to see what they have left to preserve.

It will be said that a despot gives his subjects the assurance

第四章　论奴隶制度

既然任何人对他周围的人都没有天然的权威，而且又由于强力自身根本不能产生权利，那么人们之间任何具有合法性的权威都必须建立在约定的基础之上。

格劳秀斯曾说："既然一个单独的人可以转让自己的自由，使自己成为一个主人的奴隶；那么为什么整个人类就不能够转让他们的自由，使自己成为一个国王的臣民呢?"在这段话中，有一些很不明确的字眼需要我们做出解释。这里我们姑且只就其中的一个字眼——"转让"来说明。转让包含奉送和出卖两层含义。如果一个人使自己成为另外一个人的奴隶，他不是奉送他自己，他是出卖自己以求得至少是生存权作为回报。但是如果全人类都出卖自己，他们是为了求得什么作为回报呢？一个国王不但不能供养他的臣民，相反他还要从他的臣民那里获得供养，用拉伯雷的话说，国王如果没有供养也是不能生存的。难道能说臣民们是以国王拿走他们的财产为条件，而把他们自己的人身奉送给国王的吗？如果是这样，那么我看不出臣民们还剩下什么东西值得保存了。

有人可能说，一个专制君主可以为他的臣民保证整个国家的安

of civil tranquillity. Very well, but what does it profit them, if those wars against other powers which result from a despot's ambition, if his insatiable greed, and the oppressive demands of his administration, cause more desolation than civil strife would cause? What do the people gain if their very condition of civil tranquillity is one of their hardships? There is peace in dungeons, but is that enough to make dungeons desirable? The Greeks lived in peace in the cave of Cyclops awaiting their turn to be devoured.

To speak of a man giving himself in return for nothing is to speak of what is absurd, unthinkable; such an action would be illegitimate, void, if only because no one who did it could be in his right mind. To say the same of a whole people is to conjure up a nation of lunatics; and right cannot rest on madness.

Even if each individual could alienate himself, he cannot alienate his children. For they are born men; they are born free; their liberty belongs to them; no one but they themselves has the right to dispose of it. Before they reach the years of discretion, their father may, in their name, make certain rules for their protection and their welfare, but he cannot give away their liberty irrevocably and unconditionally, for such a gift would be contrary to the natural order and an abuse of paternal right. Hence, an arbitrary government would be legitimate only if every new generation were free to accept or reject it, and in that case the government would cease to be arbitrary.

定。这当然很好，但是如果由于专制君主的野心而引起了对其他政权的战争，如果专制君主总是贪得无厌，如果专制君主的官吏们对人民进行残酷的搜刮，如果这一切与人民之间和冲突相比会给人民带来更多害处的话，那么人民又会从中得到什么利益呢？如果这种国内和平的状况对人民而言本身就是一种灾难的话，人民又怎么会从中得到什么好处呢？生活在牢狱中也是很太平的，难道这就足以证明牢狱中的生活是很令人向往的吗？被囚禁在独眼巨人西克洛甫的洞穴中的希腊人也生活得很太平，但是他们只是在等待着挨个被吞噬的命运。

一个人毫不要求回报地把自己奉送给他人，这实在是一件荒谬和不可思议的事情。这样的一种行为是不合法的、无效的，因为任何一个拥有健全心智的人都不会这么做。如果说整个国家的人民都这么做，就等于说整个国家的人民都疯了，而疯狂是不能构成权利的。

即使每个单独的个人都能够转让他自己，但是他却不能转让他的孩子。因为孩子生下来就是一个人，他们天生是自由的，他们拥有属于他们自己的自由；除了他们自己，任何人都无权来处置他们的自由权利。当然，孩子们在达到拥有判断力的年龄之前，他们的父亲可以以孩子的名义制定一些原则，来保护孩子的生存和孩子的福利，但是他不能不可挽回地、毫无条件地把孩子们的自由奉送别人，因为这样一种作为礼物的奉送违反了天然的秩序，而且是对父亲权利的滥用。因此，一个专制独裁的政府要成为一个合法的政府，其条件是每一个新一辈的人都能自由地选择承认它或者放弃它；但是，如果这样的话，这样的政府就不再是一个专制独裁的政府了。

To renounce freedom is to renounce one's humanity, one's rights as a man and equally one's duties. There is no possible *quid pro quo* for one who renounces everything; indeed such renunciation is contrary to man's very nature; for if you take away all freedom of the will, you strip a man's actions of all moral significance. Finally, any covenant which stipulated absolute dominion for one party and absolute obedience for the other would be illogical and nugatory. Is it not evident that he who is entitled to demand everything owes nothing? And does not the single fact of there being no reciprocity, no mutual obligation, nullify the act? For what right can my slave have against me? If everything he has belongs to me, his right is *my* right, and it would be nonsense to speak of my having a right *against* myself.

Grotius and the rest claim to find in war another justification for the so-called right of slavery. They argue that the victors having the right to kill the vanquished implies that the vanquished has the right to purchase his life at the expense of his liberty— a bargain thought to be the more legitimate because it is advantageous to both parties.

But it is clear that this so-called right to kill the vanquished cannot be derived from the state of war. For this reason alone, that men living in their primitive condition of independence have no intercourse regular enough to constitute either a state of peace or a state of war; and men are not naturally enemies. It is conflicts over things, not quarrels between men which constitute war, and the state of war cannot arise from mere personal relations, but only from property

放弃自由就是放弃一个人的人性，就是放弃他作为人的权利，同样也是放弃了自己的义务。对于一个放弃了一切的人来说，是根本没有办法“做出补偿”的。事实上，这样一种放弃是与人的天赋本性相违背的。因为如果你剥夺了一个人的意志自由，实际上就等于剥夺了这个人的行为的道德性。任何一个条约，如果它规定了缔约一方的绝对权威和另一方的绝对服从，那么这个条约将是不合逻辑的和无效的。对于一个有权利规定任何事情的人，他就将不必对任何事情负有责任，这一点难道不是显而易见的吗？这种既没有互惠性，又没有彼此间互相承担义务的约定，岂不是本身就会使这种行为不具有有效性吗？既然我的奴隶所有的一切都是属于我的，那么他的权利实际上也就是“我”的权利，那么他凭什么权利来反对我呢？而且说我拥有一种“反对”我自己的权利，这不是一句毫无意义的废话吗？

格劳秀斯和其他的一些人声称在战争中为奴役奴隶这种所谓的权利找到了另一个理由。他们争辩说，战争的胜利者有权利杀死战争的失败者，这本身就意味着战败者有权利以放弃他的自由为代价来换取他的生命。这种约定被认为是更加合理合法的，因为这对双方都有利。

但是，很显然，战胜者可以杀死被征服者这种所谓的权利，根本不可能是战争状态带来的结果。因为当人类生存于原始的独立状态中的时候，他们之间的相互交往关系还不能稳定到足以构成一种和平状态或者一种战争状态，所以人与人之间不是天生的敌人。造成战争的，是财富上的冲突而不是人与人之

relations. Private wars between one man and another can exist neither in a state of nature, where there is no fixed property, nor in society, where everything is under the authority of law.

Private fights, duels, encounters, do not constitute any kind of state; and as for the private wars that were permitted by the ordinances of Louis IX, King of France, and suspended by the Peace of God, these were no more than an abuse of feudal government, an irrational system if there ever was one, and contrary both to natural justice and to all sound polity.

War, then, is not a relation between men, but between states; in war individuals are enemies wholly by chance, not as men, not even as citizens,[1] but only as soldiers; not as members of their country, but only as its defenders. In a word, a state can have as an enemy only another state, not men, because there can be no real relation between things possessing different intrinsic natures.

---

① The Romans, who understood and respected the rights of war better than any other nation, carried their scruples on this subject so far that a citizen was forbidden to volunteer without engaging himself expressly against the enemy and against an enemy specifically named. When the legion in which the younger Cato fought his first campaign under Popilius was re-formed, the elder Cato wrote to Popilius saying that if he wished his son to continue to serve under him, he should administer a fresh military oath, on the grounds that his son's first oath was annulled, and that he could no longer bear arms against the enemy. Cato also wrote to his son warning him not to go into battle without first taking the oath.

I realize that the siege of Clusium and other incidents from Roman history may be quoted against me, but I am citing laws and customs. No nation has broken its own laws less frequently than the Romans, and no nation has ever had such excellent laws.

间的争吵。战争的状态不可能出自于单纯的人与人之间的关系，而只能是源自于实物财产上的关系。那种发生于一个人与另一个人之间的私人战争既不可能在尚没有固定财产权的自然状态中存在，也不可能在一切都被置于法律权威之下的社会状态中存在。

单独的个人之间的搏斗、决斗或者冲突根本不能构成一种战争状态。至于被法兰西国王路易九世的法令所允许、但是却被“上帝之和平”所禁止的私人之间的战争，只不过是对封建政府之职权的滥用。如果真的曾经存在这种制度的话，它也是一种非理性的制度，而且它还是与自然的正义及一切合理政体相违背的。

那么，战争就绝不是人与人之间的关系，而是国家间的关系。在战争中，人与人之间不是以个人身份，也不是以公民身份①，而是以士兵的身份，纯粹是偶然而成为敌人的；他们不是以国家成员的身份，而是以国家保卫者的身份才成为敌人的。总之，一个国家只能把另外一个国家作为它的敌人，而不能把一个人作为它的敌人，因为内在本性根本不同的事物之间不可能有真正的确定联系。

---

① 罗马人在对战争的权利的理解和尊重方面比其他任何民族做得都要好，他们对这个问题非常审慎，以至于如果一个公民没有明确地表示他要反抗敌人或者指名道姓地要反抗某一个敌人，他是不会被允许作为志愿者参加战争的。年轻的卡图在波比留斯的古罗马军团经历了他生平第一次战争。当这个军团被改编的时候，他的父亲老卡图写信给波比留斯说，如果波比留斯希望他的儿子小卡图继续在军团服役的话，那么小卡图就必须重新进行一次战争宣誓。因为小卡图的第一次战争宣誓现在已经无效了，小卡图不能再一次拿起武器反抗敌人。老卡图同样也给他的儿子小卡图写信，告诫他在没有进行战争宣誓之前不要参加战斗。

我知道有人会拿克鲁修姆被围之事或者罗马历史上其他一些偶然事件作为例子来反驳我，但是我所说的是法律和习俗。罗马与任何国家相比都是最少违背自己的法律的，而且也没有一个国家能有如此完备的法律。

This principle conforms to the established rules of all times and to the constant practice of every political society. Declarations of war are warnings not so much to governments as to their subjects. The foreigner— whether he is a king, a private person or a whole people— who robs, kills or detains the subjects of another prince without first declaring war against that prince, is not an enemy but a brigand. Even in the midst of war, a just prince, seizing what he can of public property in the enemy's territory, nevertheless respects the persons and possessions of private individuals; he respects the principles on which his own rights are based. Since the aim of war is to subdue a hostile state, a combatant has the right to kill the defenders of that state while they are armed; but as soon as they lay down their arms and surrender, they cease to be either enemies or instruments of the enemy; they become simply men once more, and no one has any longer the right to take their lives. It is sometimes possible to destroy a state without killing a single one of its members, and war gives no right to inflict any more destruction than is necessary for victory. These principles were not invented by Grotius, nor are they founded on the authority of the poets; they are derived from the nature of things; they are based on reason.

The right of conquest has no other foundation than the law of the strongest. And if war gives the conqueror no right to massacre a conquered people, no such right can be invoked to justify their enslavement. Men have the right to kill their enemies only when they cannot enslave them, so the right of enslaving cannot be derived from the right to kill. It would therefore be an iniquitous barter to make the vanquished purchase with their liberty the lives over which the victor has no legitimate claim. An argument basing the right over life and death on the right to enslave, and the right

这一原则也符合以前所有时代所确立的准则，符合任何一个文明的政治社会一贯的实践。宣战不只是对那个政府的警告，更主要是对那个国家臣民的警告。一个外国人（不管他是一个国王、或是一个单独的个人、抑或是一整个民族）如果没有向另外一个国王宣战，就对那个国王的臣民进行抢劫、杀戮或是拘役，那他就不能被称为敌人，而只是强盗。即使是在战争当中，一个正义的君主也会一方面尽可能多地占有敌国领土上的所有公共财物，另一方面他却非常尊重那个国家的个人人身及个人财产。他尊重他自己的权利赖以为基础的那些原则。既然战争目的是征服一个敌对的国家，所以一名战士就可以在敌对国家的保卫者手中握有武器的时候杀死他们；但是一旦这些保卫者放下他们手中的武器投降，他们就不再是敌人或者敌对国家的工具，他们又成了单纯的人，这时任何人都不再有权利杀死他们。有时候完全可能不杀死对方的一个人而摧毁一个敌对的国家。战争绝不允许造成那些为了胜利而必需的破坏之外的任何破坏。这些原则既不是由格劳秀斯发明的，也不是以诗人的权威作为基础，它们是从事物的本性中得出来的，而且是以理性为基础的。

关于征服者的权利，除了所谓最强者的法则之外，它没有其他任何基础。如果说战争并没有赋予征服者大规模屠杀被征服者的权利的话，那么他们奴役被征服者的权利也是无法产生的。一个人只有在无法使他的敌人变为他的奴隶的时候，才有权利杀死他，所以把敌人变成奴隶的权利根本不能从杀死敌人的权利中产生出来。因此，让被征服者用他们的自由来换取生命（这种生命权战胜者根本无权占有）就是一场不公平的交易。在这场争论中，既要把生死的权利建立在奴役权的基础之上，又要把奴

to enslave on the right over life and death, is an argument trapped in a vicious circle.

Even if we assumed that this terrible right of massacre did exist, then slaves of war, or a conquered people, would be under no obligation to obey their master any further than they were forced to do so. By taking an equivalent of his victim's life, the victor shows him no favour; instead of destroying him unprofitably, he destroys him by exploiting him. Hence, far from the victor having acquired some further authority beside that of force over the vanquished, the state of war between them continues; their mutual relation is the effect of war, and the continuation of the rights of war implies that there has been no treaty of peace. An agreement has assuredly been made, but that agreement, far from ending the state of war, presupposes its continuation.

Thus, however we look at the question, the 'right' of slavery is seen to be void; void, not only because it cannot be justified, but also because it is nonsensical, because it has no meaning. The words 'slavery' and 'right' are contradictory, they cancel each other out. Whether as between one man and another, or between one man and a whole people, it would always be absurd to say: 'I hereby make a covenant with you which is wholly at your expense and wholly to my advantage; I will respect it so long as I please and you shall respect it so long as I wish.'

役的权利建立在生死权的基础之上，这样的争论岂不是陷入了恶性循环之中吗？

即使我们假设那种可怕的屠杀的权利是存在的，我还是要说，战争中的奴隶或者那些被征服的人民除了要被迫服从他们的主人之外，他们对主人没有其他任何义务。既然征服者取走了被征服者生命的等价物，那么征服者对被征服者而言就没有任何的恩惠；只是他们不再不问所得地杀害被征服者，而是用剥削的方式摧毁被征服者。因此除了对被征服者的强权之外，战胜者根本不能获得任何更多的权威，征服者和被征服者之间的战争状态继续存在着。他们之间的这种相互关系是战争的结果，而战争权的继续行使就意味着任何和平条约都是不存在的。他们之间的确曾经有过协定，但是这种协定远不能结束战争状态，而只能预示着战争状态的继续。

这样，无论我们如何来看待这个问题，奴役别人的权利看上去都是无效的。它之所以无效，不仅仅因为它是非正义的，还因为它是荒谬的，它是无意义的。“奴隶制”和“权利”这两个词是互相矛盾的，它们互相排斥。不管是一个人和另一个人之间，抑或是一个人和全体人民之间，如果说“我和你定立一个条约，使损失完全归你而使利益完全归我；只要我高兴的话，我就遵守这个条约，而且只要我希望的话，你也得遵守这个条约。”这都是荒谬的。

CHAPTER 5

That We Must Always Go Back To An Original Covenant

Even if I were to concede all that I have so far refuted, the champions of despotism would be no better off. There will always be a great difference between subduing a multitude and ruling a society. If one man successively enslaved many separate individuals, no matter how numerous, he and they would never bear the aspect of anything but a master and his slaves, not at all that of a people and their ruler; an aggregation, perhaps, but certainly not an association, for they would neither have a common good nor be a body politic. Even if such a man were to enslave half the world, he would remain a private individual, and his interest, always at variance with that of the others, would never be more than a personal interest. When he died, the empire he left would be scattered for lack of any bond of union, even as an oak crumbles and falls into a heap of ashes when fire has consumed it.

'A people,' says Grotius, 'may give itself to a king.' Therefore, according to Grotius a people is *a people* even before the gift to the king is made. The gift itself is a civil act; it presupposes public deliberation. Hence, before considering the act by which *a* people submits to a king, we ought to scrutinize the act by which people become a people,

第五章　论我们必须追溯最原始的约定

即使现在我对以上我曾反驳过的一切论点都予以肯定，专制主义拥护者的处境也不会好到哪里去。在征服一群人和治理一个社会这两者之间总是有着巨大差别的。假若一个人成功地奴役了很多独立的个人，但是不管这些人的数量是多么庞大，这个人和他的奴役者都只能是主人和奴隶的关系，而根本不可能是人民和他们的统领者之间的关系。他们可能共同构成一群聚集的人，但是完全不是一个人们的联合体，因为他们之间既没有共同的利益，也不是一个政治团体。这样一个人即使奴役了半个世界，他也将仍然是一个单独的个人，他的利益区别于其他人的利益，也就仅仅是个人的利益。当这个人死后，他所留下来的帝国将会因为缺乏联合体的联系性而土崩瓦解，就像一颗橡树被火焚烧而崩倒并化为一堆灰烬一样。

格劳秀斯曾说："人民可以把他自己送给一位国王。"这样，根据格劳秀斯的观点，人民在把他们自己当作礼物奉送给君主之前就已经是人民了。这种赠送的行为本身就是政治的行为，它假定这经过了公众的深思熟虑。因此，在考察人民使自己服从于一位君主的行为之前，我们首先应该仔细考察人民是通过一种什么

for that act, being necessarily antecedent to the other, is the real foundation of society.

Indeed, if there were no earlier agreement, then how, unless the election were unanimous, could there be any obligation on the minority to accept the decision of the majority? What right have the hundred who want to have a master to vote on behalf of the ten who do not? The law of majority-voting itself rests on a covenant, and implies that there has been on at least one occasion unanimity.

样的行为使自己成为人民的，因为既然这种成为人民的行为先于服从于一位君主的行为，那么它才是社会真正的基础。

事实上，如果没有事先约定的话，除非这种选举是全体一致同意的，否则那些少数人为什么会有义务来接受多数人的决定呢？一百个想要主人的人有什么权利代表那十个不想要主人的人投票呢？少数服从多数的规则本身就依赖于一项契约，它意味着对此至少曾经在某种场合下有过全体一致的同意。

CHAPTER 6
The Social Pact

I assume that men reach a point where the obstacles to their preservation in a state of nature prove greater than the strength that each man has to preserve himself in that state. Beyond this point, the primitive condition cannot endure, for then the human race will perish if it does not change its mode of existence.

Since men cannot create new forces, but merely combine and control those which already exist, the only way in which they can preserve themselves is by uniting their separate powers in a combination strong enough to overcome any resistance, uniting them so that their powers are directed by a single motive and act in concert.

Such a sum of forces can be produced only by the union of separate men, but as each man's own strength and liberty are the chief instruments of his preservation, how can he merge his with others' without putting himself in peril and neglecting the care he owes to himself? This difficulty, which brings me back to my present subject, may be expressed in these words:

'How to find a form of association which will defend the person and goods of each member with the collective force of all, and under which

第六章　论社会公约

我设想人类发展到这样一种状况，此时在自然状态中妨害人们自我保存的种种障碍，其力量已经被证明是远远大于每个人在那种状态下所具有的自我保存能力。从此以后，那种自然的状态便不能继续存在下去，因为如果人类不改变它的这种生存方式，那么人类就会灭亡。

既然人类不能够创造新的力量，只能够结合和控制那些已经具有的力量，那么人类能够保存自己的唯一方式就是把他们分散的力量联合成一种强大到足以克服任何阻力的力量；由于这种结合，他们的力量就可以被一个唯一的动机所指导从而使它能够协调一致地行动。

这样一种力量的总和，只能通过分散的人的联合才能产生，但是既然每个人自己的力量和自由是他自我保存的主要工具，那么他怎么能够在把自己的力量和自由同别人的力量和自由相结合的同时，却又不会使自己处于危险中，也不至于忽略了他对自己所应有的关怀呢？这一难题使我回到了我的主题上，它可以用以下的话来表达：

“怎样找到某种形式的结合，使这种结合能够动用全部成员的集体力量来保护其结合者的人身和利益；而且在这种结合下，

each individual, while uniting himself with the others, obeys no one but himself, and remains as free as before. ' This is the fundamental problem to which the social contract holds the solution.

The articles of this contract are so precisely determined by the nature of the act, that the slightest modification must render them null and void; they are such that, though perhaps never formally stated, they are everywhere the same, everywhere tacitly admitted and recognized; and if ever the social pact is violated, every man regains his original rights and, recovering his natural freedom, loses that social freedom for which he exchanged it.

These articles of association, rightly understood, are reducible to a single one, namely the total alienation by each associate of himself and all his rights to the whole community. Thus, in the first place, as every individual gives himself absolutely, the conditions are the same for all, and precisely because they are the same for all, it is in no one's interest to make the conditions onerous for others.

Secondly, since the alienation is unconditional, the union is as perfect as it could be, and no individual associate has any longer any rights to claim; for if rights were left to individuals, in the absence of any higher authority to judge between them and the public, each individual, being his own judge in some causes, would soon demand to be his own judge in all; and in this way the state of nature would be kept in being, and the association inevitably become either tyrannical or void.

Finally, since each man gives himself to all, he gives himself to no one;

每个人在和别人结合的时候并不是使自己服从于其他的人，而是仅仅服从于他自己，并且仍然像从前一样自由。”这便是社会契约所要解决的根本问题。

订立契约的行为其性质如此准确地决定着这种契约的条款，以至于即使是对契约最微小的修改也会使它变得无效和空洞。所以虽然这些契约条款可能从来都没有被正式地宣告过，但是它们在任何地方都是一样的，在任何地方都会被默默地承认或者接受；而且一旦这些社会契约遭到破坏，每个人将会重新获得他原初所具有的权利，并在失去他们用天然的自由所换得的契约自由的同时，又重新获得他们天然的自由。

结合体的这些条款，如果理解正确的话，可以简化为一句话，即：每个结合者自身及其所有的权利全部都转让给整个共同体。首先，既然每个人都把自己的全部奉献出来，那么这种奉献对所有人来说都是相同的；正是因为这种奉献对所有人都是相同的，所以就没有人有兴趣把它变成别人的负担了。

其次，既然转让是无条件的，那么这个结合体就将是最完美的，而且结合体中的个人也将不必再去要求什么权利。因为如果个人保存了某些权利的话，那么在个人与公众之间就没有一个更高的权威进行裁决。每个人既然在某些事情上成为他自己的裁决者，那么不久他将会要求在任何事情上都成为自己的裁决者。这样自然状态就将会持续下去，而且这种结合将会不可避免地变成暴政或者解体。

最后，既然每个人是把他自己交给全体，那么他就不是把

and since there is no associate over whom he does not gain the same rights as others gain over him, each man recovers the equivalent of everything he loses, and in the bargain he acquires more power to preserve what he has.

If, then, we eliminate from the social pact everything that is not essential to it, we find it comes down to this: 'Each one of us puts into the community his person and all his powers under the supreme direction of the general will; and as a body, we incorporate every member as an indivisible part of the whole.'

Immediately, in place of the individual person of each contracting party, this act of association creates an artificial and collective body composed of as many members as there are voters in the assembly, and by this same act that body acquires its unity, its common *ego*, its life and its will. The public person thus formed by the union of all other persons was once called the *city*,① and is now known as the *republic* or the

① The real meaning of this word has been almost entirely lost in the modern world, when a town and a city are thought to be identical, and a citizen the same as a burgess. People forget that houses may make a town, while only citizens can make a city. The Carthaginians once paid dearly for this mistake. I have never read of the title *cives* being given to the subject of any prince, not even to the Macedonians in ancient times or the English today, in spite of their being closer to liberty than any other people. The French alone apply the name 'Citizen' freely to everyone, and that is because they do not know what it means, as their Dictionaries prove; if they did know, they would be guilty, in usurping it, of *lèse-majesté*; as it is, they use the word to designate social status and not legal right. When Bodin wanted to speak of citizens and burgesses, he made the gross error of mistaking the one for the other. Monsieur d'Alembert avoids this mistake; and in his article on 'Geneva' he correctly distinguishes between the four orders of men (five, if aliens are included) which are found in our town, and of which only two compose the republic. No other French author to my knowledge has understood the real meaning of the word 'citizen'.

他自己交给某一个人，而且既然在这种结合中，别人从他这里获得的权利和他从别人那里获得的权利并非不相等，那么每个人实际上重新获得了他所失去的所有东西的等价物，而且在这一交易中，他获得了更大的力量来保护他的所有。

那么，如果把社会契约中所有非本质的东西排除掉，我们就会发现这一契约可以表述为下面的话："我们每个人都把自身以及所有的力量一起置于公意的最高指导之下，而且作为一个整体，我们把每个成员接纳为全体不可分割的一部分。"

一时间，这种结合的行为便创造了一个人为的集合体，代替了作为订约当事人的单独个人，这一团体是由在集会中投票的那些数量的成员组成的，而且结合体基于缔约的行为获得了它的统一性、它的公共的我、它的生命和它的意志。这一由所有人结合而形成的公共人格，以前被称作城邦①，现在则被称作共

---

① 在近代世界中，这个词语的真实意义几乎完全消失了，人们把城镇或城市当做城邦，把市民当做公民。人们忘记了家庭可以构成一个城镇，但是只有公民才构成一个城邦。迦太基人曾为这种错误付出了沉重的代价。我还从来没有听说过有哪一个君主统治下的臣民可以被赋予"cives（公民）"这个称号，即使是古时候的马其顿人或者是今天的英国人都不可以，虽然他们比其他的人更接近于自由。法国人曾经随随便便地把"公民"的称呼加到任何人头上，那是因为他们根本不理解这个词的含义，这一点从他们的词典中就可以得到证明；如果他们真的理解，那么就要犯篡夺君权的叛逆大罪了。实际上法国人只是用这个词来指明一种社会身份，而不是一种法律权利。当鲍丹想要讨论公民和市民的时候，他犯了把两者混用的大错。达朗贝先生[1]则避免了这个错误，在他所写的《日内瓦》这一条目中，他正确地辨别了我们城市中所能找到的四种等级的人（如果异邦人也算在内的话，那就是五种人了），在这几等人中组成共和国的只有两等人。据我所了解，其他的法国作者都不能正确地理解"公民"这个词的真正含义。

[1] 达朗贝曾主持法国启蒙时期《百科全书》的编写，《日内瓦》是达朗贝为《百科全书》所写的一条。

body politic In its passive role it is called the *state*, when it plays an active role it is the *sovereign*; and when it is compared to others of its own kind, it is a *power*. Those who are associated in it take collectively the name of *a people*, and call themselves individually *citizens*, in so far as they share in the sovereign power, and *subjects*, in so far as they put themselves under the laws of the state. However, these words are often confused, each being mistaken for another; but the essential thing is to know how to recognize them when they are used in their precise sense.

和国或者政治体。当它扮演一个被动不为的角色时，人们叫它国家，而当它扮演一个主动作为的角色时，又叫它主权者；当把它和它的同类之物作比较时，把它叫做政权。这一结合体当中的结合者则被集体地称作人民，而且当这些人分享主权权威的时候，他们称自己为公民，而当他们把自己置于国家法律之下的时候，就称作臣民。然而这些词经常会被混淆，彼此错误地混用；但是最重要的事情就是当它们在其精确意义上被使用的时候，我们能知道如何去区别它们。

CHAPTER 7

The Sovereign

This formula shows that the act of association consists of a reciprocal commitment between society and the individual, so that each person, in making a contract, as it were, with himself, finds himself doubly committed, first, as a member of the sovereign body in relation to individuals, and secondly as a member of the state in relation to the sovereign. Here there can be no invoking the principle of civil law which says that no man is bound by a contract with himself, for there is a great difference between having an obligation to oneself and having an obligation to something of which one is a member.

We must add that a public decision can impose an obligation on all the subjects towards the sovereign, by reason of the two aspects under which each can be seen, while, contrariwise, such decisions cannot impose an obligation on the sovereign towards itself; and hence it would be against the very nature of a political body for the sovereign to set over itself a law which it could not infringe. The sovereign, bearing only one single and identical aspect, is in the position of a private person making a contract with himself, which shows that there neither is, nor can be, any kind of fundamental law binding on the people as a body, not even the social contract itself. This does not mean that the whole body cannot incur obligations to other nations, so long as those obligations do not infringe the contract; for in relation to foreign powers,

第七章　论主权者

以上的公式显示出，结合的行为包含了社会和个人之间相互的结约，所以任何一个人缔结契约的时候（实际上是和自己缔约），都会发现他自己负有双重义务：首先，对于个人而言，他是主权者中的一个成员；其次，对于主权者而言，他又是国家的一个成员。民法上所规定的那条准则，即任何人都可以不受到他和自己所订立的契约的限制约束，在这里并不能适用，因为在对自己负有义务和对自己作为其中一员的整体负有义务之间存在着巨大的差别。

由于对每个人都必须从两个角度加以考察，所以我们必须补充的是，公众的决定可以赋予臣民服从主权者的义务，但是，与之相反，公众的决定却不可以赋予主权者服从其自身的义务；如果主权者给自己设定了一条它自己不能违背的法律，那这将会违背政治体的本性了。对于主权者，由于它只是结合体中唯一的同一个方面，所以主权者在此就处于一种像一个单独的个人同自己订立契约一样的状况，这就表明没有、也不可能有任何一种根本的法律来限制人们的共同体，即使是社会契约本身也不行。这并不意味着，在不破坏这一契约的情况下，这个统一的共同体也不能对其他的国家负有义务；因为就这一共同体与外面其他政权的关系来讲，

the body politic is a simple entity, an individual.

However, since the body politic, or sovereign, owes its being to the sanctity of the contract alone, it cannot commit itself, even in treaties with foreign powers, to anything that would derogate from the original act of association; it could not, for example, alienate a part of itself or submit to another sovereign. To violate the act which has given it existence would be to annihilate itself; and what is nothing can produce nothing.

As soon as the multitude is united thus in a single body, no one can injure any one of the members without attacking the whole, still less injure the whole without each member feeling it. Duty and self-interest thus equally oblige the two contracting parties to give each other mutual aid; and the same men should seek to bring together in this dual relationship, all the advantages that flow from it.

Now, as the sovereign is formed entirely of the individuals who compose it, it has not, nor could it have, any interest contrary to theirs; and so the sovereign has no need to give guarantees to the subjects, because it is impossible for a body to wish to hurt all of its members, and, as we shall see, it cannot hurt any particular member. The sovereign by the mere fact that it is, is always all that it ought to be.

But this is not true of the relation of subject to sovereign. Despite their common interest, subjects will not be bound by their commitment unless means are found to guarantee their fidelity.

它只不过是一个单一的实体、一个个体而已。

然而，既然这一政治共同体或者称为主权者存在的根基仅仅是在于契约的神圣性，那么它就绝对不能使自己从事任何有损于最初的结合行为的事情，即使是以和外国政权签订条约的形式也不行。例如，这一共同体不能转让自己的任何一部分，或者是使自己服从于另外一个主权者。对共同体赖以存在的行为的破坏，将会消灭共同体本身，而不复存在的东西是不能够产生出任何东西的。

一旦人们这样结合成一个单一的共同体，那么对共同体任何一个成员的伤害必然意味着对整个共同体的伤害，而对于共同体的即使是更为微小的伤害也会使所有的成员都感受得到。义务和自身的利益就同样地迫使缔结契约的双方彼此互相帮助，而且同样是这些人也应该努力在这种双层联系中，把所有与之相关系的利益都结合起来。

既然主权者完全是由组成主权者的单个的人所构成，那么主权者就没有、而且也不会有任何与构成主权者的人们利益相反的利益。因此主权者也就不必要给予它的臣民任何保证，因为主权者的共同体不可能想要伤害它的所有成员，而且我们后面也会看到，它也不能够伤害任何一个个别的成员。主权者只要基于它是主权者这一简单的事实，它就会永远是它所应当是的样子。

但是臣民之于主权者的关系却并非如此。尽管有着共同的利益，臣民却不一定能履行他们的义务，除非可以找到一些方法来保证他们的忠诚。

For every individual as a man may have a private will contrary to, or different from, the general will that he has as a citizen. His private interest may speak with a very different voice from that of the public interest; his absolute and naturally independent existence may make him regard what he owes to the common cause as a gratuitous contribution, the loss of which would be less painful for others than the payment is onerous for him; and fancying that the artificial person which constitutes the state is a mere rational entity (since it is not a man), he might seek to enjoy the rights of a citizen without doing the duties of a subject. The growth of this kind of injustice would bring about the ruin of the body politic.

Hence, in order that the social pact shall not be an empty formula, it is tacitly implied in that commitment— which alone can give force to all others— that whoever refuses to obey the general will shall be constrained to do so by the whole body, which means nothing other than that he shall be forced to be free; for this is the condition which, by giving each citizen to the nation, secures him against all personal dependence, it is the condition which shapes both the design and the working of the political machine, and which alone bestows justice on civil contracts— without it, such contracts would be absurd, tyrannical and liable to the grossest abuse.

因为每个单独的个人作为一个人完全可以有个别的意志，而这个个别意志与一个人作为一个公民所具有的公意是相对立的或是不同的。他的个人利益可能会使他发出一种非常不同于公共利益的声音；他的绝对的、自然独立的生存方式可能会使他认为他对于公共事业所担负的义务完全是一种无偿的贡献，而抛弃这种义务对他人所造成的伤害远小于承担这项义务为自己带来的沉重负担；而且他会设想，构成国家的那个人为的人，既然不是一个个人，而只不过是一个理性的实体，那么他可能会尽力地去享受作为一个公民的权利，而不去承担一个臣民所应当担负的义务。这种不公平发展下去将会带来整个政治体的毁灭。

因此，为了使社会契约不至于变成一个空洞的公式，这个契约中必须默含这样一项约定（唯有这一项约定才能给予其他各项以力量），那就是如果任何人拒绝服从公意，那么全体就应该强迫他服从，这不过是说人们强迫他自由而已；因为这是使每个公民拥有国家，从而保护他避免人身依附的条件，也是形成政治机器并保证它正常运转的条件；而且唯有这项规定才赋予了社会契约合法性——如果没有这一项规定，社会契约将会是荒谬的、残暴的，而且容易遭到最严重地滥用。

CHAPTER 8
Civil Society

The passing from the state of nature to the civil society produces a remarkable change in man; it puts justice as a rule of conduct in the place of instinct, and gives his actions the moral quality they previously lacked. It is only then, when the voice of duty has taken the place of physical impulse, and right that of desire, that man, who has hitherto thought only of himself, finds himself compelled to act on other principles, and to consult his reason rather than study his inclinations. And although in civil society man surrenders some of the advantages that belong to the state of nature, he gains in return far greater ones; his faculties are so exercised and developed, his mind is so enlarged, his sentiments so ennobled, and his whole spirit so elevated that, if the abuse of his new condition did not in many cases lower him to something worse than what he had left, he should constantly bless the happy hour that lifted him for ever from the state of nature and from a narrow, stupid animal made a creature of intelligence and a man.

Suppose we draw up a balance sheet, so that the losses and gains may be readily compared. What man loses by the social contract is his natural liberty and the absolute right to anything that tempts him and that he can take; what he gains by the social contract is civil liberty and the legal right of property in what he possesses.

第八章　论公民社会

从自然状态过渡到公民社会，人类产生了一个显著的变化：正义取代了本能而成为人们行为的准则，而且人们的行为也具有了前所未有的道德的品性。只有到了这个时候，即义务的呼声取代了生理的冲动、权利取代了欲望的时候，那些从前只会为自己着想的人发现他自己被迫要依照另外的一些原则来行动，并且在考虑他自己的喜好之前，首先要求助于自己的理性。虽然在公民社会中，人们放弃了一些在自然状态下拥有的利益，但是作为回报，他却获得了远比这些利益大得多的利益；他的能力得到了如此大的锻炼和发展，他的思想变得如此开阔，他的情操变得如此高尚，他的灵魂被如此地提升了，以至于如果不是在某些情况下，他对于这些新条件的滥用使他堕落得比他原来的状况更坏的话，那么对于使他从自然状态中提升出来，使他从一个狭隘、愚蠢的动物一变而成为智能的生物，一变而成为一个人的那个幸福的时刻，他一定会永远感恩戴德的。

假如我们绘制一张收支平衡表，对所得和所失就可以容易地进行比较了。由于社会契约，人类失去的是他的自然的自由，以及对诱惑他的和他能得到的任何东西的绝对权利，而通过社会契约他所得到的是社会的自由，以及对于他所占有的财产的合法权利。

If we are to avoid mistakes in weighing the one side against the other, we must clearly distinguish between *natural* liberty, which has no limit but the physical power of the individual concerned, and *civil* liberty, which is limited by the general will; and we must distinguish also between *possession*, which is based only on force or 'the right of the first occupant', and *property*, which must rest on a legal title.

We might also add that man acquires with civil society, moral freedom, which alone makes man the master of himself; for to be governed by appetite alone is slavery, while obedience to a law one prescribes to oneself is freedom. However, I have already said more than enough on this subject, and the philosophical meaning of the word 'freedom' is no part of my subject here.

如果我们希望在权衡人类的所得和所失时避免犯错误，我们就必须明确地区分只以个人身体的力量为界限的自然的自由，和以公意为限的社会的自由；而且我们还必须区分只是建立在强力或者“最先占有权”基础上的占有权，和建立在合法名义基础上的所有权。

我们可能还应该补充一点，即在公民社会中人类获得了道德的自由，唯有这种自由使人类成为他自己的主人；因为仅仅为欲望所支配的状态是奴隶状态，而人类只有遵从自己为自己制定的法律，才是自由的。然而，对于这个主题，我已经谈得太多太多，而对于“自由”一词哲学上的含义，在这里就不是我的主题的组成部分了。

CHAPTER 9
Of Estate

Every member of the community gives himself to it at the moment it is brought into being just as he is— he himself, with all his resources, including all his goods. This is not to say that possession by this act changes its nature in changing hands and becomes property in the grasp of the sovereign; but rather, that as the resources of the nation are incomparably greater than those of an individual, public possession is in simple fact more secure and more irrevocable than private possession, without being any more legitimate — at any rate, in the eyes of foreigners; for the state, *vis-à-vis* its own members, becomes master of all their goods by virtue of the social contract, which serves, within the state, as the basis of all other rights; while *vis-à-vis* other nations, the state has only the 'right of the first occupant', which it derives from individuals.

The 'right of the first occupant', although more real than the 'right of the strongest', does not become a true right until the institution of property. Every man has a natural right to what he needs; but the positive act which makes a man the proprietor of any estate excludes him from everything else. His share having once been settled, he must confine himself to it, and he has no further right against the community. Thus we see how 'the right of the first occupant',

第九章　关于财产权

这个共同体的每一个成员在共同体形成的那个时刻，就把那一时刻下的他——包括他的自身，他所有的力量，以及他所有的财物——完完全全地交给了共同体。这并不是说由于这一行为，个人的占有权在转手的那一刻就改变了它的本性而变成了被主权者所掌握的所有权。但是实际上，由于国家的力量无可比拟地要远大于一个单独的个人的力量，所以一个简单的事实是，公共的占有要比个人的占有具有更大的安全性和更大的不可变更性，虽然没有更多的合法性（至少在外邦人眼中看来如此）。因为就国家与它的构成成员的关系而言，国家基于在国家中作为其他一切权利的基础的社会契约，而成为其成员的所有财物的主人；然而就国家对其他国家的关系而言，国家只是基于它得自个人的对于财物的“最先占有权”才成为所有财物的主人的。

虽然“最先占有者的权利”要比“最强者的权利”更加真实，但是它也只有在所有权确立之后才成为一种真正的权利。任何一个人对于他所需要的东西都拥有天然的权利，但是使一个人成为某种财产的所有者这种积极的行为，就排除了他对于其他的所有东西的所有权。他的那一份一旦被确定，他就必须把自己局限于此，而且他不能再向共同体要求更多的权利。这样，我们便看

weak as it is in the state of nature, compels in political society the respect of all men. What this right makes one aware of is less what belongs to others than what does *not* belong to oneself.

As a general rule, to justify the right of the first occupant to any piece of land whatever, the following conditions must obtain: first, that the land shall not already be inhabited by anyone else; secondly, that the claimant occupies no more than he needs for subsistence; thirdly, that he takes possession, not by an idle ceremony, but by actually working and cultivating the soil — the only sign of ownership which need be respected by other people in the absence of a legal title.

It can, indeed, be said that tying 'the right of the first occupant' to need and work is stretching it as far as it will go. Can one really avoid setting limits on the right? Is it enough to put one's feet on a piece of common land in order to claim it at once as one's own? Is it enough to have the power to keep other men off for one moment in order to deprive them of the right ever to return? How could a man or a people seize a vast territory and keep out the rest of the human race except by a criminal usurpation since the action would rob the rest of mankind of the shelter and the food that nature has given them all in common? When Nunez Balbao stood on the shore and took possession of the southern seas and of South America in the name of the crown of Castille, was that enough to dispossess all the inhabitants and to exclude all the other princes of the world? If so, such idle ceremonies would have had no end; and the Catholic King might without leaving his royal chamber have taken possession of the whole universe, only excepting afterwards those parts of his empire already belonging to other princes.

到了在自然状态下非常脆弱的“最初占有者的权利”在政治社会中是如何得到所有人的尊重的。这种权利使我们看清楚的，与其说是哪些东西是别人的，不如说是哪些东西不是我们的。

一般来说，要确定对于任何一块土地的最初占有者的权利，以下所列的条件是必须具备的：首先，这块土地还不曾被任何人居住过；第二，他要求占有的数量不应该超过他维持生存所必需的数量；第三，他获得占有权，不是通过一种空洞的形式，而是通过在这块土地上实际地劳动和耕作，这是在缺乏合法名义的情况下，能够得到其他人尊重的所有权的唯一标志。

可以说，根据需要和劳动赋予“最初占有者的权利”，实际上已经把这种权利扩展到了它所可能达到的最大极限了。人们不应该为这种权利设定一个界限吗？是不是只要涉足于一块公共土地之上，一个人就足以立刻宣布这块土地为他所有？是不是只要有力量把其他的人从一块土地上暂时赶走，就足以永远剥夺他们重新回到这块土地的权利？除非使用罪恶的篡夺方式，一个人或者一个民族怎么能够攫取大片领土并把其他的民族排除在此领土之外呢？——因为这种攫取的行为将会剥夺其他人的居住地和食物，而这些是大自然赋予他们共同享有的。当努涅兹·巴尔波站在海岸边上并且以卡斯提王冕的名义宣布对南部海洋以及南美洲的占有权的时候，这是不是就足以剥夺当地居民的土地并把全世界其他国王都排除在这片领土之外呢？如果是这样的话，这种空洞的仪式就会被无休止地使用；而且那位天主教的国王不必离开他高贵的寓所就可以占有整个世界，只要随后把那些已经为其他国王所占领的土地排除在他的帝国版图之外就可以了。

We can see how the lands of private persons, when they are united and contiguous, become public territory; and how the right of sovereignty, extending from the subjects to the soil they occupy, covers both property and persons; it makes the owners all the more dependent, and turns their own strength into the guarantee of their fidelity. This advantage seems to have eluded the ancient monarchs, who, in calling themselves simply the King of the Persians or the Scythians or the Macedonians, appear to have regarded themselves rather as rulers of men than as masters of their countries. Monarchs of the present day call themselves more shrewdly the King of France, or of Spain, or of England and so on; in holding thus the land, they are very sure of holding the inhabitants.

What is unique about the alienation entailed by the social contract is that the community in accepting the goods of an individual is far from depriving him of them; on the contrary it simply assures him of their lawful possession; it changes usurpation into valid right and mere enjoyment into legal ownership. Since every owner is regarded as a trustee of the public property, his rights are respected by every other member of the state, and protected with its collective force against foreigners; men have, by a surrender which is advantageous to the public and still more to themselves, acquired, so to speak, all that they have given up— a paradox which is easily explained by the distinction between the rights which the soverign has and which the owner has over the same property, as will be seen later.

It may also happen that men begin to unite before they possess anything, and spreading over a territory large enough for them all, proceed to enjoy it in common, or, alternatively, divide it among themselves either equally or in shares determined by the sovereign.

我们可以看到，当个人的土地相连或者邻近的时候，它们是如何变成公共领土的；也可以看到随着主权权利从臣民本身扩展到他们占有的土地，它是如何变得既包含财产权，又包含人身权的。这使得土地的所有者具有更大的人身依附性，而且又把他们自身的力量转变成他们的忠心的保证。这样的好处好像并没有被古代的君主们认识到，他们仅仅是称自己为波斯人的王、赛西亚人的王或者马其顿人的王，好像他们只是把自己看作是这些人的统治者，而没有把自己看成是整个国家的主人。今天的君主就更加聪明地把自己称作法兰西的王、西班牙的王或者英格兰的王等等了。这样，通过把持土地，他们非常确定地掌握了这些土地上的居民。

社会契约所规定的这一转让，其独特之处就在于，共同体在接受个人财物的时候远不是剥夺了个人的财物，恰恰相反，它只是确保了个人对于他的财物的合法占有；它把据有变成了正当的权利，仅仅是把享有转变成了合法的所有权。既然每个所有者都被看成是公共财产的保管人，那么他的权利就得到了国家中其他每个成员的尊重，并且受到集体力量的保护以对抗外邦人；人们通过一种既有利于公众，同时更加有利于个人的转让行为而重新获得了他所放弃的一切。以后我们就会看到，只要我们区分了对于同一份财产，主权者的权利和所有者的权利之间的不同，这种看似矛盾的说法就很容易得到解释。

可能也会有这样的情况，人们在尚未占有任何东西的时候就已经开始结合了，之后再去占据一块足够大的领土以供整个集体所用；他们或者继续共同享用这块土地，或者做出另外一种选择：他们可以平等地、也可以根据主权者规定的比例在他们中间划

In whatever manner this acquisition is made, the right of any individual over his own estate is always subordinate to the right of the community over everything; for without this there would be neither strength in the social bond nor effective force in the exercise of sovereignty.

I shall end this chapter — and Book I — with an observation which might serve as a basis for the whole social system: namely, that the social pact, far from destroying natural equality, substitutes, on the contrary, a moral and lawful equality for whatever physical inequality that nature may have imposed on mankind; so that however unequal in strength and intelligence, men become equal by covenant and by right. ①

① Under a bad government, this equality is only an appearance and an illusion; it serves only to keep the poor in their wretchedness and sustain the rich in their usurpation. In truth, laws are always useful to those with possessions and harmful to those who have nothing; from which it follows that the social state is advantageous to men only when all possess something and none has too much.

分这块土地。但不管这种获得是以何种方式进行的，个人对于他自己的那份财产的权利永远要从属于共同体对于所有财产的权利；因为若是没有这一点，社会的联系就将会没有任何稳固性，主权权利的行使也不会有有效的力量。

我要通过对于作为整个社会系统基础的观察，来结束本章、本卷书，即：社会契约远不是破坏了自然的平等，恰恰相反，它用道德的和法律的平等取代了自然状态强加给人类的任何身体上的不平等，所以不管人与人之间在体力上和智能上如何的不平等，通过契约、通过权利，人们变得平等了①。

① 在一个坏的政府之下，平等仅仅是一种表象、一种虚幻；它只能使穷人一直处于悲惨的状况，而保持富人处于据有的状态。事实上，这时法律只是有利于那些占有财富的人，而不利于那些什么东西都没有的人。由此可以得出以下结论：只有当社会中所有的人都能占有一些东西，而且又没有人能够占有太多东西的时候，社会状态才会对整个人类有利。

BOOK II

CHAPTER I

That Sovereignty Is Inalienable

The first and most important consequence of the principles so far established is that the general will alone can direct the forces of the state in accordance with that end which the state has been established to achieve— the common good; for if conflict between private interests has made the setting up of civil societies necessary, harmony between those same interests has made it possible. It is what is common to those different interests which yields the social bond; if there were no point on which separate interests coincided, then society could not conceivably exist. And it is precisely on the basis of this common interest that society must be governed.

My argument, then, is that sovereignty, being nothing other than the exercise of the general will, can never be alienated; and that the sovereign, which is simply a collective being, cannot be represented by anyone but itself— power may be delegated, but the will cannot be.

For indeed while it is not impossible for a private will to coincide with the general will on some point or other, it is impossible for such a coincidence to be regular and enduring; for the private will inclines by its very nature towards partiality, and the general will towards equality. It is even more inconceivable that there should be a guarantee of harmony between the private and the general will, even if it were to continue always, for such lasting

第二卷

第一章　论主权是不可转让的

前面所确立起来的那些原则，第一位的而且最重要的结果就是：唯有公意才能够根据建立国家所要追求的那个目标（即公共利益）来指导国家的力量。因为如果说，由于私人利益之间的冲突使得公民社会的建立成为必需的话，那么，正是那些私人利益之间的协调一致之处才使得公民社会的建立成为可能。正是这些不同利益的共同之处产生了社会的联系，如果这些个别利益没有一致之处的话，社会的存在就不可想象了。故此社会的管理必定正是以这些共同利益为基础的。

那么，我的观点是：主权不是别的，它就是公意的行使，所以它永远都不能被转让；而且，既然主权者不过是一个集体的存在，那么除了它自己，任何人都不能代表它。权力虽然可以被代表，但是意志却不能。

事实上，虽然使个别意志和公意在某些点上达到一致不是不可能，但要使两者的这种一致能够频繁出现并且持久却是不可能的。因为个别意志由于它的天然本性而总是倾向于偏私，而公意则会倾向于平等。我们更不太可能保证个别意志和公意之间的和谐一致，因为即使它总是应该存在的，但这种持续的和谐状

harmony would be the result of chance and not of design. The sovereign could say: 'What I want at present is precisely what this man wants, or at least what he says he wants'; but no sovereign could say: 'What this man is going to want tomorrow I too shall want', for it is absurd that anyone should wish to bind himself for the future, and it is a contradiction in terms to say that any human being should wish to consent to something that is the reverse of his own good. If a people promises simply and solely to obey, it dissolves itself by that very pledge; it ceases to be a people; for once there is a master, there is no longer a sovereign, and the body politic is therefore annihilated.

This is not to say that the commands of leaders may not pass for the general will if the sovereign, being free to oppose them, does not do so. In such a case the silence of the people permits the assumption that the people consents. This will be explained more fully in a later chapter.

态也只不过是机遇的结果，而非人为的设计。主权者可以说“现在我想要的恰恰就是这个人想要的，至少是他说他想要的”，但是却不能说“这个人明天想要的也是我明天应该要的”。因为说一个人应该希望他自己为未来所约束是荒谬可笑的，而且说任何一个人都应该希望自己赞同那些与他自己的幸福相违背的事情也是自相矛盾的。如果人民仅仅是一味地答应服从，那么它就会由于这种应诺的行为而使它自己解体，它就不再是人民了；因为一旦出现了一个主人，就不再有主权者了，而且政治体也会因此而消灭。

这并不是说，对于首领的命令，在主权者有反对的自由但并没有这样做的情况下，就不能被看作是公意了。在这种情况下，人民的沉默允许被假设为人民的赞同。这一点在后面的章节中我们会充分地解释。

CHAPTER 2

That Sovereignty Is Indivisible

Just as sovereignty is inalienable, it is for the same reason indivisible; for either the will is general[①] or it is not; either it is the will of the body of the people, or merely that of a part. In the first case, a declaration of will is an act of sovereignty and constitutes law; in the second case, it is only a declaration of a particular will or an act of administration, it is at best a mere decree.

Nevertheless, our political theorists, unable to divide the principle of sovereignty, divide it in its purpose; they divide it into power and will, divide it, that is, into executive and legislative, into the rights of levying taxation, administering justice and making war, into domestic jurisdiction and the power to deal with foreign governments. Sometimes our theorists confuse all the parts and sometimes they separate them. They make the sovereign a creature of fantasy, a patchwork of separate pieces, rather as if they were to construct a man of several bodies— one with eyes, one with legs, the other with feet and nothing else. It is said that Japanese mountebanks can cut up a child under the eyes of spectators,

---

① For the will to be general, it does not always have to be unanimous; but all the votes must be counted. Any formal exclusion destroys its universality.

第二章　论主权是不可分割的

正如主权是不可转让的，基于同样的原因，主权也是不可分割的；因为意志或者是公意，或者不是；它或者是人民共同体的意志①，或者只是其中一部分人的意志。在第一种情况下，这种意志的宣布是主权的行为，从而制定了法律；而在第二种情况下，它仅仅是一种个别意志的宣布或者是行政的行为，顶多也只是一道政令而已。

然而，我们的政治理论家们，因为不能根据主权的原理来区分主权，所以只能根据主权的对象来区分主权。他们把主权分为力量和意志，就是说，把主权划分为行政权和立法权，分为税收权、司法权和战争权，分为内政权和外交权。我们的政治理论家们有时候把这些部分混淆起来，有时候又把它们分裂开来。他们把主权者变成了一个由一些分散的部分拼凑起来的怪物，就好像他们用几个人的肢体拼凑了一个人一样，其中一个用眼睛，一个用腿，另一个用脚，除此之外再没有其他的部分。据说日本的一些行骗术者能够在观众的眼皮底下把一个小

---

① 意志要成为公意，并不总是必须要全体一致的，但是所有的选票都必须被统计在内。任何形式的例外都会破坏它的普遍性。

throw the different parts into the air, and then make the child come down, alive and all of a piece. This is more or less the trick that our political theorists perform after dismembering the social body with a sleight of hand worthy of the fairground, they put the pieces together again anyhow.

The mistake comes from having no precise notion of what sovereign authority is, and from taking mere manifestations of authority for parts of the authority itself. For instance, the acts of declaring war and making peace have been regarded as acts of sovereignty, which they are not; for neither of these acts constitutes a *law*, but only an application of law, a particular act which determines how the law shall be interpreted and all this will be obvious as soon as I have defined the idea which attaches to the word ‘law’.

If we were to scrutinize in the same way the other supposed divisions of sovereignty, we should find that whenever we thought that sovereignty was divided, we had been mistaken, for the rights which are taken to be part of that sovereignty prove in fact to be subordinate to it, and presuppose the existence of a supreme will which they merely serve to put into effect.

This want of precision has obfuscated immeasurably the conclusions of our legal theorists when they have come to apply their own principles to determine the respective rights of kings and of peoples. Every reader of the third and fourth chapters of the first Book of Grotius can see how that learned man and his translator, Barbeyrac, are trapped in their own sophisms, frightened of saying either too much or alternatively too little (according to their prejudices) and so offending the interests

孩子肢解，并把他肢体的各个部分抛上天空，然后又让这个孩子完完整整地活着从天上掉下来。这或多或少就是我们的政治理论家所玩的把戏了——他们用他们那种完全可以当众表演的熟练手法肢解了社会整体，然后不知用何种方法又把这些碎片拼凑在了一起。

这种错误来源于对于主权权威没有精确的概念，也源自于把主权权威的表现当成了主权权威本身的组成部分。例如，宣战和媾和的行为被当成了主权的行为，而实际上并不是如此。因为这些行为都不能制定法律，而只不过是对法律的运用，是一种确定应该如何解释法律的个别行为。只要我们确定了“法律”一词的相关思想，这一点就会非常明显了。

如果我们以同样的方式去仔细考察对主权的其他一些设想出来的划分，我们就会发现，每当我们认为我们划分了主权的时候，我们就已经犯错误了。因为那些被认为是主权的组成部分的权利总被证明实际上只是从属于主权的，而且它们要以最高意志的存在为前提条件，而它们只不过是在实施这些最高意志而已。

当这些研究法律的理论家们运用他们的原则去确定国王和人民各自相应的权利的时候，他们对于精确性的缺乏就使他们的结论极为模糊。读过格劳秀斯的第一本书[1]的第三章和第四章的读者会看清楚，这个知识渊博的人和他的这部著作的翻译者巴贝拉克是如何陷入他们自己的诡辩的，他们唯恐说得太多或者是说得太少（基于他们的偏见），唯恐冒犯了他们所要协调

〔1〕 指《战争与和平法》。

they wish to flatter. Grotius, a refugee in France, discontented with his own country and out to pay court to Louis XIII, to whom his book is dedicated, spares no pains to rob peoples of all their rights and to invest those rights, by every conceivable artifice, in kings. This would have been very much to the taste of Barbeyrac, who dedicated his translation of Grotius to the King of England, George I. But unfortunately the expulsion of James II— which Barbeyrac calls an 'abdication'— obliged him to speak with a marked reserve, to hesitate and equivocate, so as not to suggest that William III was a usurper. If these two writers had adopted sound principles, all their difficulties would have vanished, and their arguments would have been logical; but then they would, alas for them, have told the truth and paid court only to the people. The truth brings no man a fortune; and it is not the people who hand out embassies, professorships and pensions.

的种种利益。格劳秀斯不满意于他自己的国家而流亡到法国，他想要讨好路易十三，他的这本书就是要献给路易十三的，所以他不遗余力地剥夺了人民所有的权利，并运用种种想得到的花招把这些权利赋予国王。这应该非常适合于巴贝拉克的胃口，他翻译了格劳秀斯的这本著作，以献给英格兰的国王乔治一世。但是不幸的是，詹姆士二世的被驱逐（巴贝拉克称此为“让位”）迫使他说起话来不得不有所保留，吞吞吐吐，含糊其词，以避免把威廉三世暗示成一个篡夺者。如果这两位作者都能够采取合理的原则的话，他们所有的难题就都会消失的，而且他们的论辩也就会是合乎逻辑的了。但是，那样的话，令他们难过的是他们就必须说出事实真相，而且仅仅是去讨好人民了。可是，真理不会给一个人带来财富，并且人民也不能给予他们大使的头衔、教授的身份以及养老金。

BOOK II

CHAPTER 3

Whether The General Will Can Err

It follows from what I have argued that the general will is always rightful and always tends to the public good; but it does not follow that the decisions of the people are always equally right. We always want what is advantageous but we do not always discern it. The people is never corrupted, but it is often misled; and only then does it seem to will what is bad.

There is often a great difference between the will of all [what all individuals want] and the general will; the general will studies only the common interest while the will of all studies private interest, and is indeed no more than the sum of individual desires. But if we take away from these same wills, the pluses and minuses which cancel each other out, the sum of the difference is the general will. ①

From the deliberations of a people properly informed, and provided its members do not have any communication among themselves, the great number of small differences will always produce a general will and the decision will always be good.

---

① 'Every interest,' says the Marquis d' Argenson, 'has its different principles. Harmony between two interests is created by opposition to that of a third.' He might have added that the harmony of all interests is created by opposition to those of each. If there were no different interests, we should hardly be conscious of a common interest, as there would be no resistance to it; everything would run easily of its own accord, and politics would cease to be an art.

第三章　论公意是否会错

由我的以上论述可以得出如下结论：公意永远是公正的，而且总是追求公众的利益；但是我们却不能由此得出结论说，人民的决定永远是同等地正确的。我们总是希望得到那些有利的东西，但是我们并不总能认清什么是有利的。人民永远不会被腐蚀，却经常会被误导，而且唯有在这时候，人民才好像是希望得到那些不好的东西。

众意（所有个人的意图）和公意之间经常有着很大的区别；公意只考虑公共的利益，而众意则考虑私人的利益，而且众意实际上只不过是个别意志的总和。但是，如果我们从这些个别意志中除去正负相抵的那部分，剩下的那些差异的总和就是公意①。

如果那些能够充分了解情况的人民经过了深思熟虑，并且假定人民共同体的成员之间没有任何的沟通，那么从人民的那些极大数量的小差异中总能产生出公意来，而且这些决定总会是好的。

---

① 阿冉松侯爵说："每种利益都有它不同的原则，两种利益之间的和谐是由于和第三种利益之间的对立而产生的。"他还可以再补充上：所有利益之间的和谐是由于它和每种利益之间的对立而形成的。如果根本没有不同的利益，那么对于这种遇不上任何对抗的共同利益，我们几乎就不会感觉到它；一切事情都会简简单单地自行运转，政治也就不再是一种艺术了。

But if groups, sectional associations are formed at the expense of the larger association, the will of each of these groups will become general in relation to its own members and private in relation to the state; we might then say that there are no longer as many votes as there are men but only as many votes as there are groups. The differences become less numerous and yield a result less general. Finally, when one of these groups becomes so large that it can dominate the rest, the result is no longer the sum of many small differences, but one great divisive difference; then there ceases to be a general will, and the opinion which prevails is no more than a private opinion.

Thus if the general will is to be clearly expressed, it is imperative that there should be no sectional associations in the state, and that every citizen should make up his own mind for himself ① – such was the unique and sublime invention of the great Lycurgus. But if there are sectional associations, it is wise to multiply their number and to prevent inequality among them, as Solon, Numa and Servius did. These are the only precautions which can ensure that the general will is always enlightened and the people protected from error.

---

① 'Divisions,' says Machiavelli, 'sometimes injure and sometimes aid a republic. The injury is done by cabals and factions; the service is rendered by a party which maintains itself without cabals and factions. Since, therefore, it is impossible for the founder of a republic to provide against enmities, he must make the best provision he can against factions.' *History of Florence*, Book VII.

但是，如果小集团或者局部团体以牺牲更大的团体为代价而建立起来了，那么这些集团中每个集团的意志对于它的组成成员来说是公意，但是对于国家来说它只是个别意志；那么，我们就可以说，投票者的数目就不再和人口的数目相等，而只是和集团的数目相等。差异在数目上比以前减少了，而且产生的结果的普遍性也比以前减小了。最后，当这些集团中的某一个集团变得如此之大，以至于它可以支配其他的那些集团，那么结果就不再是许多小的差异的总和，而只是一个大的分裂性的分歧；这时就不再有公意了，而且占有优势地位的那个意见也只不过是一个个别意见罢了。

因此，如果要想使公意得到清楚地表达，那么极为要紧的在国家中不应有小集团存在，而且每个公民都应当提出他自己的想法①，这便是伟大的莱格古士独特而崇高的发明。但是，如果国家内存在着小集团的话，明智的做法就是使它们的数目大量增加，并且防止这些集团之间的不平等，就像梭伦、努玛、塞尔维乌斯所做的那样。这是保证公意永远光明正确以及人民不犯错误的唯一的预防措施。

---

① 马基雅弗利说：“分裂有些时候会伤害一个共和国，有些时候则会有助于一个共和国。一些阴谋小集团和小派系会对共和国造成伤害，而那些保持自己不陷于阴谋和派系的团体则会对共和国提供帮助。因此，既然共和国的创立者不能规定禁止敌对力量的存在，那么他就应该尽他最大的努力禁止派系的产生。”（《佛罗伦萨史》第七卷）

CHAPTER 4

The Limits Of Sovereign Power

If the state, or the nation, is nothing other than a legal person the life of which consists in the union of its members and if the most important of its cares is its own preservation, it must have a universal and compelling power to move and dispose of each part in whatever manner is beneficial to the whole. Just as nature gives each man an absolute power over all his own limbs, the social pact gives the body politic an absolute power over all its members; and it is this same power which, directed by the general will, bears, as I have said, the name of sovereignty.

However, we have to consider beside the public person those private persons who compose it, and whose life and liberty is naturally independent of it. Here we have to distinguish clearly the respective rights of the citizen and of the sovereign,[①] and distinguish those duties which the citizens have as subjects from the natural rights which they ought to enjoy as men.

We have agreed that each man alienates by the social pact only that part of his power, his goods and his liberty which is the concern

① Please, attentive reader, do not hasten to accuse me of contradiction. I cannot avoid a contradiction of words, because of the poverty of language; but wait.

第四章　论主权权力的界限

如果说国家或者民族只不过是一个法定的人格，它的生命就在于构成它的成员的联合，如果它最关注的就是它自身的保存，那么它就必须拥有一种普遍而且强制性的力量，以便于按照任何一种有利于全体的方式来引导或者安排它的各个部分。正像自然赋予了每个人控制他肢体的每个部分的绝对权力一样，社会契约也赋予了政治共同体控制它的成员的绝对权力；正是这种权力处在公意指导之下的时候，正如我以上所说的，就拥有了主权这个名称。

然而，除了这个公共的人格之外，我们还必须考虑到构成公共人格的那些单个的人，这些私人的生命和自由是天然地独立于这个公共人格的。这里我们必须清楚地区分公民和主权者各自的权利①，并且把公民作为臣民时所应尽的义务和他们凭人的身份所应该享有的天然的权利也区别开来。

我们已经承认，根据社会契约，每个人仅仅是转让出他的权力、他的财物以及他的自由的一部分，这部分是与共同体密切相

---

① 细心的读者，请不要急着指责我的自相矛盾。因为语言上的贫乏，使我这里难以避免用词上的自相矛盾，但是请稍等。

of the community; but it must also be admitted that the sovereign alone is judge of what is of such concern.

Whatever services the citizen can render the state, he owes whenever the sovereign demands them; but the sovereign, on its side, may not impose on the subjects any burden which is not necessary. to the community; the sovereign cannot, indeed, even will such a thing, since according to the law of reason no less than to the law of nature nothing is without a cause.

The commitments which bind us to the social body are obligatory only because they are mutual; and their nature is such that in fulfilling them a man cannot work for others without at the same time working for himself. How should it be that the general will is always rightful and that all men constantly wish the happiness of each but for the fact that there is no one who does not take that word 'each' to pertain to himself and in voting for all think of himself? This proves that the equality of rights and the notion of justice which it produces derive from the predilection which each man has for himself and hence from human nature as such. It also proves that the general will, to be truly what it is, must be general in its purpose as well as in its nature; that it should spring from all and apply to all; and that it loses its natural rectitude when it is directed towards any particular and circumscribed object— for in judging what is foreign to us, we have no sound principle of equity to guide us.

For, indeed, whenever we are dealing with a particular fact or right, on a matter which has not been settled by an earlier and general agreement, that question becomes contentious. It is a conflict in which private interests are ranged on one side and the public interest on the other; and I can see neither the law which is to be followed nor the judge who is to arbitrate. It would be absurd in such

关的，但是我们也必须承认，对于哪部分与共同体密切相关，唯有主权者才是裁断者。

对于公民所能够为国家提供的任何服务，每当主权者提出要求时，公民就应该马上提供；但是站在主权者的角度上，主权者不可以把任何一种不是为共同体所必需的负担强加于公民身上。事实上，主权者甚至不可以有这种意图，因为根据理性的规则，正如根据自然的规则，没有任何事情是没有理由的。

把我们同社会共同体联结起来的那个义务之所以是义不容辞的，只是因为这种义务是相互的；而且它们的本性也使得当一个人为了履行这种义务而为别人服务的时候，他不可能不同时也是为他自己服务。如果不是事实上所有的人都认为“每个人”这个词是适用于他自己的，而且在为全体投票的时候又考虑到他自己的话，公意怎么可能永远是公正的？所有的人又怎么可能总是希望每个人都能幸福呢？这就证明了，权利的平等以及由它所产生的正义的观念来源于每个人对他自己的偏爱，因而同样也就是根源于人的本性的。这也证明了，公意要真正成为公意，它在目标上以及在本质上必须要有普遍性；而且它必须来自于所有的人，又适用于所有的人；如果公意指向任何个别的、限定的对象的话，它就丧失了公正性——因为在我们对那些很陌生的东西做出判断时，我们没有任何可靠而公正的原则来指导自己。

事实上，每当我们处理一个特殊的事实或者权利的时候，如果它还不曾被更早的、普遍的约定所规定，事情就会变得有争议了。这是一场冲突，在这场冲突中，个人的利益站在一边，而公共的利益站在另一边；而且对此我找不到任何可以依据的法律，

a dispute to seek an express decision of the general will; for a decision could only be a conclusion in favour of one of the contending parties, and it would be regarded by the other party as an alien, partial will, a will prone to error and liable in such circumstances to fall into injustice. So we see that even as a private will cannot represent the general will, so too the general will changes its nature if it seeks to deal with an individual case; it cannot as a *general* will give a ruling concerning any one man or any one fact. When the people of Athens, for example, appointed or dismissed its leaders, awarding honours to one, inflicting penalties on another, and by a multitude of particular decrees indiscriminately exercised all the functions of an administration, then the people of Athens no longer had what is correctly understood as a general will and ceased to act as sovereign and acted instead as magistrate. All this may seem at variance with commonly accepted notions; but I must be given time to expound my own.

It should nevertheless be clear from what I have so far said that the general will derives its generality less from the number of voices than from the common interest which unites them— for the general will is an institution in which each necessarily submits himself to the same conditions which he imposes on others; this admirable harmony of interest and justice gives to social deliberations a quality of equity which disappears at once from the discussion of any individual dispute precisely because in these latter cases there is no common interest to unite and identify the decision of the judge with that of the contending parties.

Whichever way we look at it, we always return to the same conclusion: namely that the social pact establishes equality among the citizens in that they all pledge themselves under the same conditions and must all enjoy the same rights.

也找不到可以做出公断的法官。对于这样的一种争论，如果仅是求助于公意的表决，那就是荒谬可笑的；因为这种表决只能是有利于争辩双方中的一方的一个结论，这个结论会被争辩的另一方看成是外在的、偏袒的意志。这种意志很容易犯错误，而且在这种情况下很容易陷入不公正。所以，我们可以看到，正像个别意志不能代表公意一样，如果公意想去处理私人事件，那么它也将会变质；它就不能再作为公意而就任何一个人或者任何一件事做出裁决。比如，当雅典的人民任命或者废除一个首领的时候，当他们授予某个人奖赏或者施予某个人惩罚的时候，或者当他们不加选择地运用大量的个别法令来行使一个政府的全部职能的时候，他们就不再拥有得到正确理解的公意了，而且他们不再是作为主权者，而只是作为行政官员来行动了。所有这些思想好像与普遍接受的观念是不一致的，但是你们必须给我时间来详细说明我的观点。

不过，根据以上我所说的，我们可以清楚地看到：与其说公意从投票者的数量中获得它的普遍性，不如说它是从构成共同体的共同利益中获得普遍性的——因为公意是这样一种制度，在这种制度中每个人都必须使他自己服从于他强加给别人的同样的条件；利益和正义之间的这种绝妙的和谐一致，赋予了集体协商一种平等的品性，但是一旦涉及对私人问题的讨论，这种平等性就会消失，因为在后一种情况下没有一种共同的利益可以把法官的判决和争辩双方的决议结合并统一起来。

不管用什么方式观察，我们总会返回到一个相同的结论，那就是社会契约确立了公民之间的平等。在这种平等的状况下，所有的公民都保证遵守同样的条件，并且全都享受相同的权利。

Hence by the nature of the compact, every act of sovereignty, that is, every authentic act of the general will, binds or favours all the citizens equally, so that the sovereign recognizes only the whole body of the nation and makes no distinction between any of the members who compose it. What then is correctly to be called an act of sovereignty? It is not a covenant between a superior and an inferior, but a covenant of the body with each of its members. It is a legitimate covenant, because its basis is the social contract; an equitable one, because it is common to all; a useful one, because it can have no end but the common good; and it is a durable covenant because it is guaranteed by the armed forces and the supreme power. So long as the subjects submit to such covenants alone, they obey nobody but their own will; and to ask how far the respective rights of the sovereign and the citizen extend is to ask how far these two can pledge themselves together, each to all and all to each.

From this it is clear that the sovereign power, wholly absolute, wholly sacred, wholly inviolable as it is, does not go beyond and cannot go beyond the limits of the general covenants; and thus that every man can do what he pleases with such goods and such freedom as is left to him by these covenants; and from this it follows that the sovereign has never any right to impose greater burdens on one subject than on another, for whenever that happens a private grievance is created and the sovereign's power is no longer competent.

Granted these distinctions, it becomes manifestly false to assert that individuals make any real renunciation by the social contract; indeed, as a result of the contract they find themselves in a situation preferable in real terms to that which prevailed before; instead of an alienation, they have profitably exchanged an uncertain and precarious life for a better and more secure one; they have exchanged natural independence for freedom, the power to destroy others for the enjoyment of their own security;

因此，根据契约的本性，主权的每个行为，也就是真正属于公意的一切行为，都平等地约束或者关怀着所有的公民。所以主权者只能认得国家这个整体，而对构成国家的任何成员都不做出任何区别。那么，什么行为才可以被确切地称作是主权的行为呢？它不是上级和下级之间的约定，而是共同体和它的每个成员之间的约定。它是一种合法的约定，因为它的基础是社会契约；它是一个公正的约定，因为它对于所有的人都是相同的；它是一个有用的约定，因为除了共同的幸福之外它没有别的目的；它是一个持久的约定，因为它能得到武装力量和最高权力的保障。只要臣民服从于这样的契约，他们就不是在服从别人，而只是在服从他自己的意志；如果要问主权者和公民各自相应的权利能够扩展到多大的程度，那就等于在问这两者对于他们自身（每个人对全体以及全体对于每个人）能够承诺到多大的程度。

由此我们可以清楚地看到，主权权力尽管是完全绝对的、完全神圣的、完全不可侵犯的，但是它却不会超过、也不能超过公共契约的界限；并且每个人都可以根据自己所愿来处置那些依据契约留给他的财物和自由。由此可以得出结论：主权者在任何时候都无权施加给某个臣民比其他臣民更大的负担，因为每当这种事情发生时，就造成了对个人的不平，主权者的权力就不再有效。

如果我们承认这种区别，那么断言个人由于社会契约而实际放弃权利的说法就是明显错误的了；事实上，由于契约，人们会发现他们自己处在一种比过去更为优越的环境中；他们不但不是放弃权利，而是用一种不确定的、不稳固的生活非常得利地换取了一种更好的、更加安全的生活；他们是用天然的独立换来了自由，用对别人进行侵犯的权力换取了对自身安全

they have exchanged their own strength which others might overcome for a right which the social union makes invincible. Their very lives, which they have pledged to the state, are always protected by it; and even when they risk their lives to defend the state, what more are they doing but giving back what they have received from the state? What are they doing that they would not do more often, and at greater peril, in the state of nature, where every man is inevitably at war and at the risk of his life, defends whatever serves him to maintain life? Assuredly, all must now fight in case of need for their country, but at least no one has any longer to fight for himself. And is there not something to be gained by running, for the sake of the guarantee of safety, a few of those risks we should each have to face alone if we were deprived of that assurance?

的享有；他们也是用他们那种可能被别人征服的力量换取了由社会共同体保障其不可征服性的权利。他们承诺献给国家的生命，也总会得到国家的保护；即使是当他们冒着生命危险去保卫国家的时候，他们所做的不也只是把他们从国家那里得到的东西重新还给国家吗？他们所做的，不正是自然状态中，每个人在不可避免地要参与战争、并且冒着生命危险去保护那些为了维持他们的生命所必需的东西的时候，他们更加经常地冒着生命危险去做的事情吗？确实，一旦当国家需要的时候，所有的人都必须为国家去战斗，但是至少这时不必一个人再去为他自己战斗了。这时，为了保障我们的安全，我们只需承受的是如果我们被剥夺了这种保障时所必须独立面对的那很多危险中的一部分，这里我们不就是收获了一些东西吗？

CHAPTER 5
The Right Of Life And Death

It will be asked how individuals, who have no right whatever to take their own lives, can transfer to the sovereign a right they do not possess. This question looks difficult to answer only because it is badly formulated. Every man has the right to risk his own life in order to preserve it. Has it ever been said that a man who leaps out of a window to escape from a fire is guilty of suicide? Would the same crime be imputed to a man who perishes in a storm on the grounds that he knew of the danger when he embarked?

The purpose of the social treaty is the preservation of the contracting parties. Whoever wills the end wills also the means, and certain risks, even certain casualties are inseparable from these means. Whoever wishes to preserve his own life at the expense of others must give his life for them when it is necessary. Now, as citizen, no man is judge any longer of the danger to which the law requires him to expose himself, and when the prince says to him: 'It is expedient for the state that you should die', then he should die, because it is only on such terms that he has lived in security as long as he has and also because his life is no longer the bounty of nature but a gift he has received

第五章　论生死权

可能有人会问：既然个人没有处置他们自己生命的权利，那么他们怎么可能把一种他们都不具有的权利转让给主权者呢？这个问题之所以看起来难以回答，只是因为这个问题的问法不对。每个人都有为了保护他的生命而冒生命危险的权利。难道有这种说法，一个为了从火灾中逃生而从一扇窗户中跳出来的人犯有自杀之罪吗？难道一个在暴风雨中被吞噬的人因为在他上船时就知道危险的存在而可以被加上同样的罪名吗？

社会契约的目标就是保护缔结条约者。想要达到某种目的的人都需要一些手段和某些冒险，而有些牺牲与手段是分不开的。任何人如果想要以别人的生命为代价来保护他自己的生命，那么在必要的时候他必须可以为别人的生命而献出自己的生命。作为公民，没有人可以对法律要求他所冒的危险做出决断，而当君主[1]对他说“如果你牺牲，那么就会对整个国家有利”，那么他就应该去牺牲，因为正是由于这个条件他才一直生活在安全之中，也因为他的生命不再是大自然的恩赐，而是他从国

〔1〕 这里是指执政者，也就是统治者的共同体，本书中很多处“君主”都是取此意，不再一一指明。

conditionally from the state.

The death-penalty inflicted on criminals may be seen in much the same way: it is in order to avoid becoming the victim of a murderer that one consents to die if one becomes a murderer oneself. Far from taking one's life under the social treaty, one thinks only of assuring it, and we shall hardly suppose that any of the contracting parties contemplates being hanged.

Moreover, since every wrongdoer attacks the society's law, he becomes by his deed a rebel and a traitor to the country; by violating its law, he ceases to be a member of it; indeed, he makes war against it. And in this case, the preservation of the state is incompatible with *his* preservation; one or the other must perish; and when the guilty man is put to death, it is less as a citizen than as an enemy. Trial and judgement are the proof and declaration that he has broken the social treaty, and is in consequence no longer a member of the state. And since he has accepted such membership, if only by his residence, he must either be banished into exile as a violator of the social pact or be put to death as a public enemy: such an enemy is not a fictitious person, but a man, and therefore the right of war makes it legitimate to kill him.

But, it will be said, the condemnation of a criminal is an individual act. Agreed; and it follows that such duties do not pertain to the sovereign; condemnation of criminals is a right the sovereign can confer but not exercise himself. All my ideas hold together, but I cannot elaborate them all at once.

In any case, frequent punishments are a sign of weakness or slackness in the government. There is no man so bad that he cannot be

家那里收到的一份有条件的礼物。

对罪犯实施死刑可以用同样的方式来考察，正是为了防止成为凶手的牺牲品，人们才同意如果自己成了一个杀人犯的话，那么他自己就得去死。在社会契约中，人们所想的只是要保全自己的生命，而远非为了结束自己的生命。我们无法想象缔结条约者在缔结条约时只是希望自己被处以绞刑。

此外，由于任何一个做坏事的人都触犯了社会的法律，那么他就由于他的这种行为而成为国家的叛乱者或者叛徒；由于他破坏了国家的法律，所以他就不再是国家的一个成员；实际上，他发动了反对国家的战争。在这种情况下，国家的生存和他的生存就是不能相容的了，其中的一方或者另一方必须毁灭；而且如果这个有罪的人被判处死刑，那并不是以一个公民的身份，而是以一个敌人的身份。审讯和判决就是他破坏了社会协约的证据和宣告，结果他就不再是国家的一个成员。而且，既然他接受了这样一种成员的身份，至少是由于他居住于此地，那么他就必须以社会契约破坏者的身份被驱逐流放，或者以国家敌人的身份被判处死刑。这样的敌人就不是一个虚构的人，而是一个真实的人，因此战争的权利便使得杀死他成为合法的了。

但是，可能有人会说，给一个罪犯定罪是一项个别的行为。我同意这一点，而且由此可以得出的结论是，这样的一种职责并不属于主权者，给罪犯定罪是主权者可以授予但是它自己不能亲自执行的权利。我所有的观点都是前后一致的，只是我不能一下子把所有这些思想都详细阐述明白。

任何情况下，频繁的惩罚都是政府软弱或是无力的一个标志。

made good for something. No man should be put to death, even as an example, if he can be left to live without danger to society.

As for the right of pardon, or of exempting a guilty man from the penalty prescribed by law and imposed by a judge, This belongs only to that entity which is superior to both the judge and the law, namely the sovereign; but even this right is not entirely clear and it must be exercised very seldom. In a wellgoverned state there are few penalties, not because there are many pardons but because there are few criminals. In a decaying state the very multiplicity of crimes assures impunity. Under the Roman Republic neither the senate nor the consuls ever attempted to pardon criminals; nor did the people do so, though they sometimes revoked their own sentences. Frequent pardons signalize that crimes will soon need no pardon; and anyone can see what that must lead to. However, I can feel my heart whispering and restraining my pen; let us leave the discussion of these questions to the just man who has never erred and has therefore had no need of pardons.

任何一个人都不会坏到我们在任何事情上都无法使他为善。任何一个人如果他留存于世并不会对社会造成危险，那么他就不应该被处以死刑，哪怕是为了杀一儆百也不行。

至于对那些受到法律惩罚并由法官对其强制执行的罪人加以宽恕或者赦免的权利，则仅仅属于那个超越于法官和法律之上的统一体，也即主权者；但是即使这种权利也不是十分明确的，而且它也必须很少地被行使。在一个治理得很好的国家中，处罚是很少的，这不是因为赦免很多，而是因为犯罪的人很少。在一个腐朽的国家中，大量犯罪的出现则使得犯罪不再受到惩罚。在罗马共和国的统治之下，元老院或者执政官从来都没有打算赦免过罪犯；人民也从来没有这样做过，虽然有时人民会撤回自己的判决。频繁的赦免意味着犯罪行为不久以后将不再需要被赦免，每个人都能看出这必将导向什么。然而，我可以感受到我的心对自己的私语，这阻滞了我的笔；让我们把这些问题的讨论留给那些从不会犯错因而也就从不需要被赦免的正直的人吧。

CHAPTER 6

On Law

We have given life and existence to the body politic by the social pact; now it is a matter of giving it movement and will by legislation. For the primitive act by which the body politic is formed and united does not determine what it shall do to preserve itself.

What is good and in conformity with order is such by the very nature of things and independently of human agreements. All justice comes from God, who alone is its source; and if only we knew how to receive it from that exalted fountain, we should need neither governments nor laws. There is undoubtedly a universal justice which springs from reason alone, but if that justice is to be admitted among men it must be reciprocal. Humanly speaking, the laws of natural justice, lacking any natural sanction, are unavailing among men. In fact, such laws merely benefit the wicked and injure the just, since the just respect them while others do not do so in return. So there must be covenants and positive laws to unite rights with duties and to direct justice to its object. In the state of nature, where everything is common, I owe nothing to those to whom I have promised nothing, and I recognize as belonging to others only those things that are of no use to me.

第六章　论法律

通过社会契约，我们赋予了政治体以生命和存在；现在的问题就是通过立法来赋予它行动和意志。因为使政治体得以形成和结合的那个原始行为并没有决定政治体为了保存它自己而应该做些什么。

事物之所以美好，之所以合乎秩序，是由事物的本性所决定的，而与人类的契约无关。所有的正义都来自于上帝，唯有上帝才是正义的根源；只要我们懂得如何从这个神圣的根源得到正义，我们就将不再需要政府或者法律了。毫无疑问，有一种纯粹源自理性的普遍的正义，但是如果这种正义要得到所有人的承认，那么它就必须是互惠的。但是从人类的角度出发，如果没有任何天然的制裁，天然的正义法则在人类中就是虚妄无效的。事实上，如果只有正义之士尊重正义法则，而其余的人不能同样如此做来回报这些正义之士，那么这些正义的法则就只能是有利于那些邪恶的人，而伤害那些正义之士。因此，必须有契约和实际的法律来把权利和义务结合起来，并且指导正义实现它的目标。在自然状态中，任何东西都是公共的，对于那些我并没有向其做出过承诺的人，我什么都不欠他们的，而且我又只承认那些对于我而言是没有用的东西才是属于他人的。但是，在公

But this is no longer the case in civil society, where all rights are determined by law.

Yet what, in the last analysis, is law? If we simply try to define it in terms of metaphysical ideas, we shall go on talking without reaching any understanding; and when we have said what natural law is, we shall still not know what the law of the state is.

I have already said that the general will cannot relate to any particular object. For such a particular object is either within the state or outside the state. If it is outside, then a will which is alien to it is not general with regard to it; if the object is within the state, it forms a part of the state. Then there comes into being a relationship between the whole and the part which involves two separate entities, the part being one, and the whole, less that particular part, being the other. But a whole less a particular part is no longer a whole; and so as long as this relationship exists there is no whole but only two unequal parts, from which it follows that the will of the one is no longer general with respect to the other.

But when the people as a whole makes rules for the people as a whole, it is dealing only with itself; and if any relationship emerges, it is between the entire body seen from one perspective and the same entire body seen from another, without any division whatever. Here the matter concerning which a rule is made is as general as the will which makes it. And *this* is the kind of act which I call a law.

When I say that the province of the law is always general, I mean that the law considers all subjects collectively and all actions in the abstract; it does not consider any individual man or any specific action. Thus the law may well lay down that there shall be privileges, but it may not nominate the persons who shall have those privileges; the law may establish several *classes of citizen*, and even specify the qualifications which shall give access to those several classes, but it may not say that this man or that shall be admitted; the law may set up a royal government and an hereditary succession, but it may not elect a king or choose a royal family— in a word, no function which deals with the individual falls within the province of the legislative power.

民社会中，情况就不再是这样的了，那里所有的权利都是被法律加以规定的。

然而，法律归根到底是什么呢？如果我们仅仅是在形而上学的观念上来规定它，那么我们就将会持续进行一种达不到任何理解的论说；而且即使我们说明了什么是自然法则，我们也可能仍然不知道什么是国家法。

我已经说过，公意不能指向任何个别对象。因为这样一个个别对象要么在国家之内，要么在国家之外。如果它在国家之外，它的意志对国家而言因属外来便不能是公意；如果它在国家之内，它便是国家一部分，那么全体与部分之间便形成了两个单独实体的关系，部分是其中的一方，而排除了这一部分的全体是另一方。但缺少了某个部分的全体就不再是全体；而且只要这种关系存在，这里就没有全体，而只有两个不等的部分。由此导致的结果便是一方的意志就不比另一方更加是公意。

但是当作为整体的人们为作为整体的人们制定规则的时候，他们所考虑的便只是他们自己了；而且如果这里形成了任何一种关系，它都是某个视角下的整体同另外一个视角下的同一个整体之间的关系，对整体并没有任何分裂。这里人们对其做出规定的某件事就具有了公共性，正如做出这种规定的意志具有公共性一样，而且这就是我称之为法律的那种行为。

当我说法律的范围总是公共的事物的时候，我的意思是法律集体地考虑所有的臣民并抽象地考虑所有的行为；它不会考虑一个个别的人或者一个特殊的行为。因而法律完全可以规定有特权存在，但是它却不能指定哪一个人拥有那些特权；法律也可以把臣民划分为几个等级，它甚至可以详细地规定获得这些等级资格的条件，但是它却不能指明这个人或者那个人属于哪一个等级；法律还可以确立一个皇家政府以及一套世袭继承制，但是它却不能选定一个国王，或者选定一家皇室。总之，没有一项针对个别对象的职能进入立法权力的范围。

On this analysis, it is immediately clear that we can no longer ask *who* is to make laws, because laws are acts of the general will; no longer ask if the prince is above the law, because he is a part of the state; no longer ask if the law can be unjust, because no one is unjust to himself; and no longer ask how we can be both free and subject to laws, for the laws are but registers of what we ourselves desire.

It is also clear that since the law unites universality of will with universality of the field of legislation, anything that any man, no matter who, commands on his own authority is not a law; even what the sovereign itself commands with respect to a partieular object is not a law but a decree, not an act of sovereignty but an act of government.

Any state which is ruled by law I call a 'republic', whatever the form of its constitution; for then, and then alone, does the public interest govern and then alone is the 'public thing'— the *res publica*— a reality. All legitimate government is 'republican', ① I shall explain later what government is.

Laws are really nothing other than the conditions on which civil Society exists. A people, since it is subject to laws, ought to be the author of them. The right of laying down the rules of society belongs only to those who form the society, but how can they exercise it? Is it to be by common agreement, by a sudden inspiration?

---

① By this word I understand not only an aristocracy or democracy, but generally any government directed by the general will, which is law. If it is to be legitimate, the government must not be united with the sovereign, but must serve it as its ministry. So even a monarchy can be a republic. This will be clarified in Book III.

根据这个分析，我们立刻可以明白，我们可以不再问由谁来制定法律，因为法律是公意的行为；我们可以不再问君主是不是高于法律的，因为君主只是国家的一部分；我们可以不再问法律会不会不公正，因为没有一个人会对他自己不公正；我们可以不再问我们何以是自由的而又要服从法律，因为法律只不过是我们自己的愿望的记录而已。

我们还可以明了，既然法律把意志的普遍性和立法范围的普遍性联合了起来，那么任何一个人，不管他是谁，凭借他的权威对任何事发出的号令就不是法律；即便是主权者自身针对一个个别的对象发出的命令也不是法律，而只是一道政令；这不是主权的行为，而只是一项政府的行为。

对于任何一个依照法律进行统治的国家，不管它的构成形式如何，我都称之为“共和国”。因为在这里，而且只有在这里才是公共利益在统治着，只有在这里“公共事物”才成为现实。任何一个合法的政府都是共和政体的①，我后面将会解释政府是什么。

法律实际上只不过是公民社会得以存在的条件。人民由于要受法律的支配，所以他们就应当是法律的制订者。制订社会规则的权利只能属于那些构成社会的人，但是他们如何行使这种权利呢？是根据自发的认同或者突发的灵感吗？

---

① 我理解这个词语不仅仅是指贵族制或者民主制，而是通称任何一种在公意，也就是法律指导下的政府。如果一个政府要成为合法的，它就必须不得和主权者联合在一起，而只能作为执行部门为主权者服务。这样，甚至君主制也可以是共和制的。这一点将在本书的第三卷中详细说明。

Has the body politic an organ to declare its will? Who is to give it the foresight necessary to formulate enactments and proclaim them in advance, and how is it to announce them in the hour of need? How can a blind multitude, Which often does not know What it wants, because it seldom knows what is good for it, undertake by itself an enterprise as vast and difficult as a system of legislation? By themselves the people always will what is good, but by themselves they do not always discern it. The general will is always rightful, but the judgement which guides it is not always enlightened. It must be made to see things as they are, and sometimes as they should be seen; it must be shown the good path which it is seeking, and secured against seduction by the desires of individuals; it must be given a sense of situation and season, so as to weigh immediate and tangible advantages against distant and hidden evils. Individuals see the good and reject it: the public desires the good but does not see it. Both equally need guidance. Individuals must be obliged to subordinate their will to their reason; the public must be taught to recognize what it desires. Such public enlightenment would produce a union of understanding and will in the social body, bring the parts into perfect harmony and lift whole to its fullest strength. Hence the necessity of a lawgiver.

政治体有没有一个机构来表达自己的意志呢？谁赋予政治体那种必要的远见事先就能明确地表达出这些规定并且宣布它们呢？政治体又是如何在必要的时刻宣布它们呢？那些盲目的群众，他们通常并不知道他们想要什么，因为他们很少知道什么对他们是有益处的，那么他们自己又如何能从事像立法体系那样重大而且困难的事业呢？对于他们自己而言，他们总是希望得到对他们有益处的东西，但是他们自己并不能认清楚这些东西。公意永远是正确的，但是那些指引公意的判断并不总是明智的，所以它就必须被示以事情的真相，而且有些时候又必须被示以事情应该呈现的样子；必须给它指明一条它应追求的美好道路，而且要保证它不被私人的欲望所诱惑；必须赋予它对处境和理性的一种判断力，这样它才能权衡当下的切实利益与长远的隐患；个人看得到幸福却又拒绝它，公众期望幸福却又看不到它。这两者同样都需要指导。必须强迫个人使他们的欲望服从于他们的理性；必须教会公众认清他们真正希望的东西。这种公众智慧将会在社会共同体中创造理智和意志的结合体，使共同体的各部分达到和谐一致，并且使得共同体实现它的最大力量。因此，必须要有一个立法者。

CHAPTER 7
The Lawgiver

To discover the rules of society that are best suited to nations, there would need to exist a superior intelligence, who could understand the passions of men without feeling any of them, who had no affinity with our nature but knew it to the full, whose happiness was independent of ours, but who would nevertheless make our happiness his concern, who would be content to wait in the fullness of time for a distant glory, and to labour in one age to enjoy the fruits in another. ① Gods would be needed to give men laws.

The same reasoning which Caligula used empirically, Plato used philosophically in his dialogue *The Statesman* to reach a definition of civil or kingly man. But if it is true that great princes seldom appear, how much more rare must a great lawgiver be? A prince has only to follow a model which the lawgiver provides. The lawgiver is the engineer who invents the machine; the prince is merely the mechanic who sets it up and operates it.

---

① A people does not become famous until its constitution begins to decline. We do not know for how many centuries the constitution of Lycurgus gave happiness to the Spartans before there was talk about them in the rest of Greece.

第七章　论立法者

为了找到一个最适合于所有国家的社会法则，就需要有一个最高的智慧存在。这个最高的智慧能够理解人类的感情但是又不会被人类的感情左右；它与我们人类的本性没有任何关系，但是却能完全地了解人类的本性；它的幸福独立于我们的幸福，但是它却会把我们的幸福作为它的关怀；它乐意花费充足的时间去等待一个长远的荣耀；它也乐意在这个时代里辛勤劳作，而在下一个时代中去享受劳作的果实①。人类真得要神明来为他们立法了吧。

柏拉图在他的对话体著作《政治家篇》中，从哲学的角度运用了卡里古拉从经验角度运用的同样的推论，以求达到对政治人物或王者的界定。但是如果说伟大的国君很少出现的话，那么一个伟大的立法者的出现该会稀缺到什么样的程度呢？因为一个国君只不过是遵循伟大立法者所提供的模型而已。立法者是发明机器的工程师，而国王仅仅是组装机器、操纵机器的技术工人而已。

---

① 除非一个民族的制度开始衰落了，否则这个民族是不会出名的。人们往往并不知道莱格古士的制度在希腊其他各国开始谈论它们之前，早已经给斯巴达人带来了多少个世纪的幸福了。

Montesquieu says that at the birth of political societies, it is the leaders of the republic who shape the institutions but that afterwards it is the institutions which shape the leaders of the republic.

Whoever ventures on the enterprise of setting up a people must be ready, shall we say, to change human nature, to transform each individual, who by himself is entirely complete and solitary, into a part of a much greater whole, from which that same individual will then receive, in a sense, his life and his being. The founder of nations must weaken the structure of man in order to fortify it, to replace the physical and independent existence we have all received from nature with a moral and communal existence. In a word each man must be stripped of his own powers, and given powers which are external to him, and which he cannot use without the help of others. The nearer men's natural powers are to extinction or annihilation, and the stronger and more lasting their acquired powers, the stronger and more perfect is the social institution. So much so, that if each citizen can do nothing whatever except through cooperation with others, and if the acquired power of the whole is equal to, or greater than, the sum of the natural powers of each of the individuals, then we can say that law-making has reached the highest point of perfection.

The lawgiver is, in every respect, an extraordinary man in the state. Extraordinary not only because of his genius, but equally because of his office, which is neither that of the government nor that of the sovereign. This office which gives the republic its constitution has no place in that constitution. It is a special and superior function which has nothing to do with empire over men; for just as he who has command over men must not have command over laws, neither must he who has command over laws have command over men; otherwise, the laws, in ministering to the legislator's passions, would often merely perpetuate his injustices, and partial judgements would inevitably vitiate the sanctity of his works.

孟德斯鸠说，当一个政治社会诞生的时候，是共和国的领导者创造了制度，而在那之后，是由制度来塑造共和国的领导者。

我们可以说，任何一个敢于从事为一个民族创建制度的事业的人，就必须准备好改变人类的天性，准备好把一个个从其自身而言完全是完整而且独立的个人转变成一个更大的整体的一部分。从某种意义上说，这些个人就是从这个整体中获得他们的生命和存在的。为了增强民族的力量，这个民族的创立者就必须弱化他们原有的组织方式，用一种道德性的、公共性的存在方式代替人们得之于自然的那种生理的、独立的存在方式。总之，必须剥去一个人自身本有的力量，而赋予他本身之外的力量，而且对于这种本身之外的力量，如果没有别人的帮助，他就不能运用。人类自然的力量越是接近于消失或者灭绝，他们获得的力量就越强大、越持久，社会制度就越巩固、越完美。如果能达到这样的程度，即如若不通过和其余的人合作，每个公民就什么都不能做，而且如果他从整体所获得的力量等于、甚至是大于所有的人自然力量的总和，那么我们就可以说，立法就已经达到了它完美的顶点。

立法者在任何方面都是国家中的一个非凡的人。他的非凡不仅仅是由于他的天才，同样也是因为他的职务，这一职务不是行政职务，也不是主权职务。这种创立了国家机构的职务在国家机构中却不居于任何位置。它是一种独特的、超越的职能，它与对人民的统治没有任何关系；因为正像对人们下达命令的人不能制定法律一样，制定法律的人也不能对人们发号施令；否则的话，法律会被立法者的感情所左右，而要经常维护他的不公正，他的偏袒的判决就会不可避免地损害他的工作的神圣性。

When Lycurgus gave laws to his country, he began by abdicating his monarchical functions. It was the habit of most Greek cities to confer on foreigners the task of framing their laws. The modern republics of Italy have often copied this custom; the republic of Geneva did so, and found that it worked well. ① Rome in its happiest age saw all the crimes of the Tyranny revived within its borders, and came near to perishing simply because it had put both the legislative authority and the sovereign power in the same hands.

And yet even the decemvirs themselves never arrogated the right to make any law on their own authority alone. 'Nothing we propose to you,' they said to the people, 'can become law without your consent. Romans, be yourselves the authors of the laws which are to ensure your happiness.'

Thus the man who frames the laws ought not to have any legislative right, and the people itself cannot, even should it wish, strip itself of this untransferable right; for, according to the fundamental compact, it is only the general will which compels individuals and there can be no assurance that an individual will is in conformity with the general will until it has submitted to the free suffrage of the people— I have said this already, but it is worth repeating.

And so we find in the work of the lawgiver two things which look contradictory— a task which is beyond human powers and a non-existent authority for its execution.

---

① Those who think of Calvin merely as a theologian do not realize the extent of his genius. The codification of our wise edicts, in which he had a large share, does him as much credit as his *Institutes*. Whatever revolutions may take place in our church, the memory of that great man will not cease to be honoured among the adepts of that religion while the love of country and of liberty still lives among us.

当莱格古士给他的国家颁布法律的时候，他是在让出了他的王位后才开始的。大多数希腊城市的习惯是把为自己制订法律的任务授予异邦人。近代的意大利诸共和国经常模仿这种习俗，日内瓦共和国也是这样做的，并且还发现这种做法运行良好①。在罗马最辉煌的时期，我们就可以看到暴政的种种罪恶已经在它的内部复活，并且可以看到它已接近于毁灭的边缘，原因只是在于它使立法权威和主权权力掌握在同样的人手里。

而且，即使罗马十人委员会自己都从来没有仅仅凭借他们的权威就冒称他们拥有立法的权利。他们告诉罗马人民："我们向你们建议的任何事情没有你们的同意都不能成为法律。罗马人，请你们做你们自己的法律的制订者，以便保证你们的幸福。"

因而，编订法律的人就不应该拥有任何立法权，而且人民自己，就算他有此意愿，也不能剥夺自己这种不可转移的权利；因为根据基本公约，只有公意才能强制个人，而且我们又不能保证个人意志会是和公意保持一致的，除非它已经被提交全体人民自由投票表决了。这一点我已经说过了，再重复一遍也是值得的。

因此，在立法者的工作中，我们发现了两件看似矛盾的事情——一项超乎人的能力之外的任务以及把它付诸执行的权威的缺位。

---

① 那些认为加尔文只不过是一个神学家的人并没有认识到他的天才的高度。在我们明智的法令编纂工作中，他起了很大的作用，这给他带来的荣誉就同他的《体制》一书（全名为《论基督教的体制》）所带给他的荣誉一样的大。不管我们的教会中可能会发生什么样的变革，只要对国家、对自由的热爱仍然存在于我们中间，对这位伟大人物的记忆就不止不于宗教人士的尊敬。

There is another difficulty which deserves mention. Those sages who insist on speaking in their own language to the vulgar instead of in the vulgar language will not be understood. For there are thousands of ideas which cannot be translated into the popular idiom. Perspectives which are general and goals remote are alike beyond the range of the common herd; it is difficult for the individual, who has no taste for any scheme of government but that which serves his private interest, to appreciate the advantages to be derived from the lasting austerities which good laws impose. For a newly formed people to understand wise principles of politics and to follow the basic rules of statecraft, the effect would have to become the cause; the social spirit which must be the product of social institutions would have to preside over the setting up of those institutions; men would have to have already become before the advent of law that which they become as a result of law. And as the lawgiver can for these reasons employ neither force nor argument, he must have recourse to an authority of another order, one which can compel without violence and persuade without convincing.

It is this which has obliged the founders of nations throughout history to appeal to divine intervention and to attribute their own wisdom to the Gods; for then the people, feeling subject to the laws of the state as they are to those of nature, and detecting the same hand in the creation of both man and the nation, obey freely and bear with docility the yoke of the public welfare.

A sublime reason, which soars above the heads of the common people, produces those rules which the lawgiver puts into the mouth of the

这里还有一个难题值得我们关注。如果那些智者坚持要用他们自己的语言而不是用普通人的语言向普通人讲话，那么智者们就不能被普通人理解，因为有很多观念无法翻译成通俗语言。过于概括的观念和太遥远的目标同样都超出普通人的能力范围；对于那些除了关心与他自己的私人利益密切相关的政府计划，对于其他的政府计划没有任何兴味的人来讲，让他们对那些从持续的苦行中（这种苦行是良好的法律要求他们所从事的）得到的好处心存感激是很困难的。为了使一个新建立的民族能够领会那些明智的政治原则，并且遵循那些治理国家的根本准则，我们必须倒果为因：那些本来应该是社会制度的产物的社会精神将不得不反过来支配这些社会制度的创立，人们将不得不在法律出现之前就变成本来应该是由法律所塑造的那个样子。由于这些原因，立法者便既不能使用暴力，也不能运用辩论，他必须求助于另外一种权威，这种权威可以不以暴力而能强制人，不用论证而能说服人。

这就是整个历史中，所有民族的创立者都被迫求助于神明的干预，并且把他们自己的智慧归功于神明的缘故了。因为这样，人们就会觉得服从国家的法律就如同服从自然的法则一样，也会发觉人类的诞生和国家的创立掌握在同一只手中，那么他们就会自由地服从并且顺从地承担起公共福祉的重担了。

一种超乎普通人能力的崇高理性创造了种种规则，立法者把这种种规则放到不朽的神明口中，这样就可以借助于这

immortals, thus compelling by divine authority persons who cannot be moved by human prudence.[1] But it is not for every man to make the Gods speak, or to gain credence if he pretends to be an interpreter of the divine word. The lawgiver's great soul is the true miracle which must vindicate his mission. Any man can carve tablets of stone, or bribe an oracle, claim a secret intercourse with some divinity, train a bird to whisper in his ear, or discover some other vulgar means of imposing himself on the people. A man who can do such things may conceivably bring together a company of fools, but he will never establish an empire, and his bizarre creation will perish with him. Worthless authority may set up transitory bonds, but only wisdom makes lasting ones. The Law of the Hebrews, which still lives, and that of the child of Ishmael which has ruled half the world for ten centuries, still proclaim today the greatness of the men who first enunciated them; and even though proud philosophy and the blind spirit of faction may regard them as nothing but lucky impostors, the true statesman sees, and admires in their institutions, the hand of that great and powerful genius which lies behind all lasting things.

Even so, we must not conclude from this, with Warburton, that religion and politics have the same purpose among men; it is simply that at the birth of nations, the one serves as the instrument of the other.

---

① 'The truth is,' writes Machiavelli, 'that there has never been in any country an extraordinary legislator who has not invoked the deity; for otherwise his laws would not have been accepted. A wise man knows many useful truths which cannot be demonstrated in such a way as to convince other people.' (*Discourses on Livy*, Book v, Chapter xi.)

种神圣的权威来约束那些仅靠人类的审慎所不能感动的人①。但是，并不是说任何一个人都可以借助于神明立言的，也不是说一个人只要他假装是神明的话语的诠释者就可以得到人们的信任。只有立法者的伟大灵魂，才是可以证明他的使命的真正的奇迹。任何一个人都可以刻立石碑，或者收买一个神谕，或者冒称和某些神灵的秘密感通，或者训练一只小鸟在其耳边吐露神言，又或者寻找其他一些粗鄙的欺骗别人的方式。一个只能做这种事情的人有可能会纠集一群傻瓜，但是绝不能建立一个帝国，而且他的那个荒唐的创造也将会随他本人一起毁灭。毫无价值的权威可以建立一种短暂的结合，但是唯有智慧才能确立一种长久的结合。那些今天还存在着的希伯来人的法律，以及那些统治了半个世界近十个世纪的伊斯梅尔人的后嗣的法律，直到今天仍然在显示着那些首先阐明这些法律的人的伟大。即使自高自大的哲学和盲目的派系精神可能会把这些人仅仅看作是侥幸的骗子，但是真正的政治家将会在这些人的制度中，看到并且崇拜那些主导了所有持久的事物的伟大而且强力的天才手段。

即使这样，我们也不能由此得出跟华伯登一样的结论，即宗教和政治在人们中间有着相同的目标；而是应该说，在一个民族诞生的时候，一个〔1〕是被用作另一个〔2〕的工具的。

---

① 马基雅弗利写道："事实是，在任何一个国家中都从来没有一个可以不借助于神明的非凡的立法者。因为若是不借助于神明，他的法律将不会被人们接受。一个智者可能知道很多有用的真理，但却不能通过某种方式论证这些真理以使人们信服。"（《李维论》，第五卷，第十一章）

〔1〕 指宗教。

〔2〕 指政治。

CHAPTER 8

The People

Just as an architect who puts up a large building first surveys and tests the ground to see if it can bear the weight, so the wise lawgiver begins not by laying down laws good in themselves, but by finding out whether the people for whom the laws are intended is able to support them. Such reasoning led Plato to refuse to provide laws for the Arcadians or the Cyreneans, because he well knew that those peoples, being rich, would not tolerate equality. Crete, too, provides an example of good laws and bad men, for the people Milos tried to discipline were dominated by their vices.

The world has seen a thousand splendid nations that could not have accepted good laws, and even those that might have accepted them could have done so only for short periods of their long history. Nations, like men, are teachable only in their youth; with age they become incorrigible. Once customs are established and prejudices rooted, reform is a dangerous and fruitless enterprise; a people cannot bear to see its evils touched, even if only to be eradicated; it is like a stupid, pusillanimous invalid who trembles at the sight of a physician.

第八章　论人民

正像一个建筑师要建造一幢大厦，他首先就要勘测和检查地基，以检查它能否承受大厦的重量一样，一个贤明的立法者不是一开始就制订一部就其本身来说很好的法律，而是要弄清楚他为之制定法律的那些人民能不能接受这些法律。正是这种理性使得柏拉图拒绝为阿加狄亚人和昔兰尼人制订法律，因为他清楚地知道那两个民族的人非常富有，因而是不能容忍平等的。克立特就为我们提供了一个有着好的法律和坏的人民的民族例子，因为米诺斯力试图训导的乃是被邪恶所支配的人民。

世界上曾经有过上千个煊赫一时但是不能接受好法律的民族，即使是那些可以接受好的法律的民族，也只是在它们很长的历史中一个很短的时期内能够做到这一点。民族就像个人一样，只有在它们年轻的时候才是可教的；随着年龄的增长，它们就逐渐变得无可救药了。一旦习俗形成，或者偏见一旦生根，改革就将是一件危险而且毫无结果的事情。人民不能容忍别人哪怕是为了消除他们的缺点而去触碰其缺点，就像一个愚蠢而且懦弱的病人见到医生就浑身发抖一样。

I am not denying that just as certain afflictions unhinge men's minds and banish their memory of the past, so there are certain violent epochs and revolutions in states which have the same effect on peoples that psychological shocks may have on individuals; only instead of forgetting the past, they look back on it in horror, and then the state, after being consumed by civil war, is born again, so to speak, from its own ashes, and leaps from the arms of death to regain the vigour of youth. Such was the experience of Sparta at the time of Lycurgus, of Rome after the Tarquins, and, in the modern world, of Holland and Switzerland after the expulsion of the tyrants.

But such events are unusual; they are exceptional cases to be explained by the special constitution of the states concerned. It could not even happen twice to the same people; because although a people can make itself free while it is still uncivilized, it cannot do so when its civil energies are worn out. Disturbances may well destroy a civil society without a revolution being able to restore it, so that as soon as the chains are broken, the state falls apart and exists no longer; then what is needed is a master, not a liberator. Free peoples, remember this maxim: liberty can be gained, but never *regained*.

For nations, as for men, there is a time of maturity which they must reach before they are made subject to law; but the maturity of a people is not always easily recognized; and something done too soon will prove abortive. Peoples differ; one is amenable to discipline from the beginning; another is not, even after ten centuries. The Russians have never been effectively governed because the attempt to govern them was made too early. Peter the Great had the talent of a copyist; he had no true genius, which is creative

我不否认，正像某些疾病可以使人们头脑失常并且抹去他们对过去的记忆一样，在国家中也有一些动荡的时期或者革命会对人们产生影响，这种影响类似于心灵上的震惊可能会对个人产生的影响，只不过这时人们不是对忘记过去，而是对回忆过去感到惊恐。接下来那个由于内战而毁灭的国家可以说会在它的废墟上被重新建立起来，跳出死亡的拥抱而重新获得青春的活力。莱格古士时期的斯巴达，塔尔干王朝之后的罗马，以及在近代驱逐了暴君之后的荷兰和瑞士都有过这样的经历。

但是这种事例是不常见的，它们是特殊事例，需要从相关国家的特殊制度来解释。这种事情也不能在同一个民族身上发生两次，因为虽然人民处于未开化状态的时候，他们可以使自己获得自由，但是当他们的文明精神耗尽了的时候，他们就不能再做到这一点了。动乱可以完全破坏一个公民社会，而革命又不能重建它，所以一旦锁链被打碎之后，这个国家就会分崩离析而不再存在。从此，人民所需要的就会是一个主人，而非一个解放者。自由的人，请你们记住这句格言：“人们可以获得自由，但是却永远不能重新获得自由。”

对于一个国家，正如对于一个人，在他被要求去服从法律之前，必须要有一段时间使他达到成熟期，但是一个民族的成熟与否不是很容易就能认清的；而且如果有些事情被提前做了的话，那它必将会夭折。各民族是不同的，有的民族一开始就能遵守纪律，而另外的民族就算是经过了十个世纪也不能。俄罗斯人从来就没有被有效地治理过，因为对他们治理的尝试做得太早了。彼得大帝具有一种模仿的天赋，但是他没有一种真正的天才，即那种创造

and makes everything from nothing. Some of the things he did were sound; most were misguided. He saw that his people was uncivilized, but he did not see that it was unready for government; he sought to civilize his subjects when he ought rather to have drilled them. He tried to turn them into Germans or Englishmen instead of making them Russians. He urged his subjects to be what they were not and so prevented them from becoming what they might have been. This is just how a French tutor trains his pupil to shine for a brief moment in his childhood and then grow up into a nonentity. The Russian Empire would like to subjugate Europe and will find itself subjugated. The Tartars, its subjects or neighbours, will become its masters— and ours. Such a revolution seems to me inevitable. All the kings of Europe are labouring in concert to hasten its coming.

性的、能凭空创造一些事物的天才。他所做的一些事情是合理的，但大多数是举措失当的。他看到他的民族是未开化的，但是他却没有看到他的民族尚没有准备好接受治理；他试图使他的民族文明，而那时他本应该是训练他们的。他不是尽力使他的人民变成俄罗斯人，而是试图使他们成为德国人或英国人。他催促他的臣民成为他们本来不应是的样子，这样便阻止了他们成为他们本来可以变成的那个样子。这正像一个法国的指导教师训练他的学生，想使他们在幼年时代短时间内就显姓扬名，但是他们长大后却一事无成。俄罗斯帝国想要征服欧洲，但最终将会发现被征服的是它自己。它的附庸和邻居鞑靼人将会成为他们的主人——也会成为我们的主人的。这样一种革命在我看来是不可避免的，欧洲所有的国王正在协同努力以加速它的到来。

CHAPTER 9

The People: Continued

Just as nature has set bounds to the stature of a well-formed man, outside which he is either a giant or a dwarf, so, in what concerns the best constitution for a state, there are limits to the size it can have if it is to be neither too large to be wellgoverned nor too small to maintain itself. In the body politic there is a maximum of strength which must not be exceeded, and which is often fallen short of as a result of expansion. The more the social bond is stretched, the slacker it becomes; and in general a small state is relatively stronger for its size than a large one.

A thousand considerations bear witness to the truth of this. First, administration becomes more difficult over great distances, just as a weight becomes heavier at the end of a long lever. Government becomes more burdensome as the area is enlarged, for each town has its own administration, which the people pays for, and each region has its administration, which the people also pays for, then each province has one, and so on up to the greater governments, the satrapies, the viceroyalties, each costing more the higher they rise and always paid for by the unfortunate populace; and then on top of all comes the supreme administration, bearing down on everyone. Such a great number of charges added to charges continually exhausts the subjects; and far from being better governed by this hierarchy of orders,

第九章　论人民(续)

就如同大自然给一个发育正常的人的身高设定了一个界限，如果超过了这个界限他就会成为一个巨人或者侏儒；同样，与一个国家最合适的体制密切相关，国家的幅员也存在着一个界限，它不能太大，否则便不能很好地治理；它也不能太小，否则它就不能保存自己。每个政治体都有一个它不能超越的最大力量的限度，而由于领土的扩张，政治体的力量经常达不到这个最大值。社会的纽带越是延伸，它就变得越脆弱。一般来讲，小的国家由于它的幅员小，相对来说它会比一个大国更加强大。

有上千个证据可以证明这一点的正确性。首先，距离越远，管理就会变得越困难，正像一个重物越是处于一个长杠杆的底端，就会变得越重。随着行政领域的扩展，行政就会变得负担越重，因为每一个市镇都有它的行政机构，这都需要人民负担，此外每个地区又有它的行政机构，这也需要人民负担；接下来每个省还有它的行政机构，如此等等一直到更高级的行政区划，如巡抚府、总督府；而且行政等级越是上升，其开销也就越大，而所有这些花费总是要由那些不幸的平民来负担；最终到达行政区划的最高点便是最高政府，它压跨了所有的人。如此大量层层叠加的负荷榨干了臣民们，所以由于这层层的等级，人民远不是被治理得更好

they are much worse off than they would be if they had only one administration over them. As it is, there is hardly any public revenue available for emergencies, and when the state is faced with such a need, it trembles on the verge of ruin.

Nor is this all. Not only is the government less vigorous and swift in enforcing respect for the law, in preventing nuisances, correcting abuses and thwarting any seditious movements that may arise in distant quarters, but at the same time the people has less feeling for governors whom it never sees, for a homeland that seems as vast as the world, and for fellow-citizens who are mostly strangers. The same laws will not suit so many various provinces, which, with their different customs and contrasting climates, cannot tolerate the same form of government. Having different laws only creates misunderstanding and confusion among peoples who live under the same governors and are in continuous communication with one another; they intermingle and intermarry, but if different sets of rules prevail, they will not even know if what they call their patrimony is really their own. Talents are hidden, virtues are ignored and vices remain unpunished when such a multitude of men, who do not know one another, is brought together in the same place by one single seat of supreme administration. The governors have too much to do to see everything for themselves; their clerks rule the state. And the measures needed to maintain a general authority, which so many scattered officials try to evade or exploit, absorb all political attention, so none is left to study the people's happiness, and hardly any left for its defence in case of need. This body which is too big for its constitution collapses and perishes, crushed by its own weight.

了，如果只有一个行政机构管理他们的话，那么人民会比现在生活得更好。实际上，国家几乎没有任何可以动用的公共收入以应付突发的事件，当国家面对这样一种告急的情况时，它就会在灭亡的边缘摇摇欲坠了。

这还不是全部。不仅仅政府在坚持对法律的尊重上、在防止动乱上、在纠正滥用权力上以及在反对可能由某个遥远的地区爆发的任何妨碍社会治安的运动上是不够强壮和灵敏的；与此同时人民对于他们从来没有见过的管理者对于广阔如整个世界的广大领土对于与他们几乎是完全陌生的同胞公民，也很少有感情。同一个法律不能适用于如此多的不同地区，因为这些不同地区有着各自不同的习俗和迥然相反的气候，他们不能承受同一种形式的政府。而有不同的法律则会在人民中间产生误解和混乱，因为这些人民生活在同一个管理者的管理之下，并且彼此之间不断地交往着；这些人民互相结合、互相通婚，如果他们顺从了别人的种种习俗，那么他们就会甚至不知道他们所谓的世袭遗风是否真正是他们自己的了。当这样一大群彼此互不相识的人由于一个至高的行政职位而被聚集在同一个地方的时候，他们的天赋就会被湮没，德行会被忽视，邪恶也会得不到惩罚。管理者有太多的事情要做，以至于他们不能亲自留心政事，而他们的职员统治了这个国家。为维护一个公共的权威（这个权威正是那么多边远地区的官员们竭力要逃避或者窃取的）所必须要采取的措施就占去了所有政治上的精力，如此一来便没有剩余的精力再去关心人民的福祉了，而且在一旦需要的时候，也几乎没有剩余的精力去保卫人民。这样一个相对于体制来讲过于庞大的政治体就会在其自身重力的压迫之下分崩离析并毁灭。

On the other hand, a state if it is to have strength must give itself some solid foundation, so that it can resist the shocks that it is bound to experience and sustain the exertions that it must make to preserve itself; for all peoples generate a kind of centrifugal force, by which they brush continuously against one another, and they all attempt to expand at the expense of their neighbours, like the vortices of Descartes. Thus the weak are always in danger of being swallowed up, and indeed no people can well preserve itself except by achieving a kind of equilibrium with all the others which makes the pressure everywhere the same for all.

This shows us that there are reasons for expansion and reasons for contraction; and indeed it is not the least part of political wisdom to judge, as between the one and the other, the precise balance which is most conducive to the preservation of the state. In general one might say that any reasons for expansion, which are exterior and relative, ought to be less compelling than the reasons for contraction, which are internal and absolute. A strong and healthy constitution is the first thing to look for because the strength which comes from good government is more reliable than the resources which large territories yield.

One may add that there have been states whose political structure was such that the necessity of conquest was part of their very constitution, states which, in order to maintain themselves at all, were obliged to enlarge themselves unceasingly. Possibly they have congratulated themselves on this, as a fortunate necessity; but reflection on the same necessity must also have shown them that at the end of their greatness lay the inevitable moment of their fall.

另一方面，一个国家如果想要拥有强大的力量，就必须赋予自己某种坚固的根基，如此一来，它才能够经受得住那些它必须要经历的种种震荡，并且保持住那些为了保护它自己而必须要做的种种努力；因为所有的民族都有一种离心力，由于这种离心力，它们彼此之间会持续不断地产生摩擦，而且他们都试图以牺牲他们的邻居为代价进行扩张，就像笛卡儿所说的漩涡。因此那些弱小的民族总是会处于一种被吞并的危险当中，而且事实上，除非所有的民族能够达到一种均衡的状态，使得在任何地方大家的压力都是相等的，否则任何民族都不能保存自己。

这告诉我们，扩张有其理由，而收缩同样有其理由；如果能够在扩张和收缩之间找到一种精确的均衡，使之最能有益于国家保存自己，事实上那将是政治智慧中极为重要的方面。一般地，我们可以说，扩张的理由是外在的、相对的，而收缩的理由则是内在的、绝对的，所以扩张的理由比收缩的理由具有较少的强制性。寻求一种强大而健康的体制是首先要做的一件事，因为一种源自于良好政府的力量要比广阔的领土所能提供的丰富资源更加可靠。

有人可能会补充说，曾经存在过这样政治结构的国家，即征服的必要性就是它们体制的一部分，这样的国家仅仅是为了保存它们自己就被迫无休止地扩张。可能它们曾经为自己这种幸运的必要性而大加庆贺，但是对这种必要性的深思会告诉它们，在它们的鼎盛之极，暗藏着它们不可避免的垮台时刻。

CHAPTER 10

The People: Continued

There are two ways of measuring a body politic, by the extent of its territory and by the number of its people; and there must be a certain balance between these two dimensions if the state is to achieve its best size. Men make the state and the soil nourishes men; thus the right balance requires that there be land enough to feed the inhabitants and as many inhabitants as the land can feed. It is in this proportion that the maximum strength of a given number of persons is brought forth; for if there is too much territory, defence is burdensome, cultivation inadequate and produce excessive; and this soon becomes the cause of defensive wars; while if, on the other hand, there is too little land, the state must live on what it can import at the discretion of its neighbours, and this soon becomes the cause of offensive wars. Any people which has to choose between commerce and war is essentially weak; it depends on its neighbours; it depends on contingencies; it will never have more than a short, uncertain existence; either it conquers and ends its predicament, or it is conquered and exists no more. It can safeguard itself in freedom only by means of littleness or bigness.

One cannot specify the exact mathematical proportion there should be between the area of the land and the number of inhabitants, because of the different characteristics of different places, differences in degrees of fertility, in the nature of the produce, in the effects of climate;

第十章　论人民(续)

我们有两种方式来衡量一个政治体，即通过它的领土面积以及通过它的人口数量。如果一个国家要达到它的最佳大小，那么就必须在这两个衡量尺度之间实现一种平衡。人构成了国家，而土地养活了人；因此，这两者间的合理均衡要求有足够多的土地来养活它的居民，同时居民的数量又要正好等于土地所能供养的人口。只有在这个比例上，一定数量的人口才能实现它的最大力量。因为如果领土过多，那么防御就会成为负担，土地的耕种就会不充分而且产出也会过剩，这不久就会引发防御性的战争；如果情况相反，领土过少，那么这个国家就要看邻国的脸色依赖于从他们那里进口，而这不久将会导致侵略性的战争。任何一个民族如果只能在贸易或者战争之间做出选择，那么它本质上就是脆弱的。它要依赖于它的邻国，它要依赖于局势，它的存在就只能是短暂而且不稳固的；它或者是通过征服别人而结束自己的困境，或者被别人征服而归于灭亡。也就是说只有借助于使自己变得渺小或者伟大，它才能保护自己的自由。

没有人能够详细地指出在土地的面积和居民的数量之间应该有怎样一个精确的比例，这不仅是因为不同地方有不同特点，土地的肥沃程度各不相同，物产性质不同以及气候影响上有差异；

and also because of the differences there are between the temperaments of men who inhabit the different territories, some consuming little in a fertile country and others living well off a frugal soil. Again we should have to consider the greater or lesser fecundity of the women, the distinctive features of the land, whether more or less favourable to population; the number of immigrants that the lawgiver might hope to attract by his institutions. From this it follows that he must make his decisions in the light not of what he sees, but of what he foresees, calculating not so much the number of the existing population as the number which the population must naturally reach. Finally, there are a thousand occasions when some particular accident of situation demands or allows the assimilation of more land than appears necessary. In a mountainous country, where the type of cultivation — woodland and pastures— requires less work, where the women are shown by experience to be more fecund than in the plains, and where the steep slopes of hills leave only a marginal degree of that flat land which alone can be relied on for vegetation, men will spread out more widely. The contrary is the case on the edge of the sea, where men will draw together in a small area, even among rocks and sands that are almost barren; for fishing can make up for much of the deficiency of agricultural produce; and being close together enables such men the better to resist pirates; and they can easily rid themselves by overseas settlement of any surplus population.

There is yet another condition for the institution of a people, one condition which no other can replace and without which all the rest are unavailing: a plenitude of peace must be enjoyed; for the period of the formation of a state, like that of the lining up of a regiment, is the time when it is least capable of resistance and most open to destruction. A state can defend itself more effectively amid total chaos than during the time of fermentation, when everyone is thinking about his own position and not about the common danger.

而且也是因为居住在不同领土上的居民在气质上存在着差异，比如一些居住在肥沃的国土上的人消耗甚少，而另外一些居住在贫瘠国土上的人却消耗甚多。再者我们还必须考虑到女人生育能力的大小，土地各自的特性、它是否或多或少地会对人口有利，以及立法者借助于它的体制希望吸引的外来移民的数量。由此我们可以得出结论，立法者不应该根据他所见到的，而必须根据他所能预见到的来做出决定，他不应该只考虑到现有人口的数量，他更应该考虑到人口自然会达到的数量。最后，还会有上千种的情况，如在一些特别的突发情况下会要求或者允许人民占有多于必需的土地。在多山的国家中，那里的耕地类型主要是森林和牧场，因而就需要较少的劳动，经验证明，这些地方的女人比平原上的女人具有更强的生育能力。同样在这些地方，由于在陡峭的山坡上只有很小部分的平地可望用于耕种，所以人们便向外散布得更广。相反的情况是在海边，人们聚集在很小的区域内，即使那里是贫瘠不毛的岩石或者沙滩。这是因为渔业能够大量弥补农业产出上的不足；也因为密切地聚集在一起使他们能够更好地抵御海盗；还因为他们可以通过海外殖民很容易就摆脱人口过剩的负担。

一个民族体制的建立还要有其他的条件，有一个条件是其他任何条件都不能代替的，而且如果没有了这个条件，其他所有的条件都将是无效的。这个条件就是：人民必须享受充分的和平。因为一个国家在创立时期，就如同一支军队初编的时期一样，是一个国家最没有抵抗力、最易于被破坏的时期。一个国家即使是在混乱当中也比在酝酿时期更能有效地保护自己，因为在酝酿时期，每个人都在考虑他自己在国家中的地位，而不会去

If there is a war, famine or sedition during this critical period, the state will inevitably be overthrown.

It is true that many governments have been set up during such disturbances, but then it is the governments themselves which destroy the state. Usurpers always choose troubled times to enact, in the atmosphere of general panic, laws which the public would never adopt when passions were cool. One of the surest ways of distinguishing the work of a lawgiver from that of a tyrant is to note the moment he chooses to give a people its constitution.

Which people, then, is fit to receive laws? I answer: a people which, finding itself already bound together by some original association, interest or agreement, has not yet borne the yoke of law; a people without deep-rooted customs or superstitions; one which does not fear sudden invasion, and which, without intervening in the quarrels of its neighbours, can stand up to any of them, or secure the help of one to resist another; a people in which every member may be known to all; where there is no need to burden any man with more than he can bear; a people which can do without other peoples and which other peoples can do without;① one which is neither rich nor poor, but has enough to

---

① If two neighbouring peoples cannot do without one another the situation is hard for the one and dangerous for the other. Any wise nation, in such a case, will hasten to deliver the other from its dependence. The republic of Thlascala, an enclave within the Mexican Empire, preferred to do without salt rather than buy it from the Mexicans, rather even than take it from them when it was offered as a gift. The wise Thlascalians saw the trap concealed in the Mexican generosity. They kept their freedom; and their little state, locked within the territory of a great Empire, was in the end the instrument of that Empire's ruin.

考虑公共的危险。如果在这个关键时期有一场战争、一场饥馑或是一场动乱，国家不可避免地将会被颠覆。

的确，曾经有许多政府在这样动乱的时期中建立起来，但是接下来正是这些政府自己破坏了国家篡位者总是选择动乱不安的时刻来颁布法律，因为这些法律在人民冷静时是不会被采纳的。所以区分立法者的创作和暴君的创作的一个最为明确的方式，就是看他们所选择的为人民立法的时间。

那么，什么样的民族才适合接受法律呢？我的回答是：一个虽然发现自己已经由于某种原初的联合、利益或者约定而联系在一起了，但是还未曾承受过法律约束的民族；一个没有根深蒂固的传统或者迷信的民族；一个不惧怕突然的入侵，并且不会干预四邻争端的民族，这个民族能够勇敢地抵抗周围的任何一个民族，并且能够借助一个民族的帮助来抵制另外一个民族；一个其中任何一个成员都被所有的成员所认识，而且不需要对其中的任何一个成员强加其所不能承受的负担的民族；一个不需要其他的民族就能生存，而且其他的民族不需要它也能生存的民族①；一个既不太富裕也不太贫穷，但却有足够的东西供给自己的

① 如果两个相邻的民族彼此相分离便不能生存，这种情况对其中的一个民族就会太艰难，而对另一个民族则太危险。任何一个明智的民族，在这种情况下，将会尽快把另外一个民族从它的依赖状态中解放出来。处于墨西哥帝国包围中的一块领土上的斯拉斯加拉共和国，宁可不食食盐度日，也不愿从墨西哥人那里购买食盐，更不愿在墨西哥人把食盐作为礼物送给他们时从墨西哥人那里接受它。明智的斯拉斯加拉人看到了隐藏在墨西哥人慷慨背后的陷阱。他们保持了他们的自由，而这个被封锁在墨西哥大帝国领土之内的小国家，最终却成为毁灭墨西哥帝国的工具。

keep itself; and lastly one which combines the cohesion of an ancient people with the malleability of a new one. What makes the task of the lawgiver so difficult is less what has to be established than what has to be destroyed; and what makes success so rare is the impossibility of finding the simplicity of nature together with the needs that society creates. It is difficult to combine all these conditions; and that is why so few wellconstituted states exist.

There is still one country in Europe which is fit to receive laws, and that is the island of Corsica. The valour and fidelity with which this brave people has recovered and defended its freedom entitle it to be taught by some wise man how to preserve that freedom. I have a presentiment that this little island will one day astonish Europe.

民族；最后，还是一个结合了古老的民族的稳定性和新生民族的可塑性的民族。立法者的任务之所以艰难，更多的不在于必须建立什么，而在于必须破坏什么；而使得立法成功如此少见的原因，则在于天然的朴素性和社会产生的需要结合在一起是不太可能见到的。把上面所有的条件都结合在一起是很困难的，这就是为什么很少有体制良好的国家存在的原因了。

在欧洲仍然有一个国家是可以为之立法的，这就是科西嘉岛。这个勇敢的民族在恢复和保卫他们的自由时十分英勇和忠诚，这使他们有资格由一位贤明的人来教导他们保卫其自由。我有一个预感，有一天这个小岛会使欧洲为之惊讶的。

CHAPTER 11

Various Systems Of Law

If we enquire wherein lies precisely the greatest good of all, which ought to be the goal of every system of law, we shall find that it comes down to two main objects, *freedom* and *equality*: freedom because any individual dependence means that much strength withdrawn from the body of the state, and equality because freedom cannot survive without it.

I have already explained what civil freedom is; as for equality, this word must not be taken to imply that degrees of power and wealth should be absolutely the same for all, but rather that power shall stop short of violence and never be exercised except by virtue of authority and law, and, where wealth is concerned, that no citizen shall be rich enough to buy another and none so poor as to be forced to sell himself; this in turn implies that the more exalted persons need moderation in goods and influence and the humbler persons moderation in avarice and covetousness. ①

Such equality, we shall be told, is a chimera of theory and could

---

① Do you want coherence in the state? Then bring the two extremes as close together as possible; have neither very rich men nor beggars, for these two estates, naturally inseparable, are equally fatal to the common good; from the one class come friends of tyranny, from the other, tyrants. It is always these two classes which make commerce of the public freedom: the one buys, the other sells.

第十一章　论种种不同的法律系统

如果探究那个应该成为所有法律体系目标的全体成员的最高幸福究竟在哪里，我们会发现它可以归结在两个目标上：自由和平等。自由是目标，因为任何个人的依赖性都意味着一部分力量被从国家共同体中抽掉了；平等是目标，则是因为没有平等，自由便不能存在。

我已经解释过什么是公民的自由；至于平等，这个词绝不能用来指所有的人在权力和财富上的绝对相等所应该达到的程度，而要用来指权力应该不至于变成暴力以及只能凭借威望和法律才能行使权力；就财富而言，平等是指没有一个公民能够富裕到可以购买另一个公民，而且没有一个公民贫穷到被迫出卖他自己；从而平等便又意味着位高势尊的人应该在财富和影响上保持节制，而地位相对卑下的人则应该在贪婪和妄羡上保持节制①。

可能有人会对我们说，这种平等只是一种理论上的幻想，在

---

① 你希望国家内的和谐一致吗？那么就要使这两极尽可能地接近；既没有非常富裕的人，也没有乞丐。因为这两个天然不可分离的阶层对于公共的幸福来说同等致命；从这两个阶层中的一个产生暴政的支持者，而从另一个则产生暴君。经常是在这两个阶层之间进行着对公共自由的交易：一个购买自由，另一个出售自由。

not exist in reality. But if abuse is inevitable, ought we not then at least to control it? Precisely because the force of circumstance tends always to destroy equality, the force of legislation ought always to tend to preserve it.

However, these general objectives of all institutions must be modified in each country to meet local conditions and suit the character of the people concerned. It is in the light of such factors that one must assign to each people the particular form of constitution which is best, not perhaps in itself, but for that state for which it is destined. For example, is your soil meagre and barren or the territory too narrow for its inhabitants? Then look to industry and crafts, so that manufactured goods may be exchanged for the natural resources that are lacking. Suppose, on the other hand, you have rich plains and fertile slopes, good land too little inhabited. Then concentrate on agriculture, to increase the population, and eschew artisanry, which invariably depopulates the countryside and brings the few inhabitants there are together in certain urban centres. ① Have you a long and convenient coastline? Then fill the sea with ships, develop trade and navigation, and you will have a brilliant if short existence. Does the sea, along your shores, wash against almost inaccessible rocks? Then remain ichthyophagous barbarians; you will live more peacefully, better perhaps, and certainly more happily. In short, apart from those principles which are common to all, each people has its own special reasons for ordering itself in a certain way and for having laws that are fitted to itself alone. Thus it was, in the

---

① Any branch of foreign trade, says the Marquis d'Argenson, brings only an illusory advantage to the kingdom in general; it may enrich a few individuals, even a few big towns, but the nation as a whole gains nothing and the people is none the better for it.

现实中根本不能存在。但是如果权力的滥用是不可避免的，那么我们不是至少应该控制它吗？正是因为环境的力量总是倾向于破坏平等，所以立法的力量应该总是倾向于保持这种平等。

然而，所有制度的这一共同目标，在每个国家中则必须做出调整以适应于当地的条件以及相应的民族的特点。正是基于这些因素，立法者应该赋予每个民族特殊形式的体制，这种体制就其自身来讲可能并不是最好的，但是对于这一体制所针对的国家来讲却是最好的。比如，你们的土壤太荒凉、太贫瘠吗？你们的领土对于居民来说太狭小吗？那么你们就转向工业和手工业吧，这样你们就可以用你们的工业产品来换取你们所缺乏的自然资源了。相反，假设你们拥有富饶的平原和肥沃的山川，你们有上等的土地但人口稀少，那么你们就集中从事农业以增加人口，而且要抛弃工艺业，因为它总是会使乡村的人口减少，而把这些本来就少的人口都集中在一定的城市中心①。你们有绵长且便利的海岸线吗？那么就在海面布满船舶，来发展贸易和航海业吧，你们将会得到一个短暂但却辉煌的生命。沿着你们的海岸，海水冲洗着那些不可接近的岩石吗？那么你们就继续做吃鱼为生的野蛮人吧，你们将会生活得更加安宁，也许更加美好，但肯定更加幸福。总之，除了那些对所有的民族而言是共同的原则之外，每个民族都有它特殊的理由以某种特定的方式来筹划他们自己的生活，有理由拥有那些只适合于他们自己的法律。正是因此，所以古代的

---

① 阿冉松爵士说，一般来说，对外贸易的任何部门都只能给王国带来虚假的好处；它虽然可以使一些人，甚至是一些大的城市变得富裕，但是国家作为一个整体并不能从中得到什么，而且人民也不会因此生活得更好。

past, that the Hebrews, and more recently the Arabs, took religion as their chief object, while the Athenians had literature, Carthage and Tyre trade, Rhodes seafaring, Sparta war, and Rome civic virtue. The author of *L' Esprit des lois* has shown with scores of examples how the art of the lawgiver directs the constitution towards each of its ends.

What makes the constitution of a state really strong and durable is such a close observance of conventions that natural relations and laws come to be in harmony on all points, so that the law, shall we say, seems only to ensure, accompany and correct what is natural. But if the lawgiver mistakes his object and builds on principles that differ from what is demanded by the circumstances; if his principle tends towards servitude while circumstances tend towards liberty, the one towards wealth and the other towards increased population, the one towards peace and the other towards conquest, then the laws will be weakened imperceptibly, the constitution will deteriorate, and the state will continue to be disturbed until it is finally destroyed or transformed, and invincible Nature regains her empire.

希伯来人以及更为近代的阿拉伯人选择了宗教作为他们的目标，而雅典人选择了文艺，迦太基和梯尔选择了贸易，罗德岛选择了航海业，斯巴达选择了战争，罗马选择了公民的德行。《论法的精神》一书的作者已经通过大量的事实证明了立法者的艺术是如何引导体制分别指向这每个目标的。

能够使一个国家的体制真正强大和持久的原因，就在于人们能够密切结合不同的习俗，以使自然的联系和法律在所有的点上能协调一致，以至于我们可以说，法律只不过是在确保、陪伴和纠正着自然的东西。但是如果立法者搞错了他的目标，而采取了同实际情形不相符合的原则：如果他的原则倾向于奴役，而实际情形则倾向于自由，如果一个追求财富而另一个追求人口增长，一个追求和平而另一个追求征服，那么法律就会不知不觉地被削弱，制度将会变质，而且国家也将持续处于紊乱状态，直到最后被推翻或者改变，从而不可征服的自然又重新获得了它的统治。

CHAPTER 12

Classification Of Laws

For everything to be well ordered and the best possible form given to the republic, there are various relations to be considered. First, there is the action of the whole body politic on itself, that is to say, the relation of all with all, or of the sovereign with the state, and this relation, as we shall see, is made up of relations between intermediate terms.

The laws which regulate this relation bear the name of Political Laws, and are also called Fundamental Laws— not unreasonably, if the laws are wise ones. For if in each state there is only one good way of regulating it, the people which has found that way ought to keep to it. But if the established order is bad, why should the laws which prevent its being good be regarded as fundamental? Besides, a people is in any case entirely at liberty to alter its laws, even its best laws; and if it chooses to do itself an injury, who has the right to prevent it from doing so?

The second relation is that of the members of the body politic among themselves, or of each with the entire body: their relations among themselves should be as limited, and relations with the entire body as extensive, as possible, in order that each citizen shall be at the same time perfectly independent of all his fellow citizens and excessively dependent on the republic— this result is always achieved by the same means, since

第十二章　法律的分类

为了使所有的事务都井然有序，并且赋予公共事务尽可能好的形式，我们需要考虑各种各样的关系。首先是整个政治体对于它自身的行为，就是说全体与全体的关系，或者说主权者与国家的关系，而且以后我们将会看到，这个关系是由中间条件之间的联系构成的。

规定着这种联系的法律就叫做政治法，如果这个法律是明智的，我们也不无理由称之为根本法。因为，如果在每个国家中都只有一种最好的方式来规定它的秩序的话，那么找到这种规定方式的人民就应该坚持它。但是，如果一种确立了的秩序是不好的，那么妨碍这种秩序成为好秩序的法律为什么还应该被看作是根本法呢？此外，一个民族在任何情况下都有完全的自由来改变它的法律，即使这个法律是最好的法律；而且如果一个民族选择了自己伤害自己，那谁又有权利阻止它这么做呢？

第二种联系是政治共同体的成员之间的联系，或者是共同体的成员和共同体之间的联系：共同体成员之间的联系应该受到最大程度的限制，而成员与共同体之间的联系应该尽可能地增大，以使得每个公民都完全地独立于他所有的同胞公民，同时却又极端地依赖于共和国。这种结果总是通过同样的手段实现，因

it is the power of the state alone which makes the freedom of its members. It is from this second relationship that Civil Laws are born.

We may consider a third kind of relation between the person and the law, namely that of disobedience and its penalty. It is this which gives rises to the establishment of Criminal Laws, though at bottom these are less a specific kind of law than the sanction behind all laws.

To these three sorts of law must be added a fourth, the most important of all, which is inscribed neither on marble nor brass, but in the hearts of the citizens, a law which forms the true constitution of the state, a law which gathers new strength every day and which, when other laws age or wither away, reanimates or replaces them; a law which sustains a nation in the spirit of its institution and imperceptibly substitutes the force of habit for the force of authority. I refer to morals, customs and, above all, belief: this feature, unknown to our political theorists, is the one on which the success of all the other laws depends; it is the feature on which the great lawgiver bestows his secret care, for though he seems to confine himself to detailed legal enactments, which are really only the arching of the vault, he knows that morals, which develop more slowly, ultimately become its immovable keystone.

Among these various classes of law, it is only Political Laws, which constitute the form of government, that are relevant to my subject.

为只有国家的权力才能使它的成员获得自由。正是通过第二种联系，才产生了民法。

我们可以认为有第三种联系，即个人和法律之间的联系，它是一种不服从和对此惩罚的联系。正是这种联系导致了刑法的产生，虽然刑法在根本上与其说是一种特殊的法律，不如说是对其他所有法律的制裁。

除了以上三种法律，还必须要加上第四种，这第四种法律是所有法律中最重要的，它不是刻在大理石上或铜表上的，而是刻在人民心里的，它形成了国家真正的体制，它每天都会积聚新的力量，而且在其他法律衰亡的时候，它激励或者代替它们；它使一个民族的制度精神得以保存，并且不知不觉地用习惯的力量取代权威的力量。我这里就是在说道德、习俗，而且最重要的是信仰：这些未能为我们的政治理论家所认识的重要方面，正是其他所有法律所赖以成功的基础；伟大的立法者所秘密关注的正是这些东西，因为虽然立法者看上去好像把自己局限于具体法律的制定，而这些具体法律实际上只是拱顶上的拱架而已，他知道只有那些发展缓慢的道德才是拱顶不可移动的基石。

这些不同种类的法律之中，只有决定政府形式的那些政治法，才是与我的主题相关的。

BOOK III

Before speaking of the various forms of government, let us try to fix the precise meaning of this word, which has not hitherto been very well explained.

CHAPTER I

Of Government In General

I Must warn the reader that this chapter should be read with care, for I have not the skill to make myself clear to those who do not wish to concentrate their attention.

Every free action has two causes which concur to produce it, one moral — the will which determines the act, the other physical — the strength which executes it. When I walk towards an object, it is necessary first that I should resolve to go that way and secondly that my feet should carry me. When a paralytic resolves to run and when a fit man resolves not to move, both stay where they are. The body politic has the same two motive powers and we can make the same distinction between will and strength, the former is *legislative power* and the latter *executive power*. Nothing can be, or should be, done in the body politic without the concurrence of both.

We have seen that the legislative power belongs, and can only belong, to the people. On the other hand, it is easy to see from principles established above [Book II, Chapters 4 and 6]

第 三 卷

在讨论各种不同形式的政府之前，让我们首先尽量确定“政府”这个词的准确含义，因为它的含义迄今为止还没有被清楚地解释过。

第一章　政府总论

我必须告诫我的读者，你们一定要仔细阅读本章，因为对于那些不打算集中他们的注意力的人，我是没有办法给他们讲清楚的。

每个自由的行为都由两种原因共同使它产生，一种是道德上的，即决定行为的那个意志；另一种是物理上的，即执行这种行为的力量。当我走向一个目标的时候，我首先必须决定要走向那里，其次是使我的脚必须能把我带过去。如果一个瘫痪的人决定要跑，或者一个健康的人却不想动，那么他们都只能待在原地。政治共同体也有相同的两种动力，而且我们可以同样地把它们区分为意志和力量，前者就是立法权力，而后者就是行政权力。没有两者的共同出现，人们就不可能、也不应该在政治体中做出任何事情来。

我们已经看到立法权力属于而且只能属于人民。另一方面，我们也可以很容易地从上文（本书的第二卷，第四、第六章）所确

that executive power cannot belong to the generality of the people as legislative or sovereign, since executive power is exercised only in particular acts which are outside the province of law and therefore outside the province of the sovereign which can act only to make laws.

The public force thus needs its own agent to call it together and put it into action in accordance with the instructions of the general will, to serve also as a means of communication between the state and the sovereign, and in a sense to do for the public person what is done for the individual by the union of soul and body. This is the reason why the state needs a government, something often unhappily confused with the sovereign, but of which it is really only the minister.

What, then, is the government? An intermediary body established between the subjects and the sovereign for their mutual communication, a body charged with the execution of the laws and the maintenance of freedom, both civil and political.

The members of this body are called magistrates or *kings*, that is to say *governors*, and the whole body bears the name of *prince*.① Thus, those theorists who deny that the act by which a people submits itself to leaders is a contract are wholly correct. For that act is nothing other than a commission, a form of employment in which the governors, as simple officers of the sovereign, exercise in its name the power it has placed in their hands, a power which the sovereign can limit, modify and resume at pleasure, since the alienation of such a right would be incompatible with the nature of the social body and contrary to the purpose of the social union.

I therefore call 'government' or 'supreme administration' the

---

① Thus in Venice the ruling college is called the Most Serene Prince even when the Doge is not present.

立的原则中看出，行政权力不能属于作为立法者和主权者的人民全体，因为行政权力只能通过个别的行为来行使，而这种个别的行为已经超出了法律的范畴，因而也超出了只能制定法律的立法者的范畴。

因而公共的力量就需要一个自己的代理机构把它凝聚起来，并且根据公意的指导把公共力量付诸实行，以作为在国家和主权者之间进行交流的手段，而且也可以为公共人格做事，在某种意义上正如灵魂和肉体的结合体对个人所做的事情一样。这就是为什么国家需要一个政府的原因，虽然这个政府经常会被不幸地误认为是主权者，而实际上它只不过是主权者的臣属而已。

那么，什么是政府呢？政府就是在臣民和主权者之间建立的、以便于两者之间互相交流的中介体，一个负责法律的执行以及维护个人的和社会的自由的中介体。

这个中介体的成员被称为行政官员或者国王，也就是管理者，而这个中介体作为一个整体则被称为君主”①。所以那些理论家否定人民服从首领时所依据的那种行为是一项契约，这是完全正确的。那种行为只不过是一种委托，一种雇用形式，在这里，管理者仅仅是作为主权者的执行官员，以主权者的名义来行使主权者委托给他们的权力；而对于这种权力，主权者可以随其所愿加以限制、修改以及收回。这些都是因为对这种权利的转让是和社会共同体的本性不能调和的，而且也是违背了政治联合的目标的。

因此，我把对于行政权力的合法行使称为“政府”或者“最高

---

① 因此，在威尼斯，即使在总督不出席的时候，大议会仍然被称为“最尊敬的君主”。

legitimate exercise of the executive power, and I call 'prince' or 'magistrate' the man or the body charged with that administration.

It is in the government that we may discern those intermediary forces whose relations constitute those of all with all, or of the sovereign with the state. This last relation can be depicted as one between the extremes of a continuous proportion, of which the geometrical mean is the government. The government receives from the sovereign the orders which it gives to the people; and if the state is to be well balanced, it is necessary, all things being weighed, that the product and power of the government considered in itself should equal the product and power of the citizens who are sovereign in one sense and subjects in another.

Furthermore, no one of these three factors can be changed without destroying the balance. If the sovereign seeks to govern, or if the magistrate seeks to legislate, or if the subjects refuse to obey, then order gives way to chaos, power and will cease to act in concert, and the state, disintegrating, will lapse either into despotism or into anarchy. Lastly, as there is only one geometrical mean between two extremes, there is only one good government possible for any state; but as a thousand events may change the relations within a nation, different governments may not only be good for different peoples, but good for the same people at different times.

To try to give some idea of the various relations which may exist between the two extremes, I shall take as an example the number of the people, as this is a relation easily expressed.

Suppose the state is made up of ten thousand citizens. The sovereign can only be considered collectively and as a body, but every member as a subject has to be considered as an individual. Thus the sovereign is to the subject as ten thousand is to one, that is to say,

行政”，并且又把负责行政的个人或者团体称为“君主”或“行政官员”。

正是在政府中，我们可能会发现这些中介的力量，这些力量之间的联系构成了人民全体对人民全体的联系，或者说主权者与国家之间的联系。主权者与国家之间的关系可以被描绘成一个连续比例的首尾两项的关系，而政府则是它们的几何平均数。政府从主权者那里接受了向人民发布的命令，而且如果想使一个国家处于良好的平衡状态，在考虑到所有的事情之后，就必须使政府自身的乘积或者幂，等于作为主权者的公民和作为臣民的公民的乘积或者幂。

此外，以上三个因素中的任何一个发生了改变，这个比例就会被破坏。如果主权者要进行统治，或者如果行政官员想要立法，或者如果臣民拒绝服从，那么秩序就会被混乱所代替，力量和意志就不能协同一致，而且国家就会解体，就会堕落为专制或者无政府状态。最后，由于在连续比例的首尾项之间只有一个比例中项，所以对于任何一个国家都只可能有一个好的政府；但是由于成千种事务可能会改变一个民族内部的一些联系，所以不仅不同的民族应该有不同的政府，即使同一个民族在不同的时期也应该有不同的政府。

为了说明可能存在于连续比例的首尾两项之间各种不同的关联，我举人口数目作为一个例子，因为这个关联是比较容易说明的。

假定一个国家中有一万名公民。由于主权者只能作为一个整体来看待，但是每个成员作为臣民却又必须作为个人来看待，因而主权者对人民的比例就是一万比一。这就是说，国

each single member of the state has for his own share only a ten-thousandth part of the sovereign authority, although he submits himself entirely to it. Now if the people is increased to a hundred thousand men, the position of the subject is unaltered, for each bears equally with the rest the whole empire of the laws, while as sovereign his share of the suffrage is reduced to one hundred-thousandth, so that he has ten times less influence in the formulation of the laws. Hence, as the subject remains always one single individual, the ratio of sovereign to subject increases according to the number of citizens. Whence it follows that the more the state is enlarged, the more freedom is diminished.

When I say that the ratio increases, I mean that it is farther removed from parity. So the greater the ratio in the geometrical sense, the smaller the ratio in the popular sense; for in the former, the ratio, considered according to quantity, is measured by the quotient, whereas in the latter, the ratio, considered according to identity, is judged by similarity.

The smaller the ratio between the particular wills and the general will, that is, between the people's morals and the law, the more will repressive force have to be employed. Hence, for the government to be good, its strength must be increased to the extent that the people is more numerous.

In proportion as the enlargement of the state means offering the holders of public authority more temptations and more opportunities to abuse their power, it follows that the more power the government needs to control the people, the more power the sovereign needs, in its turn, to control the government. I am speaking here not of an absolute power, but of the relative power of the different elements in the state.

It follows from this double ratio that the continuous proportion between sovereign, prince and people is by no means an arbitrary idea, but a necessary consequence of the nature of the body politic. It follows further that since one of the extremes,

家中每个单独的成员自己只能分享主权权威的一万分之一，虽然他还必须完全地服从于主权者。现在，假设人口增加到十万，臣民的地位没有改变，因为每个臣民同其他所有的臣民一样都要平等地承担全部的法律；然而作为主权者，他分享到的表决权却缩减到十万分之一，于是在法律的制定过程中，他的影响减小了十倍。由于臣民总是作为一个单一的个体，所以主权者对臣民的比率根据公民人口的增加而增加。由此可以得出结论，国家越是扩大，自由就越是缩小。

当我说比率增大的时候，我的意思是说离开平等更远了。所以在几何意义上这一比率越大，而在普通意义上这一比率就越小；因为在前者，比率是根据数量来考虑的，是以商的大小来衡量的，而在后者，这一比率是根据平等性来考虑的，是以相似性来判断的。

个别意志和公意之间的比率越小，就是说公民的是非原则和法律之间的比率越小，就必须要使用越大的强制性力量。因此，为了使一个政府成为好的政府，随着公民人口数量的增多，政府的力量就必须增强到相应的程度。

根据比率，由于国家的扩大意味着给予了公共权威的掌控者更大的诱惑和更多的滥用权力的机会，所以如果政府需要越多的权力来控制人民，那么主权者就需要越多的权力来控制政府。我这里并不是说一种绝对的权力，而是说国家不同部分的相对权力。

从这个双重比率可以看出，主权者、君主以及人民之间的连续比例绝不是一个臆造的观念，而是政治共同体之本性的必然结论。我们更可进一步得出结论，既然连续比例的首尾项中的

namely the people as subject, is represented by unity, every time the double ratio is increased or diminished, the simple ratio increases or diminishes in the same way, and the middle term is in consequence changed. This shows that there is no one unique and absolute constitution of government, but that there may be as many different kinds of government as there are states of different sizes.

If anyone, wishing to ridicule this system, suggested that in order to find the geometrical mean and construct the body of the government one need only on my view take the square root of the number of the people, I should reply that I am here using that number only as an example; and the ratios of which I speak are not measured merely by the number of men but more generally by the amount of activity, which results from the concurrence of innumerable causes; I should add that although I have borrowed momentarily for the sake of expressing myself in fewer words, the language of geometry, I am still well aware that geometrical precision has no place in moral calculations.

The government is in small what the body politic (which includes it) is in large. It is a fictitious person endowed with certain faculties, active like the sovereign, passive like the state; and it can be broken down into similar relations; in consequence these relations yield a new ratio; and within each we can continue the process of analysis according to the order of the magistracies until we reach a single indivisible middle term, that is, a single chief or supreme magistrate, who may be shown at the centre of this pattern, as the unity between the series of fractions and the series of whole numbers.

Without burdening ourselves with such a multiplication of terms, let us simply consider the government as a new body within the state, distinct from both people and sovereign and intermediary between the two.

一项，即作为臣民的公民，总是表现为“一”，所以随着双重比率的每次增大或者缩小，单项比率也会同样地增大或者缩小，而比例中项作为其中的一项因而也会发生改变。这表明从不存在一个唯一的、绝对的政府体制；由于国家的大小不同，可以存在许多不同形式的政府。

如果有人要嘲笑我的这个方法，而且认为，要找到首尾项的几何平均值并且建立一个政府，照我的观点只需要计算出人口数字的平方根就可以了，我的回答是：我在这里仅仅是举人口数量作为一个例子，而且我所说的比率并不能仅仅靠人口数目来衡量，而且更一般地是要根据大量的行为来衡量的，这些行为又是由数不清的原因导致的。我要补充的是，虽然这里为了更简洁地表达我的观点，我借用了几何学的语言，但是我依然十分清楚，几何学的精确性在对道德衡量中是不太适用的。

政府是那个包含了政府在内的大型政治共同体的小型存在。政府是一个被授予了一定能力的虚拟的人，它既像主权者一样是主动的，又像国家一样是被动的；它可以被分解出类似的比例关系，而这些比例关系进而产生新的比率；而且在其中我们可以根据行政官员的等级继续进行分析，直到分解出一个单一的、不可分割的比例中项，即一个唯一的首领或者一个最高的行政长官，他可以被看作是这一比例系列模式的中心，是这一系列分数和一系列整数之间的那个“一”。

为了不使我们自己在如此繁多的比例项目中纠缠不清，让我们简单地把政府看成是国家中一个新的团体，它区别于人民、

There is this essential difference between the two bodies— the state exists in itself while the government exists only through the sovereign. Thus the dominant will of the prince is, or ought to be, only the general will or the law, and his force nothing other than the public force concentrated in his hands; as soon as he resolves to perform on his own authority some absolute and independent act, the union of all begins to slacken. And if in the end it comes about that the prince has a particular will more active than that of the sovereign, and if, to enforce obedience to this particular will, he uses the public force which is in his hands, with the result that there are, so to speak, two sovereigns, one *de jure* and the other *de facto*, then the social bond vanishes at once and the body politic is dissolved.

Even so, for the body of the government to have an existence, a real life distinct from the body of the state, and for all its members to be able to act in concert and serve the purpose for which the government has been set up, it must have a particular *ego*, a consciousness common to its members, a force, a will of its own tending to its preservation. Such a particular existence implies assemblies, councils, a power to deliberate and determine, rights, titles, and privileges which belongs exclusively to the prince, and which should make the position of the magistrate the more honourable in proportion to the extent to which it is the more arduous. The difficulty is to find a method of ordering this subordinate whole within the greater whole, so that it does not weaken the general constitution while strengthening its own, and so that its private force, designed for its own preservation, shall always be distinct from the public force, designed for the preservation of the state; in short, so that it will always be ready to sacrifice the government to the people and not the people to the government.

Moreover, even though the artificial body of the government is the

主权者，是在这两者之间的中介体。

国家和政府这两者之间存在着本质的区别，即国家因它自身而存在，然而政府却只能通过主权者而存在。因而君主的统治意志就只能是，而且也只应该是公意或者法律；君主的力量也只能是集中在他手中的公共力量。一旦他试图运用他的权威进行绝对的、独立的行为，那么所有人构成的共同体就会因此开始松散。而且如果到最后，君主有了一个比主权者的意志更为活跃的个别意志，如果君主为了使人民服从于他的个别意志而使用了他手中的公共力量，这样，可以说就有了两个主权者，一个是法律上的，另一个是事实上的，那么这个社会结合体就会立即消亡，政治共同体也就解体了。

虽然如此，但为了使政府这个团体成为真正的存在，即拥有一个区别于国家共同体的真实生命，为了使政府的所有成员都能协同一致地行动，并服务于政府建立时所追求的那个目标，政府就必须成为一个特别的“自我”，拥有一种其成员所共有的意识，拥有自我保存的意志和力量。这样一种特别的存在就意味着要有大会、委员会、审议和决定的权力、各种权利、荣誉头衔、专属于君主的种种特权，以及那种能够使得行政官员随着职责的辛劳程度的增加，其地位便愈加荣耀的特权。但困难就在于，在国家这个更大的整体内找到一种安置政府这一附属整体的方式，以使得政府在强化自己体制的时候，不至于削弱国家的公共体制，并使得我们能够把以保存政府自身为目的的力量和以保存国家为目的的力量区别开来。简言之，使政府总是会准备着为了人民而牺牲政府，而不是为了政府而牺牲人民。

此外，即使政府这一人为的团体是另外一个同样的人为

work of another equally artificial body, and even though it has only a kind of borrowed and subordinate life, this does not prevent its being able to act with greater or less vigour and speed, and enjoying, so to speak, a health that may be more robust or less. Lastly, without departing directly from the purposes for which it has been set up, it may deviate from them in varying degrees according to the manner in which it has been constituted.

It is all these differences which give rise to the various relations that ought to exist between the government and the body of the state, in accordance with the fortuitous and particular relations by which this same state is changed. For often the government which is in itself the best becomes the most evil unless its relations with the state are modified to meet the defects of the body politic to which it belongs.

团体[1]的产物，即使政府只能有一种借来的、从属的生命，但这并不妨碍它能够凭借或多或少的活力和敏捷性采取行动，可以说也不妨碍它能够享有一种或多或少是强有力的健康状态。最后，政府虽不会直接背离人们建立政府时的目标，但是它却可能根据它自身的建构方式而在某种程度上偏离这个目标。

正是所有这些区别，导致政府和国家共同体之间，根据那些使同一个国家发生变化的偶然的、特殊的比例关系，而应当存在着各种各样的比例关系，尽管本身是最好的政府，常常因为它与国家的比例关系被改变以迎合它所属于的政治共同体的缺点，而变成了最坏的政府。

〔1〕 指国家。

CHAPTER 2

The Constitutive Principle Of The Different Forms Of Government

To explain the general reason for these differences, it is necessary to distinguish here between the prince and the government, as I have already distinguished between the state and the sovereign.

The body of the magistrates may be composed of a greater or lesser number of members. We have already observed that the ratio of sovereign to subjects is greater to the extent that the people are more numerous, and by an obvious analogy we can say the same of the government in relation to the magistrates.

As the total power of the government is at all times that of the state, it never varies; and from this it follows that the more force the government exerts over its own members, the less there remains for it to use over the whole people.

Hence the more numerous the magistrates, the weaker the government. As this principle is fundamental, let us try to make it clearer.

We may distinguish in the person of the magistrate three essentially different wills. First, there is the will which belongs to the individual, and tends only to his personal advantage. Secondly, there is the collective will of the magistrates; this is concerned only with the advantage of the prince, and might be called the corporate will, since it is general *vis-à-vis* the government and particular *vis-à-vis* the state of which the government is a part.

第二章　论政府的不同形式的建构原则

为了解释这些区别的一般原因，这里有必要对君主和政府进行区分，正像我曾经在国家和主权者间做过区分一样。

行政官员的团体可以由数量或多或少的成员构成。我们已经注意到，随着人口数量的增加，主权者对于臣民的比率也会增长到相应的程度，而且通过一个明显的类比，我们可以说，政府和行政官员之间也有同样的关系。

政府的全部权力在任何时候都等于国家的全部力量，它从来都不会改变；由此可以得出结论，政府在它的成员身上耗费越多的力量，那么余下来应用到全体人民身上的力量就会越少。

因此，行政官员的人数越多，政府就会越弱。由于这条原则是根本性的，那么就让我们尽量地把它表达清楚吧。

我们可以在行政官员个人的身上分出三种本质上不同的意志。首先，是只属于个人的意志，这种意志只会倾向于个人的利益。第二，是行政官员们的集体意志，这种意志只关心君主的利益，我们也可以把它称为团体的意志，因为对于政府而言，它是公共的，而对于政府只是其中的一部分的国家而言，它又是个别的。

Thirdly, there is the will of the people or the sovereign will, which is general both with regard to the state considered as a whole and with regard to the government considered as part of the whole.

In a perfect system of legislation, the individual or particular will would be nonexistent, the government's own corporate will very subordinate, and the general or sovereign will therefore always dominant and always the sole regulator of all the others.

In the order of nature, on the contrary, these different wills become the more active as they are the more concentrated. Hence, the general will is always the weakest, the corporate will takes second place, and the particular will comes first of all; so much so, that within the government, each member is primarily a private self, secondly a magistrate, and thirdly a citizen. This sequence is exactly the reverse of what the social order demands.

That being so, let us suppose that the government is in the hands of a single individual. Then the particular will and the corporate will will be perfectly united, and the corporate will accordingly raised to its highest possible degree of intensity. Now, since the exercise of power depends on the degree of will, and since the absolute power of the government is invariable, it follows that the most active government is that of one man.

If, on the other hand, we combine the government and the legislative authority, make the prince the sovereign, and each citizen a magistrate— then the corporate will, being merged in the general will, will be no more active than the general will, and so leave the particular will to command the totality of power. Thus the government, having always the same absolute power, will be left with a minimum of relative strength and activity.

These relations are indisputable, and other considerations add further confirmation. It is clear, for example, that each magistrate

第三，是人民的意志或者说主权者的意志，这种意志无论对被看作一个整体的国家来说，还是对被看作是国家整体的一部分的政府来说，都是公共的。

在一个完美的立法体系下，个别的或者特殊的意志是没有地位的，政府自己的团体意志将会居于次要的地位，而公意或者说主权者的意志因而总是居于主导地位，并且总是其他所有意志的唯一的校准者。

相反，在自然的秩序中，这些不同的意志越是集中，它们就变得愈加活跃。因此，公意总是活跃度最弱的，团体意志居于第二位，而那些个别意志则是所有意志中最活跃的；因此，在一个政府中，每个政府成员都首先是个人自己，其次是一个行政官员，第三才是一个公民。这种次序是和社会秩序所要求的次序完全相反的。

弄清楚了这一点，再让我们假定政府是掌握在唯一的一个个人手中的。那么他的个别意志和政府的团体意志将会达到完美的结合，而且政府的团体意志也相应地达到它最大可能的强度。现在，由于权力的行使依赖于意志的强度，而且又由于绝对权力是不变的，所以结论便是，最活跃的政府是唯一一个人的政府。

相反，如果我们把政府和立法权威合并起来，使主权者就是君主，使每个公民就是一个行政官员，那么团体意志就会和公意合并在一起，因而团体意志就不会比公意更加活跃，并且让个别意志仍然掌握着全部的权力。这样，总是拥有同样绝对权力的政府，其相对力量和活跃程度便处于最低点。

这些关联是无可争辩的，而且其他方面的考察可以给予它更进一步的证明。比如，很明显，在一个政府共同体中的每个行政

is more active within the body of the government than is each citizen within the body of the state, and hence that the particular will has more influence over the acts of the government than it has over those of the sovereign, for every magistrate is nearly always entrusted with some distinct function of government, while no citizen, taken singly, has any distinct function of sovereignty. Besides, the more the state expands, the more its real strength is increased, though not in proportion to its expansion; but while the state remains the same size, the magistrates can be multiplied without the government gaining thereby any real strength, since its strength is that of the state, which is always the same. In this way the relative strength or activity of the government diminishes without there being any possibility of its absolute or real power increasing.

Again, there is no doubt that the dispatch of public business becomes slower in proportion as there are more persons responsible for it; attaching too much importance to prudence, large bodies attach too little to luck; they miss opportunities, and they deliberate so long that they lose the profits of deliberation.

I have just shown that the government slackens to the extent that the magistrates are multiplied, and I showed earlier that the more numerous the people, the more the repressive force must increase. From this it follows that the ratio of magistrates to government should be the inverse of the ratio of subjects to sovereign; that is to say, the more the state is enlarged, the more the government must reduce its ranks, so that the number of magistrates diminishes in proportion to the increase of the people.

I should add that I am speaking here of the relative strength of the government and not the quality of its behaviour; for, on the contrary, the more numerous the magistrates, the closer their corporate will approaches the general will, while under a single magistrate that same corporate will is, as I have said, only a particular will. Thus there is lost on the one side what could be gained on the other;

官员都会比在一个国家共同体中的每个公民更活跃，因此个人意志对于政府行为的影响要比它对于主权者的影响要大，因为几乎每个行政官员都被赋予了某种确定的政府职能，然而就单个的公民来讲，却没有一个人被赋予某种特定的主权职能。此外，国家越是扩展，它的实际力量也就越增大，虽然实际力量的增强与地域的扩张并不是成比例的；但是在国家保持一定规模的时候，行政官员的数目成倍地增加，政府却不会因此获得任何实际的力量，因为它的力量就是国家的力量，而这个国家力量没有变化。通过这个方式，政府的相对力量和活跃程度减小，而其绝对权力或者实际权力却没有任何增加的可能性。

还有一点是无疑的，即随着负责的人越来越多，公共事务的处理就会变得越来越慢；大机构过于强调审慎，而忽视运气，他们失去机会，他们如此长时间地深思熟虑，以至于失去了深思熟虑的好处。

我刚才说明了随着行政人员的增加，政府就会相应地变得松弛，而且早些时候我也说明了人口的数量越多，强制性力量就越是需要增加。由此可以得出结论，行政官员对政府的比率与臣民对主权者的比率应该是成反比的；就是说，国家越是扩大，政府就越应该缩减它的行政等级，从而使得行政官员的数目随着人口的增加成比例地减少。

我要补充的是，我这里谈论的是政府的相对力量，而不是它的行为的性质；因为，相反的情况是，行政官员的数目越多，他们的团体意志就越接近于公意，然而在一个唯一的行政官员的掌控下，政府的团体意志就像我已经说过的，只能是一个个别意志。因而从一方面说有所失，从另一个方面讲便是有所得；立法者的

and the art of the lawgiver is to know how to settle the point at which the strength and the will of the government, which always stand in inverse ratio, can be combined in the proportion most beneficial to the state.

艺术就在于知道如何确定一个合适的点，在这个点上，总是成反比的政府的力量和意志能够根据最有利于国家的比例结合在一起。

CHAPTER 3
Classification Of Governments

In the preceding chapter we saw why the different types or forms of government are distinguished according to the number of members who compose them; it remains to be seen in the present chapter how this classification is made.

First, the sovereign may put the government in the hands of the whole people, or of the greater part of the people, so that there are more citizen-magistrates than there are ordinary private citizens. This form of government is known as *democracy*.

Alternatively, the sovereign may confine the government to the hands of a few, so that there are more ordinary citizens than there are magistrates: this form of government is called *aristocracy*.

Yet again, the sovereign may concentrate the entire government in the hands of one single magistrate, from whom all the others will derive their power. This third form of government is the most common, and is called *monarchy* or royal government.

It should be noticed that all these forms, or at any rate the first two, can be had in greater or lesser degrees; they have a fairly marked elasticity. Democracy may include all the people or it may be limited so as to include only half. Aristocracy in its turn may extend to half the people or be limited to the smallest possible number. Even royal government can to some extent be shared.

第三章　论政府的分类

在前面一章中，我们清楚了为什么要根据构成政府的成员的数量来划分政府的不同类型或者形式。在这一章中，我们将会看到这种划分是如何进行的。

首先，主权者可以使政府掌握在全体人民或者绝大多数人民的手中，这样，作为行政官员的公民的数量就会比作为普通个人的公民要多。这种政府形式我们称之为民主制。

或者，主权者可以使政府仅掌握在一少部分人手中，这样国家中普通公民就会比行政官员要多，这种政府形式就被称为贵族制。

再者，主权者可以使整个政府都集中在一个唯一的行政官员手中，其他所有的人都从这个行政官员手中获得他们的权力。这第三种政府形式是最普遍的，它被称为君主制或者皇室政府制。

我们应该注意到，所有的这些政府形式，至少前两种政府形式自身可以有程度或大或小的变动，它们甚至有相当显著的变动幅度。民主制可以包括全体的人民，它也可以被限制到只包含一半的人民。相应地，贵族制可以包括半数人民，也可以被限制到尽可能最少的人数。即使是皇室政府在某种程度上也可以被分享。

Sparta had always two kings according to its constitution, and the Roman Empire is known to have had as many as eight Emperors at once without it being true to say that the Empire was divided. Thus there is always a point at which each form of government overlaps the next form; and it is clear that although government has only three names, it is actually open to as many variations of form as the state has citizens.

Moreover, since a government is able in certain respects to divide itself into separate parts, one administered in one way and the other in another way, the three forms of government may be combined to yield a multitude of mixed forms, each of which it can multiply by the three simple forms.

Throughout the ages men have debated the question 'What is government?', and yet they have failed to see that each of the possible forms is the best in some cases and the worst in others.

If in each particular state the number of supreme magistrates should be in inverse ratio to the number of citizens, it follows that, in general, democratic government suits small states, aristocratic government suits states of intermediate size and monarchy suits large states. This rule follows directly from our axiom; but how are we to calculate the multitude of particular circumstances which may offer exceptions to the rule?

斯巴达根据它的宪法，总是有两个国王，我们还知道罗马帝国同时甚至可以有多达八个皇帝，我们却不能说罗马帝国此时是分裂的。任何一种形式的政府都会在某一点上和其他形式的政府是重叠的。很明显，虽然政府只具有以上三种名称，但是政府可能具有和一个国家的公民数目相同的各种不同的政府形式。

此外，既然一个政府在一些特定的方面又能够把自己分成若干部分，一个部分通过一种方式进行管理，而另一个部分则通过另一种方式进行管理，所以政府的这三种形式可以被结合起来而产生大量的混和形式，每种混合形式都可以从三种简单形式中产生出来。

在各个历史时期，人们一直都在争论这个问题："什么是最好的政府?"但是，他们都没能看到每一种可能的政府形式在一些情况下都可以是最好的，而在另外的情况下却又是最坏的。

如果说在每个国家中，最高行政官员的数目应该和公民的数目成反比，那么一般说来，民主制政府适合于小国家，贵族制政府适合于中等程度的国家，而君主制政府则适合于大的国家。这个规律直接地得自于我们的公理；但是，我们该如何考量那些对这个规律而言是例外的大量特殊情况呢?

CHAPTER 4
Democracy

He who makes the law knows better than anyone how it should be executed and interpreted. So it might seem that there could be no better constitution than one which united the executive power with the legislative; in fact, this very union makes that form of government deficient in certain respects, for things which ought to be kept apart are not, and the prince and the sovereign being the same person constitute, so to speak, a government without government.

It is not good that he who makes the law should execute it or that the body of the people should turn its attention away from general perspectives and give it to particular objects. Nothing is more dangerous in public affairs than the influence of private interests, and the abuse of the law by the government is a lesser evil than that corruption of the legislator which inevitably results from the pursuit of private interests. When this happens, the state is corrupted in its very substance and no reform is possible. A people which never misused the powers of government would never misuse independence, and a people which always governed itself well would not need to be governed.

In the strict sense of the term, there has never been a true democracy,

第四章　论民主制

既然那个制订法律的人比其他任何人都更清楚如何执行法律和解释法律，所以看上去似乎没有一种比结合了行政权力和立法权力的体制更好的体制了；但是事实上，正是这种结合使得这种政府形式在某些方面是不完善的，因为这里一些应该被分开的东西却没有被分开，而且可以说，如果君主〔1〕和主权者成了同一个人，那么建构起来的就是一个没有政府的政府。

让那个制订法律的人来执行法律，或者说让全体人民把他们的注意力从普遍的对象上移开而投放到个别的目标上，这并非是一件好事。在公共事务中，没有比私人利益的影响更为危险的了，这里政府对于法律的滥用不会比立法者的腐败危害更大，而立法者的腐败却是对私人利益追求的不可避免的结果。如果这样的腐败发生了，国家就会从根基上被败坏了，任何改革就都是不可能的了。一个从来都不会滥用政府权力的民族永远都不会滥用独立自主，一个总是能够把自己治理得很好的民族永远都不需要被别人统治。

从“民主制”这个词的严格意义上讲，从来都不曾有过真实的

〔1〕 指行政者，也就是统治者的共同体。

and there never will be. It is contrary to the natural order that the greater number should govern and the smaller number be governed. One can hardly imagine that all the people would sit permanently in an assembly to deal with public affairs; and one can easily see that they could not appoint commissions for that purpose without the form of administration changing.

I believe indeed that one can lay down as an axiom that when the functions of government are divided between several commissions, those with the fewest members acquire sooner or later the greatest authority, if only because the facility of dispatching business leads naturally in that direction.

Besides, how many things that are difficult to have at the same time does the democratic form of government not presuppose? First, a very small state, where the people may be readily assembled and where each citizen may easily know all the others. Secondly, a great simplicity of manners and morals, to prevent excessive business and thorny discussions. Thirdly, a large measure of equality in social rank and fortune, without which equality in rights and authority will not last long. Finally, little or no luxury; for luxury is either the effect of riches or it makes riches necessary; it corrupts both the rich and the poor; it sells the country to effeminacy and vanity; it deprives the state of all its citizens by making some the slaves of others and all the slaves of opinion.

This is why a celebrated author has made virtue the cardinal principle of a republic; for all the conditions that I have named cannot prevail without virtue. But this same great genius, having failed to make the necessary distinctions, was often wrong and sometimes obscure, and failed to see that since the sovereign authority is everywhere the same, the same principles should have a place in every well-constituted state, though to a greater or lesser extent, assuredly, according to the form of the government.

民主制，而且永远也不会有，因为大多数人进行统治而少数人被统治的状态是与自然秩序相违背的。任何一个人都不能想象所有的人坐在一起无休止地开会以处理公共事务；而任何一个人都可以很容易地懂得他们根本不可能在为了处理公共事务而任命一些代理人的时候，却没有改变政府的管理形式。

事实上，我相信我们可以把这一点作为一个公理，即如果政府的职能被许多代理机构分别掌握了，那么那些成员较少的代理机构迟早会取得最大的权威，仅仅是在处理公务上的方便就自然地会引导到这个方向。

此外，民主制的政府形式同时预设了太多苛刻的条件。首先，得是一个非常小的国家，在这里人民可以很容易地集会，并且每个公民都可以很容易地认识其他的公民。其次，要有非常简朴的风尚和道德，以防止产生过多的事务和棘手的争论。第三，在社会等级和财富上要达到高度的平等，没有这种平等，权利和权威上的平等就不会持久。最后，又要极少有甚至是没有奢侈，因为奢侈或者是财富的结果，或者使财富成为必需；这既腐蚀富人，又腐蚀穷人；它也会把国家出卖给娇弱和虚荣；它还会通过把一些人变成另外一些人的奴隶，或者通过把所有的人变成公众舆论的奴隶，而把全体公民从国家中剥夺了去。

这就是一个著名的作家曾经把德行作为一个共和国的根本原则的原因了，因为如果没有德行，以上我所说的所有条件都根本不能维持。但是，同样是这个伟大的天才却不能做出必要的区分，因而经常犯错误，有些时候又是模糊不清的，而且他也没有看到既然主权权威在任何地方都是相同的，那么这个原则在任何一个体制良好的国家中都应该是适用的——当然，这要或多或少地依据于政府形式。

We may add that there is no government so liable to civil war and internecine strife as is democracy or popular government, for there is none which has so powerful and constant a tendency to change to another form or which demands so much vigilance and courage to maintain it unchanged. It is under this constitution, before all others, that the citizen must be armed with strength and fidelity, and repeat from the bottom of his heart every day of his life the words a virtuous Palatine[①] once spoke in the Diet of Poland: '*Malo periculosam libertatem quam quietum servitium.*'

If there were a nation of Gods, it would govern itself democratically. A government so perfect is not suited to men.

---

① The Palatine of Posen, father of the King of Poland and Duke of Lorraine.

我们应该补充一点，从没有一种政府像民主制政府或者人民政府那样易于发生内战或者内部冲突了，因为没有一种政府有如此强烈而且持久的倾向要使自己改变成另一种形式，也没有一种政府需要如此多的警惕和勇气以保持自己的形式不被改变。正是在这种体制下，公民必须用力量和坚定来武装自己，并且在生命的每一天中都要从心底里记诵着一位道德高尚的侯爵[①]在波兰议会上曾经说过的一句话："我宁可要伴随着危险的自由，也不要被奴役下的和平。"

如果有一个神明的城邦的话，它可能会用民主制来治理。一个如此完美的政府是不适合于人类的。

① 波兹南侯爵，1704～1735年曾为波兰国王，后逊于位于洛林公爵。

CHAPTER 5 Aristocracy

We have here two distinct artificial persons, namely the government and the sovereign, and therefore two general wills, one belonging to all the citizens, and the other to members of the administration only. Thus, although the government may regulate its interior discipline as it pleases, it can never speak to the people except in the name of the sovereign, that is, in the name of the people itself— something that must never be forgotten.

The first societies were governed aristocratically. The heads of families deliberated on public business among themselves; the young people yielded willingly to the authority of experience. Hence the names of *priests*, *elders*, *the senate*, *gerontes*. The savages of North America still retain today this method of government, and they are very well governed.

But to the extent that artificial inequality came to prevail over natural over natural inequality, riches and power① came to be preferred to age, and aristocracy became elective. Lastly, the bequeathing of power together with goods by fathers to their children made families patrician and so made government hereditary; and then there appeared senators aged twenty.

---

① It is clear that the word *Optimates*, for the ancients, did not mean the best but the strongest.

第五章　论贵族制

这里我们有两种区别明显的虚拟人格，分别叫做政府和主权者，因而也就有两种公意，一种是属于所有的公民的，而另外一种是仅属于行政机构的成员的。这样，虽然政府可以随其所愿地调整它的内部纪律，但是除非它以主权者的名义，也就是以人民自己的名义，否则它便不能对人民发布命令——这一点我们必须永远不可忘记。

最原始的社会形态是根据贵族制来治理的。家族的头领们彼此共同商讨公共事务，年轻人心甘情愿地服从于经验的权威，因此就有了长老、长者、元老、尊长这些称呼。北美洲的野蛮人今天仍然保存着这种治理方式，而且他们治理得非常好。

但是到了一定的程度，人为的不平等逐渐战胜了自然的平等，财富和权力①与年龄相比开始更被看重，贵族制也就变成推选的。最后，与财富一起，权力开始由父到子地继承，这使得某些家庭成为贵族，从而使得政府成为世袭制的，由此便出现了年龄只有二十岁的元老。

---

① 很明显，对于古人来说，“贵族”这个词并不是指最好的，而是指最强有力的。

There are thus three types of aristocracy, natural, elective and hereditary. The first is suited only to primitive peoples; the third is the worst of all governments; the second is the best, and this is aristocracy in the true sense of the word.

Aristocracy has not only the advantage of distinguishing between the sovereign and the government, it has also the advantage of selecting its magistrates. Under popular government all the citizens are born magistrates, while this other system limits itself to a small number of magistrates, every one of whom is elected,① a method which makes honesty, sagacity, experience and all the other grounds of popular preference and esteem further guarantees of wise government.

Besides, assemblies can be more easily arranged, business can be better discussed and be dispatched with more order and diligence; the credit of the state is better upheld in the eyes of foreigners by venerable senators than it is by an unknown and despised multitude.

In a word, it is the best and most natural arrangement for the wisest to govern the multitude, if we are sure that they will govern it for its advantage and not for their own. One ought never to multiply devices uselessly, or employ twenty thousand men to do what a hundred picked men could do much better. But it must be noted that the corporate interest begins at this point to direct the national energies less strictly in accordance with the general will,

---

① It is of the utmost importance that the law should regulate the procedure of election of magistrates, for if this is left to the will of the prince, there will be no avoiding a decline into hereditary aristocracy, as happened in the Republics of Venice and Berne. The first of these two states has long since fallen into decay, while the other preserves itself only by the extreme wisdom of its senate — a very honourable and very dangerous exception to the rule.

这样，就有三种类型的贵族制：自然的、推选的和世袭的。第一种只适用于原始的人类；第三种是所有政府中最坏的一种；而第二种则是最好的，而且这才是就“贵族制”这个词的真实意义而言的贵族制。

贵族制不仅具有把主权者和政府明确区分开来的优点，而且它还具有选举它的行政官员的优点。在人民政府之下，所有的公民都天生是行政官员，然而贵族制则把行政官员限制为少数人，其中的每个人都是由选举产生的①，这种方式使得诚实、贤明、经验以及其他所有被人们普遍看重和尊敬的品质，成为一个明智政府的更进一步的保证。

此外，会议可以更容易地召集，事务可以更好地讨论，进而人们可以更加有序且勤勉地处理这些事务；在外邦人的眼中，与那些不知名的、受人轻视的群众相比，值得尊敬的长老可以更好地维持国家的声望。

总之，如果我们能够确定他们是为了群众的利益而不是为了他们自己的利益而治理群众的话，那么让最明智的人治理广大群众便是最好而且最自然的安排了。我们不应该毫无益处地增加机构，也不应该雇用两万人去做由一百个挑选出来的人就可以做得更好的工作。但是我们必须注意，在这里团体的利益开始更少

① 最重要的是，法律应该规定行政官员选举的程序，因为如果把这一程序留给君主的意志来决定的话，那么政府将不可避免地沦为世袭贵族制了，正像在威尼斯共和国和伯尔尼共和国曾经发生过的那样。这两个国家，前者已经腐朽了很长时间了，而后者则仅仅是通过它的元老院的极端贤明才使自己保存了下来——这是一个非常光荣但却危险的例外。

and that a further inevitable tendency is for a part of the executive power to escape the domain of law.

As for the circumstances which suit this form of government, it is not necessary to have the state so small or the people so simple and upright that the execution of the law follows directly from the public will, as is the case in a good democracy. Nor must the nation be so large that the magistrates, being widely scattered, have to take upon themselves some of the powers of the sovereign, each in his own region; and so begin by making themselves independent and end by becoming masters.

But if aristocracy calls for rather fewer virtues than does popular government, it still calls for virtues of its own, such as moderation among the rich and contentment among the poor; for it seems that strict equality would be out of place; it was not observed even in Sparta.

Moreover, if this form of government involves a certain inequality of wealth, that is simply so that the administration of public affairs may be entrusted to those who can best give all their time to it, and not, as Aristotle asserted, so that the rich should always be chosen. On the contrary, it is necessary that an opposite choice should occasionally teach people that merit is a more important qualification than riches for preference.

地严格按照公意来指导国家力量了，而且一个不可避免的更进一步的倾向是：一部分行政权力逃避了法律的约束。

至于最适合于这种政府形式的外部环境，它不必要求国家是一个小的国家，人民是简朴而正直的人民，以便使得法律的执行能直接地遵循公共意志，而这些是一个良好的民主制所必须的条件。国家也不必是很大的，因为国家很大会导致四散分布很广的行政官员能够在他们自己的辖地内攫取一些主权者的权力，并使得他们开始时是寻求独立自主，最终变成了主人。

但是，如果说贵族制与人民政府相比，对德行要求较少的话，它却仍然要求一些它自身的德行，比如富人的节制，以及穷人的知足；因为看上去严格的平等在这里是不合时宜的，这一点即使在斯巴达也不曾见过。

此外，如果说这种政府形式内含了财富上的不平等的话，这也只是为了能够把对公共事务的管理授予那些最能够为此奉献全部时间的人，而不是如亚里士多德所断言的，是为了使富人总是能够被选中。反之，通过相反的选择时不时地教育人民：与财富相比，优良品质是应该被看重的一个更为重要的资格，也是十分必要的。

CHAPTER 6
Monarchy

So far we have considered the prince as a collective and artificial person, unified by the force of the law and acting as trustee of executive power in the state. We have now to consider that power being held in the hands of a natural person, a real man, one having the sole right to exercise it according to the law. Such a man is known as a monarch or king.

Contrary to the other administrations, where a collective being represents an individual, in this one an individual represents a collective being; so that the moral unity which constitutes the prince is at the same time a physical unity, naturally bringing together those faculties which the law brings together with such difficulty in the other forms of administration.

Thus the will of the people and the will of the prince, the public force of the state and the individual power of the government, all respond to the same mover; all the levers of the machine are in the same hands; all act towards the same end; there are no conflicting movements to counteract one another, and we cannot imagine any constitution where more action would be produced by less effort.

第六章　论君主制

以前我们曾经把君主当作一个集体的、人为的人格来考察，它是由法律的力量才结合起来的，并且在国家中作为行政权力的保管人。现在我们必须考虑权力掌握在一个自然人、一个真实的人手中的情况，即只有这个唯一的人才能根据法律来行使这个权力。这样的一个人就是一个君主或者国王。

与其他的由一个集体人格来代表一个个人的管理形式不同，在这种政府中，是由一个个人来代表一个集体的人格，因而构成君主的那个道德上的统一体[1]，同时也就是一个肉体上的统一体[2]，在其他的政府形式中法律要花费很大的困难才能使之结合起来的种种才能，在此很自然地就结合在一起了。

因而，人民的意志和君主的意志、国家的公共力量和政府的个别的权力，都只向同一个人负责；国家机器的所有控制杆都掌握在同一双手中；所有的行为都指向同样的目标；这里根本没有相互冲突的行为，使得两者相互抵消，我们不能想象任何别的体制能够通过更少的努力而产生更多的效果。阿基米德静静

〔1〕 即是指行政者的整体。

〔2〕 即是指一个个人，国君。

Archimedes sitting quietly on the shore and effortlessly launching a large ship is the model of a skilful monarch governing his vast kingdom from his chamber and making everything move while he himself seems motionless.

But if there is no government more vigorous than monarchy, there is also none where the particular will has more command, and more easily dominates the other wills. Everything moves towards the same end, it is true, but that end is not the public happiness; and the very strength of the administration operates continuously to the disadvantage of the state.

Kings want to be absolute, and from afar men cry out to them that the best way of becoming absolute is to make themselves loved by their people. This is a fine precept; and even in some respects a very true one. Unfortunately, it will always be laughed at in courts. The power which rests on the love of the people is undoubtedly the greatest, but is precarious and contingent; and princes will never be satisfied with it. The best kings want to be able to be bad if they feel like it without ceasing to be masters; a political sermonizer may well tell kings that since the people's force is the king's force, a king's best interest is to have the people flourishing, numerous and formidable; but kings know very well that this is not true. Their personal interest is primarily that the people should be weak, wretched and never able to resist them. I admit that if the subjects were always perfectly submissive, then it would be to the interest of the prince for the people to be strong, so that the people's strength, being also the prince's strength, should make him feared by his neighbours; but since this is only a secondary and subordinate advantage, and since strength is incompatible with submissiveness, it is natural that princes always prefer the doctrine that is more immediately useful to them. This is what Samuel put forcefully to the Hebrews,

地坐在海岸上毫不费力地使一条大船发动，正可以象征着一位技巧极高的君主只要待他的内阁中就可以统治他的辽阔王国，他自己看上去是一动不动的，但是却驱动着所有的东西。

但是，如果说没有任何政府能比君主制政府更加有活力的话，那么同样没有任何别的政府，其个别意志具有更大的支配性，能更加容易地控制其他的意志。的确，这里所有的东西都朝向同一个目标，但是这个目标却不是公众的幸福，而且正是这个行政权力又持续不断地变成对国家的损害。

国王想成为绝对的统治者，人们从遥远的地方向他们大声呼吁：成为绝对统治者的最好方式就是让自己得到人民的爱戴。这是一个很好的准则，而且在某些方面，它甚至是非常真实的准则。不幸的是，在宫廷中它总是遭到嘲笑。以人民的爱戴为基础的权力毫无疑问是最伟大的，但也是不稳定的和短暂的，而君主永远不会对此感到满意，就是最好的国王也希望如果他们愿意就可以做坏事，同时又依然是主人。一个政治布道者可以明白地告诫国王：既然人民的力量就是国王的力量，那么一个国王最大的利益就是使人民繁荣兴盛、人口众多、力量强大；但是国王又清楚地知道这并不是事实。他们的个人利益首先在于：人民应该是软弱的、悲惨的，而且永远都不能反抗他们。我承认，如果臣民永远能完全顺从的话，那么使人民强大起来也可能会和君主的利益是相符合的，因为这就使得人民的力量也就成为君主的力量，从而使他们令周围的邻居所畏惧；但是既然这只是第二位的、次要的利益，又因为力量和顺从总是不相容的，所以很自然地，君主们总是会更喜欢那些对他们来说更加直接有用的原则。这就是塞缪尔向希伯来人强烈表达过的、也是马基雅弗利明

and what Machiavelli has proved very clearly— under the pretence of instructing kings, he has taught important lessons to the people. Machiavelli's *Prince* is a handbook for republicans. ①

We have seen from the discussion of general proportions that monarchy is suited only to large states, and we find this again when we examine monarchy in itself. The more numerous the public administrators, the more the ratio between prince and subjects diminishes and approaches parity, coming to a point where the ratio is one to one, or equality itself, in democracy. This same ratio is greater to the extent that the government contracts, and reaches its maximum when the government is in the hands of a single man. Then there is too great a distance between the prince and the people and the state lacks bonds of union. For such bonds to be formed there must be intermediary ranks, with princelings, grandees, and a nobility to fill them. But all this is unsuited to a small state, which would be ruined by so many social orders.

But if it is difficult for a large state to be well governed, it is still more difficult for it to be well governed by a single man; and everyone knows what happens when a king rules through deputies.

An essential and inevitable defect, which will always make monarchical government inferior to republican government, is that whereas in republics the popular choice almost always elevates to the highest places only intelligent and capable men, who fill their office with honour,

---

① Machiavelli was a gentleman and a good citizen; but being attached to the house of Medici, he was forced during the oppression of his country to disguise his love of liberty. The very choice of an execrable hero reveals his secret intention, and the antithesis between his principles in his book *The Prince* and those in his *Discourses on Livy* and *The History of Florence* proves that this profound political thinker has so far had only superficial or corrupted readers. The Pope's court strictly prohibited his book, which I can well believe, since that was the Court he depicts most plainly.

确地证明过的——马基雅弗利以向国王提供指导作为伪装，把这些教训教给了人民。他的《君主论》成为共和党人的手册[①]。

我们由前面对一般比率的探讨中已经看到，君主制仅仅适用于大的国家，这里就君主制本身再进行考察的时候，我们又一次发现了这一点。公共行政人员的数量越多，君主和臣民之间的比率就越缩小，并且越接近于相等；到了某一点上，即民主制中，这个比率是一比一，或者说比例项完全相等。而随着政府的精简，这个比率则会相应地逐渐增大，当政府掌握在唯一一个人手中的时候，这个比率达到它的最大值。这时，君主和臣民之间有着太大的距离，国家也就没有了联系的纽带。要使这种纽带形成，国家中就必须有包含了王子、王公、贵族的中间等级。但是所有这些对于一个小的国家都是不合适的，小国会因为这么多的等级而毁灭的。

但是，如果说治理好一个大的国家很困难的话，那么由一个人治理好一个大国就将会更加困难；而且每个人都知道当一个国王通过代理机构进行统治的时候将会发生什么。

一个根本的、不可避免的缺陷使得君主制政府总是不如共和制政府，这个缺陷就是在共和国中公共的选择几乎总是只把那些有智慧的、有能力的人提拔到那些最高的位置上，这些人也会

---

① 马基雅弗利是一个君子，也是一个好公民；但是由于依附于梅狄奇家族，所以在国家的压力下，马基雅弗利被迫掩饰了他对自由的热爱。他在此书中选择一个令人憎恨的主人公便揭示了他的秘密企图，而且他在《君主论》一书中的原则和他在《李维论》、《佛罗伦萨史》等书中的原则的互相对立，也证明了这位渊博的政治思想家到目前为止还只是拥有一些肤浅的、堕落的读者。罗马宫廷严禁了他的书，对此我完全相信，因为他最清晰地描绘了罗马宫廷。

those who rise under monarchies are nearly always muddled little minds, petty knaves and intriguers with small talents which enable them to rise to high places in courts, but which betray their ineptitude to the public as soon as they are appointed. The people is much less often mistaken in such choices than is a prince, and a man of real merit is almost as rare in a royal ministry as a fool at the head of a republican government. Thus, when by some happy chance a born ruler takes the helm of affairs in a monarchy that is almost wrecked by swarms of egregious administrators, then everyone is amazed at the resources he discovers, and his reign marks an epoch in the history of the country.

For a monarchy to be well governed, its size and extent ought to be proportionate to the talents of those who govern. It is easier to conquer than to administer. With enough leverage, a finger could overturn the world; but to support the world, one must have the shoulders of Hercules. However small the state may be, princes are almost always inadequate. When, on the other hand, it happens that the state is too small for its ruler, a very rare thing, then it is even worse governed, because such a ruler, in following his own broad vision, forgets the people's interest; and he makes them no less miserable by the misuse of his superabundant abilities than a mediocre ruler would make them through the defects of an insufficient talent. It is as if kingdoms ought, so to speak, to expand or contract with each successive reign, according to the capacity of the prince. In a republic, on the other hand, where the talents of the senate are of a more settled measure, the state can have fixed boundaries without the administration working any less well.

The most perceptible disadvantage of government by one man is the lack of that continuity of succession which provides an

光荣地履行他们的职责；但是在君主制下，得到提升的几乎总是那些缺乏头脑的人、卑鄙的骗子、阴谋家，这些人凭借一点小聪明使他们在宫廷中爬到很高的位置，但是一旦他们得到任命，他们的不称职也就马上暴露在公众面前。在这种人员选择中，人民会比君主犯少得多的错误；而在一个皇室政府中，能有一个具有真正的优良品质的人，就像在共和制政府的首领中有一个傻子一样少见。因而，如果由于某种幸运的机会，一个天生的统治者在一个几乎被一大群极端的执政者们败坏了的君主制政体中掌握了权力的话，那么我们就都会为他提出的应对办法而吃惊，而且他的统治将会在这个国家的历史上开辟一个新纪元。

要使一个君主制国家得到良好的治理，它的大小和领土范围应该是与统治者的才能成比例的。征服一个国家比治理一个国家更加容易。只要有足够的杠杆作用，一个手指就可以颠倒整个世界；但是要维持这个世界，人们就必须有赫居里士的肩膀了。但是，不管这个国家如何的小，对它来说，国君也几乎总是力量不足的。然而，假若真有这种情况，即国家对于统治者来说真是太小了（这是极少见的事情），那么这个国家甚至会治理得更糟，因为这样一个统治者会为了追求他的宏图大略而忘记了人民的利益；由于他对自己才能的过分滥用而给人民带来的不幸，并不比一个普普通通的君主由于才能的缺乏而带来的不幸更小。可以这么说，一个王国每朝每代都应该根据君主的能力来扩大或者缩小其领土。相反，在共和制国家中，由于议院的才能有着一个更为确定的度量，所以国家可以有固定的边界，而不会使国家的治理变坏。

由一个人治理的政府其最显而易见的缺点就是缺乏继承上的连续性，而在其他两种政府体系中，有一种继承上的连续性为社会

uninterrupted bond of union in the other two systems. When a king dies, another is needed; elections leave a dangerous interval; they are stormy; and unless the citizens have more disinterestedness and integrity than is usual under such governments, there will be bribery and corruption. It is difficult for one to whom the state has been sold not to sell it in his turn, and recover from the weak the gold which the strong have extorted from him. Sooner or later, under such an administration everything becomes venal; and the peace which is enjoyed under kings is worse than the disturbances of interregnums.

What has been done to prevent this evil? Thrones have been made hereditary in certain families, and an order of succession thus set up to prevent any dispute on the death of the king— that is to say, by substituting for the disadvantages of elections, the disadvantages of regencies, apparent peace has been preferred to wise administration, and the risk of having children or monsters or imbeciles for rulers preferred to having to dispute the choice of a good king. People do not realize that in exposing themselves to the hazards of these alternatives, they are gambling against all the odds. It was a very shrewd remark that the young Dionysus made to his father, when his father, reproaching him for a dishonourable action, said: 'Did I set you such an example?' 'Ah,' replied the son, 'your father was not a king.'

When someone is brought up to command others, everything conspires to rob him of justice and reason. Great pains are taken, we are told, to teach young princes the art of ruling; but it does not appear that this education does them any good. It would be better to begin by teaching them the art of obeying. The greatest kings known to history were not among those brought up to rule, for ruling is a science that is least well mastered by too much practice;

结合体提供了永不间断的纽带。当一个国王去世后，就需要选举一个新的国王，而选举会导致一个危险的间断期。这种间断期会充满狂风暴雨，而且除非在这种政府下的公民能比平常具有更大的无私和正直，否则就会出现贿赂以及腐败。那些收买了国家的人，很难得接下来不再出卖国家，难得不从弱者那里夺回自己以前被强者勒索去的金钱。在这样一种管理之下，迟早有一天一切事情都会成为贪污腐败的。人们在国王统治下享受到的这种和平要比空位时期的混乱更糟糕呢。

人们曾经做过什么来防止这种邪恶的产生呢？人们曾经使王位在某些特定的家族中世袭，并且确定了继承的次序以防止由于国王的去世而引起的争端。这就是说，通过用摄政的缺陷来取代选举的缺陷，表明人们宁愿要短暂的和平，而不愿要贤明的行政管理；宁愿冒险让小孩、怪物、智障者作为统治者，也不愿为了选择一个好的国王而产生争端。人们没有意识到当他们冒着危险做这种选择的时候，他们已经使得一切机会都不利于自己了。小狄俄尼索斯的父亲曾因为一件非常可耻的事而责备小狄俄尼索斯说："我为你做过如此的榜样吗？"小狄俄尼索斯说："哦，可是你的父亲并不是国王啊。"小狄俄尼索斯对他父亲说的这句话是很精明的。

当一个人被培养到能号令别人的时候，一切就都会合力来剥夺他的正义感和理性了。据说要教会一个年轻的王子统治的艺术是要费很大力气的，但是结果显示这种教育对他们并没有任何益处，如果开始时就教育他们服从的艺术的话会更好的。历史上那些有名的、伟大的国王并不是培养出来的，因为统治乃是这样的一门科学：练习得越多，掌握的便越少；而且一个人通过服从，比通

it is one a man learns better in obeying than in commanding. *Nam utilissimus idem ac brevissimus bonarum malarumque rerum delectus, cogitare quid aut nolueris sub alio Principe aut volueris.*

One consequence of this lack of coherence is the instability of royal government, which, being sometimes directed according to one plan and sometimes according to another, depending on the personality of the king who rules, or of those who rule for him, cannot long have a fixed objective or a consistent policy; this unsettledness makes the state drift from principle to principle, and from project to project, a defect not found in those forms of government where the prince is always the same. Thus we see that, in general, if there is more cunning in a royal court, there is more wisdom in a republican senate, and that republics have a more stable and effective guidance — something which cannot obtain where every revolution in the administration means a revolution in the state — for it is the universal rule of all ministers and nearly all kings to reverse the policy of their predecessors.

This same lack of cohesion gives the lie to a sophism which is very common among royalist political thinkers, that is, not only of comparing civil government to household government and the prince to the father of a family — a fallacy I have already refuted — but also of generously attributing to a royal ruler all the virtues he has need of, and always assuming that the prince is everything he should be. With the help of these assumptions, royal government becomes manifestly preferable to all other kinds, because it is incontestably the strongest, and needs only a corporate will more in harmony with the general will to be also the best form of government.

But if, according to Plato, a born king is a very rare being — how often do Nature and Fortune combine to enthrone such a man? And if

过发号施令，对此人们会学习得更好。“辨别什么是好的和什么是坏的最有效的且最简便的方式就是想象一下，当由别的人而不是你自己来做国王的时候，你会希望发生什么。”

这种缺乏连贯性的一个后果就是皇室政府的变化无常，它们有时用这种计划来指导自己，有时又用另一种计划来指导自己，而这完全取决于进行统治的国王或者代国王统治的人的个性，因而他们不能长时期地有一个确定的目标，也不能有一个一贯的政策。这种变化无常总是使政府由一种原则转到另一种原则，由一个计划转到另一个计划；而这种缺陷在其他形式的政府中是没有的，因为在那些政府形式中君主是同一的。这样，我们会看到，通常情况下，如果在一个皇家宫廷中有越多的诡诈，那么在共和政体的元老院中就有越多的智慧，因而共和政体就能有一个更加稳定而且有效的指导。在那些政府的变革就意味着整个国家的革命的地方是不可能得到这种结果的，因为所有的大臣和几乎所有的国王都会颠覆他们前任的政策，这是一条普遍的准则。

同样是这个一贯性的缺乏，驳斥了保皇主义的政治思想家普遍坚持的一个诡辩，那就是，他们不仅把国家政治比拟于家庭政治，把君主比拟于一家之主（这个谬论我已经反驳过了），而且他们还慷慨地给一个皇家统治者加上他们应该具有的所有美德，并总会假定君主的确就是他们应该是的那个样子。借助于这些假定，皇室政府变得明显优越于其他各种类型的政府，因为它无可争辩地是最强的政府，而且只要它的团体意志能更加符合于公意，它们甚至就可以是最好的政府形式。

但是如果根据柏拉图的观点，一个天生的国王是十分罕见的，自然和命运要花费多久才能结合起来把王位授予这样的一个人呢？

a royal education necessarily corrupts those who receive it, what must be expected of a succession of men brought up to rule?

It is deliberate self-deception to confuse royal government with the government of a good king. To understand what this form of government is inherently, one must consider it as it is under mediocre or evil princes, for either princes will be such when they accede to the throne or such is what occupying the throne will make them.

Although these difficulties do not escape our authors, they have never been in the least embarrassed by them. The remedy, they say, is to obey without a murmur. God in his wrath inflicts bad kings on us, so they must be endured as a divine punishment. This argument is undoubtedly edifying; but I fancy it is more suited to the pulpit than to a book of political theory. What would be said about a physician who promised miracles, and whose whole art was to teach the sick to practise patience?

We all know that we have to put up with a bad government when it is bad; the problem is to find a good government.

如果皇家教育必然地会腐蚀那些接受这种教育的人，那么我们对于那些被培养出来继承统治的人又能期望什么呢？

把皇室政府和一个明君治理的政府混为一谈，这是一种故意地自我欺骗。要理解皇室政府这种政府形式本质上究竟如何，我们必须考虑：当它由一个平庸或者邪恶的君主统治的时候，它会是什么样子，因为君主们不是在登上王位的时候就已经是平庸或是邪恶的，就是王位会使得他们变得平庸或者邪恶。

我们的作家们并不是没有看到这些难题，但是这些难题一点也没有使他们感到困窘，他们说解决的办法就是默不做声地服从。愤怒的上帝使坏的君主降临到我们头上，所以作为上帝的惩罚，我们必须忍受这些坏的君主。毫无疑问，这种论辩是很有教训意义的，但是我认为它更适合于在布道坛中讲，而不是在一本政治理论书中讲。如果一个医生对病人许诺了奇迹，而他所能做的就只是告诉这个病人要耐心，我们会怎样评价这个医生呢？

我们都知道当一个政府变坏的时候，我们不得不忍受它，但是问题是要寻求一个好的政府。

CHAPTER 7

Mixed Forms Of Government

Strictly speaking, no government of a simple form exists. A single head of state has to have subordinate magistrates; a people's government must have a head. Thus in the division of executive power there is always a gradation from the larger number to the smaller— with this difference, that sometimes the many depend on the few, and sometimes the few depend on the many.

Sometimes there is an equal division, either when the constitutive parts are mutually dependent, as in the government of England, or when the authority of each part is independent but imperfect, as in the case of Poland. This latter form is bad, because there is no unity in the government, and the state lacks bonds of union. Which is better: a simple form of government or a mixed one? This is a question much debated by political theorists, and one to which I myself must give the answer I gave earlier about all forms of government.

In itself, the simple form of government is the best, precisely because it is simple. But when the executive power is not sufficiently subordinate to the legislative— that is to say, when the ratio of prince to sovereign is greater than that of people to prince— this lack of proportion has to be remedied by dividing the government, for then all the diverse elements of the government will have no less authority over the subjects, but their separation will make them less powerful against the sovereign.

第七章　论混合形式的政府

严格地说，单一形式的政府是不存在的。一个有唯一的首领的国家也必须要有附属的行政官员，一个人民政府也必须要有一个首领。因而，在行政权力的划分中总会存在着人数由多到少的等级——其不同之处只在于，有些时候是多数要依赖于少数，有些时候少数则是要依赖于多数。

有时候也会有完全相等的权力划分，这或者是在政府的各个组成部分是相互依存的时候，就像英国政府；或者是在各个组成部分虽然独立但却并不完备的时候，比如波兰政府。后一种形式是不好的，因为这样的政府中没有团结，而且国家也会缺乏黏合剂。单一形式的政府和混和形式的政府，哪种政府更好些呢？这是政治理论家争论不休的一个问题，对于这个问题，我要给出和我早些时候关于政府形式的回答相同的答案。

就其本身而言，单一形式的政府是最好的，恰是因为它是单一的。但是当行政权力并不完全依附于立法权力的时候，就是说，当君主对于主权者的比率大于人民对君主的比率的时候，这种比率的失衡必须通过对政府进行划分来补救。因为通过划分，虽然政府的各个部门对于臣民的权威并没有减少，但是对它们的分割将使它们总体上不如主权者力量强大。

The same disadvantage can also be prevented by establishing intermediate magistrates who, separated from the government altogether, serve only to balance the two powers, and uphold their respective rights. Then the government is not mixed, it is tempered.

The opposite disadvantage can be remedied by similar means; and when the government is too slack, commissions can be set up to give it concentration. In the first case, the government is divided in order to weaken it; in the second, in order to strengthen it. This is the practice of all democracies. The maximum of strength and of weakness are equally found in the simple forms of government, whereas the mixed forms provide a moderate degree of strength.

这同样的缺陷也可以通过设立居间的行政官员来防止，这些居间的行政官员从政府中分离出来，其作用只是平衡这两种权力，并且维持两者各自的权力。这样，这种政府便不是混和形式的，而只是有调节的形式。

相反的缺陷也可以通过类似的方式来挽回：即当政府太松弛的时候，可以设立一些委员会使政府变得集中。在第一种情况下，划分政府是为了削弱它；而在第二种情况下，划分政府是为了加强它。这是所有的民主制国家都在实践着的。在单一形式的政府中同时都可见到极度的强力和极度的软弱，但是混和形式的政府却能够提供比较适中的力量。

CHAPTER 8

That All Forms Of Government Do Not Suit All Countries

Freedom is not a fruit of every climate, and it is not therefore within the capacity of every people. The more one reflects on this doctrine of Montesquieu, the more one is conscious of its truth. And the more often it is challenged, the more opportunities are given to establish it with new evidence.

In every government in the world, the public person consumes but does not produce anything. Whence does it obtain the substance it consumes? From the labour of its members. It is the surplus of private production which furnishes public subsistence. From this it follows that the civil state can subsist only if men's work yields more than they themselves need.

But this surplus is not the same in every country of the world. In some it is substantial, in others middling, in some nil, in others a deficit. The proportion depends on the fertility of the climate, on the kind of labour which the soil requires, on the nature of its products, on the strength of the inhabitants, and on the degree of consumption that is necessary for them, and on various other factors which go to make up the whole proportion.

In addition, all governments do not have the same nature; some are more voracious than others; and their differences are based on this

第八章　论任何一种政府形式都不能适用于所有的国家

自由并非是任何气候条件下都能长出的果实，因而它就不是任何民族都能拥有的。人们越是能够反思孟德斯鸠提出的这个学说，就越能意识到它的真理性。这一学说越是受到人们的挑战，它就越有机会获得新的证据来证明它的准确性。

世界上每个政府中，公务人员从来都是只消费而不生产任何东西的。那么他们从哪里获得消费所需的那些东西呢？都是来自国家成员的劳动，正是个人产品的剩余供给了公共之所需。由此可以得出结论，只有当人们的劳动生产了超出他们自己所需的产品的时候，政治状态才能存在。

但是这种产品剩余在全世界不同国家中是不相同的。在一些国家中剩余是很充足的，在另外的一些国家中剩余则是适量的，在其他一些国家中剩余为零，还有一些国家中则有赤字。这个比例依赖于各国气候的好坏、土壤所需要的劳动的种类、它的产品的特性、当地居民的体力、他们所必需的消费量的大小，以及其他一些共同构成了这整个比例的各种各样的因素。

此外，并不是所有的政府在本性上都是相同的：有一些政府比其他政府更加贪婪；这些政府间的差别是建立在以下的原则之

next principle— that the further public contributions are from their source, the more burdensome they are. This burden should not be measured by the quantity of the contributions exacted, but by the distance they have to go to return to the hands from which they come; when this circulation is rapid and well established, it does not matter whether much or little is paid; the people will always be rich and finances will flourish. Correspondingly, however little the people gives, when that little does not return to it, it soon exhausts itself in continuous payments; the state is never rich and the people is always penurious.

This demonstrates that the greater the distance between the people and the government, the more onerous the taxes become; so that in a democracy the people is least burdened, in an aristocracy more burdened, and in a monarchy it bears the greatest weight of all. Monarchy is thus suited only to opulent nations, aristocracy to those of moderate wealth and size, and democracy to small and poor countries.

Indeed, the more one reflects, the more one recognizes that in this matter there are differences between free states and monarchies: in the former everything is used for the common advantage, while in the latter, private power and public power are competitive, and the one is increased only by weakening the other. As for despotism, instead of governing the subjects in order to make them happy, it makes them miserable in order to govern them.

Thus in every climate there are natural factors on the basis of which one can determine the form of government which that climate necessitates; and we can even say what sort of inhabitants each must have.

Mean and sterile places, where the product does not repay the labour, must remain uncultivated and deserted, or peopled only by savages.

上的：公共赋税距离它们的来源越远，那么赋税的负担就越重。这种负担不能通过用抽取赋税的数量来衡量，而要根据税收返回到交纳它们的纳税人手中要经过的距离来衡量。如果这一循环是很迅速的而且制度规定良好的话，那么税收的多少是无关紧要的；人民将总会是富裕的，而且财政也会是很繁荣的。相反的情况下，不管人们缴纳的税有多么少，如果这少量的税也不能返回到人民手中，人民不久就会因为持续不断地交税而使自己消耗一空；国家将永远不会富裕，人民将永远是困乏的。

这证明了人民和政府之间的距离越大，赋税就会变得愈发繁重。所以在一个民主制国家中人民的负担是最轻的，在贵族制国家中人民的负担会重一些，而在一个君主制国家中人民的负担是所有国家中最重的。因而君主制只适合于那些富裕的国家，贵族制适用于那些财富和领土中等规模的国家，而民主制则适合于小而贫穷的国家。

事实上，我们越是反思，就越能认识到在这个问题上自由国家和君主制国家之间是存在着差别的：在前者中，所有的东西都被用于公共的利益；而在后者中，私人的权力和公共的权力是相互竞争的，一个的增强要通过对另一个的削弱来达成。至于专制制度，它治理人民的目的不是使人民幸福，相反，它通过使人民生活悲惨以便于统治他们。

因而，在每种气候条件下都有一些自然因素，在这些因素的基础上就可以确定最适合于这种气候的政府形式，而且我们甚至可以说出这种气候下应该有什么样子的居民。

在环境劣等且贫瘠的地方，那里的产出根本不能偿还人们为之付出的劳动，只能放弃耕种而任其荒芜，或者让野蛮人去居住。

Places which yield only the bare necessities of men's lives must be inhabited by barbarous peoples, since no political society is possible. Places where the surplus of product over labour is moderate are suited to free peoples. Places where an abundant and fertile soil gives a lavish return for little labour will want monarchical government, so that the luxury of the prince may consume the surpius of the product of the subjects — for it is better that this surplus should be absorbed by the government than dissipated by private persons. There are exceptions, I know, but these exceptions themselves confirm the rule, in that sooner or later they produce revolutions which put things back into the order of nature.

We must always distinguish general laws from particular causes which can modify their effect. If all the South were covered with republics and all the North with despotic states, it would still be true that, in terms of climate, despotism suits hot countries, barbarism cold countries, and that a good polity suits temperate regions. I realize that this general rule may be admitted and its application disputed; it could be argued that there are very fertile cold countries and very barren southern ones. But this is a difficulty only for those who fail to see the thing in all its ramifications. One must, as I have already said, consider the factors of production, strength, consumption and so on.

Suppose there are two equal territories, one yielding five units, the other ten. If the inhabitants of the former consume four and those of the latter nine, the surplus of the one will be one-fifth and of the other one-tenth. The ratio of these two surpluses will then be the inverse of that of their products, so that the territory yielding five units will show a surplus double that of the territory yielding ten.

在那些产品仅能满足人们最起码的生活需要的地方，只能由未开化的民族去居住，因为在那里不可能存在政治社会。在那些超出于必要劳动的剩余产品比较适中的地方，则适合于自由的民族。而在那些充足而肥沃的土壤使得很少的劳动就可以获得慷慨回报的地方则需要君主制，这样，君主的奢侈就可以消费掉臣民产出的大量剩余——因为由政府来吸收这些剩余要比让这些剩余分散在个人手中好得多。我也知道有例外的情况，但是这些例外本身就确证了这个规律，即它们迟早会引发革命而使得一切事物又返回到自然的秩序中去。

我们必须时刻把一般规律和能够使一般规律的效果降低的特殊原因区分开来。即使整个南部都是共和制国家，而整个北方都是专制国家，然而，单就气候而言，专制更适合于热带国家，野蛮人适合于寒冷的国家，而良好的政治则适合于温带国家，这都仍然有其真理性。我知道人们可能会承认这一普遍规律，但是对于它的运用却颇有争议：人们可能争辩说，有很多土壤肥沃的寒冷国家，也有一些土壤贫瘠的南方国家。但这只是对于那些不能从各个方面观察事物的人来说才是一个难题。正如我已经说过的，我们必须考虑到产出、体力、消费等各种因素。

假设有两块面积相等的领土，一块产出五个单位的产品，另一块产出十个单位的产品。如果前者的居民消费掉四个单位的产品，而后者的居民消费掉九个单位的产品，那么其中一个的产品剩余就是五分之一，而另一个的产品剩余则是十分之一。那么，这两者剩余的比率就和它们产出的比率成反比，所以产出五个单位产品的那块领土的剩余就是产出十个单位产品的那块土地的剩余的两倍。

But there is no question of a double product, and I do not believe anyone could venture to equate the fertility of a cold country with that of a hot country. But let us assume such equality; let us, for example, equate England and Sicily, Poland and Egypt. Farther south there will be Africa and India; farther north, there will be nothing. What differences in agricultural technique will be needed to achieve this equality of product? In Sicily, it is enough simply to scratch the soil, while in England, how much effort is needed to work it! But where more hands are required to obtain the same product, the surplus is necessarily less.

Note a further point, that the same number of men consume much less in hot countries. The climate requires a man to be abstemious to keep fit— and Europeans who try to live in hot countries as they live at home die of dysentry and stomach disorders. 'We,' says Chardin, 'are carnivorous beasts, wolves, compared to the Asians. Some attribute the abstemiousness of the Persians to the fact that their country is less cultivated; but I, on the contrary, believe that their country is less rich in commodities because the inhabitants need less. If their frugality [he continues] were the effect of the poverty of the soil, it would be the poor alone who ate little; in fact everybody does; and instead of finding people eating less or more in each province according to the fertility of the land, one finds the same frugality throughout the kingdom. They are very proud of their way of life, and say that one has only to look at their complexions to see how superior their way is to that of other nations. And indeed, the complexion of the Persians is clear, their skin is fair, delicate and smooth, while that of the Armenians, their subjects who live in the European manner, is rough and blotchy, and their bodies are fat and heavy.'

但是这不是一个双倍产出的问题，而且我不相信，有人会把寒冷国家的土地肥沃程度等同于一个炎热国家的土地肥沃程度。但是，姑且让我们假设有这样的等同。比如，我们假设英格兰和西西里的情况是等同的，波兰和埃及的情况是等同的。向南更远的地方，有非洲和印度，向北更远的地方，就什么也没有了。要获得同等的产出，在农业技术上需要有多大的差异呢？在西西里，人们只要松松土就可以了，然而在英格兰则需要为其付出多少精力啊！在那些要获得同样的产出就需要更多人力的地方，剩余必然会减少。

我们更应该进一步注意到一点，在热带国家相同数量人口的消耗则要少得多。这里的气候要求人们节制食欲以保持健康，欧洲人在热带国家如果试图和在家乡一样的生活，那么他就会死于痢疾和消化不良。沙尔丹曾说："与亚洲人相比，我们就是食肉的野兽，是狼。有些人把波斯人的节约归因于他们国家的耕耘不善；与之相反，我却相信他们的国家之所以在日用品上不甚富裕，是因为那里的居民需求不多。如果他们的节俭，（沙尔丹接着说）是土地贫乏的结果，那就应该只有穷人才吃得少；但事实是所有的人都吃得少；而且人们并没有发现在他们的不同省份中，根据各处土地的肥沃程度，他们吃的有多有少，而是发现整个王国中人们都是同样的节俭。波斯人为他们的生活方式感到非常自豪，他们说只要看一下他们的面色就会知道他们的生活方式要比其他国家的人的生活方式优越得多。而且，事实上，波斯人的面色是匀净的，他们的皮肤美丽、细腻又光滑，然而按照欧洲人的方式生活的亚美尼亚人的皮肤则是粗糙而多斑点的，而且他们的身体肥胖又笨重。"

The closer men are to the equator, the more frugally they live. They eat hardly any meat; rice, maize, couscous, millet and cassava are their daily food. In India there are millions of men whose food costs less than a penny a day. In Europe itself we notice a marked difference of appetite between the peoples of the north and those of the south. A Spaniard could live eight days on the dinner of a German. In countries where men are more gluttonous, luxury is turned towards the things men consume. In England, it shows itself in tables loaded with meats; in Italy one is regaled on sugar and flowers.

Luxury in clothing reveals similar differences. In countries where the changes of season are swift and violent, people have better and simpler clothes; in countries where they dress only for appearance, people care more for show than utility, and clothes themselves are a luxury. In Naples you will see men strolling daily along the Posillipo in gold-embroidered jackets and no hose. It is the same thing with buildings; people attach importance to magnificence when they have nothing to fear from the climate. In Paris or London people want to be housed warmly and comfortably. In Madrid, they have superb reception rooms, but no windows that close and their bedrooms are like rat holes.

Foodstuffs are more substantial and richer in hot countries— this is a third difference and it does not fail to influence the second. Why does one eat so many vegetables in Italy? Because they are good, nourishing and of excellent flavour. In France, where they get nothing but water, they are not at all nourishing, and count for nothing at the table; but even so they take up no less ground and cost just as much to cultivate. Experiment has shown that the wheats of Barbary, otherwise inferior to those of France, yield much more flour; and that the French wheats, in turn, yield more than those of the North. From this one can deduce that

人们越是接近于赤道，他们生活得就越是节俭。他们几乎不吃肉食；大米、玉米、粗麦粉、小米、木薯是他们的日常食品。在印度有数百万的人，他们每天消耗的食品价值还不到一便士。即使在欧洲内部，在其北部的民族和南部的民族之间，我们也能发现在食欲上的明显差别。一个德国人的一顿晚餐可以让一个西班牙人吃上八天。在那些人民比较贪吃的国家，奢侈转而表现为人们所消耗的食物。在英格兰，奢侈表现在桌上摆满了肉类；而在意大利，人们只是享用糖类和鲜花而已。

人们在着装上的奢侈揭示了类似的差异。在那些季节变化迅速而且剧烈的国家，人民的穿着更加优良而且简单；而在那些穿着仅仅是为了外表的国家中，人们更看重着装的好看而非其实用性，衣着本身就成为一种奢侈。在那不勒斯，你每天都可以看到一些人沿着鲍西里普山漫步，他们穿着镶金边的上衣，却没有穿内衣。在建筑上也有类似的情况：当人们对于气候不再感到可怕的时候，人们便开始重视建筑的富丽堂皇。在巴黎或者伦敦，人们想要居住得温暖而且舒适；而在马德里，他们虽然有华丽的客厅，但是窗户大开，而且他们的卧室就像老鼠洞一样。

在热带国家，食品更加丰满而且富有营养。这是第三种差异，而且这个差异一定能影响到第二种差异。为什么在意大利人们食用那么多蔬菜呢？因为这里的蔬菜质量上乘、营养丰富而且味道又非常鲜美。而在法国，那里的蔬菜中除了水分之外什么都没有，它们一点都没有营养，因而在餐桌上根本没有什么价值；但即使这样，这些蔬菜占用的土地却一点也不少，而且也要花费同样的力气去耕种。实验已经显示，巴巴里的小麦虽然不如法国的小麦好，但是却可以产出更多的面粉；而法国的小麦产出的面粉则又比北方国家的小麦多。由此我们可以推断，沿着从赤道到极地这

a similar gradation may be observed along a line from the equator to the pole. Now is it not a tangible disadvantage to have a smaller amount of nourishment in an equal quantity of produce?

To all these various considerations, I may add another which is drawn from, and which reinforces them, that is, that hot countries need fewer inhabitants than cold countries, and can feed more— which provides a double surplus to the advantage of despotism. The wider the area that is occupied by the same number of people, the more difficult revolts become; for the inhabitants cannot get together quickly and secretly, while it is always easy for the government to discover plots and to cut communications. On the other hand, the more a numerous people is packed together, the less easily can the government infringe on the sovereign; popular leaders deliberate as securely in their private rooms as the prince in his council, and the crowd gathers as swiftly in the public squares as the troops in their barracks. It is thus to the advantage of tyrannical government to act over great distances. With the aid of strongpoints to serve as fulcra, its strength increases with distance, on the principle of leverage. ①

The strength of the people, on the contrary, is effective only if it is concentrated; it evaporates and is lost when it is dispersed, just as gunpowder scattered on the ground ignites only grain by grain. The least populous countries are thus the most fitted to tyranny; wild beasts reign only in deserts.

---

① This does not contradict what I said in Book II, Chapter 9, about the disadvantages of a large state, for there I was dealing with the authority of the government over its members, and here it is a question of the government's strength over the subjects. Its scattered members serve it as so many fulcra to exert pressure on the people from a distance, but it has no such fulcrum to exert pressure on its own members. Thus in the one case the length of the lever is its weakness; in the other, its strength.

条线我们可以观察到一种类似的分等级的现象。这样，从同等数量的产出中只能获得较少的营养，这本身不就是一个很明显的不利条件吗？

在所有这些各种各样的考虑之外，我还要补充另外一个考虑，这个考虑是从以上各项中引申出来的，但却可以强化它们；这个考虑就是热带国家与寒带国家相比需要更少的居民，却能供养更多的人民。这便提供了有利于专制政府的双重剩余。相同数量的人占有的领土面积越广，他们的反叛就变得越发困难；因为居民们不能迅速而且秘密地集合起来。然而对于政府而言，却总是可以很容易就发觉人们的密谋，并隔绝人们的联系。相反，越多数量的人聚集在一起，政府就越不容易侵犯到主权者；人民的领袖可以在他们的秘室中蓄谋，就像君主在他们的内阁中一样安全；而且人民也可以在广场上集合起来，就像军队在兵营中的集合一样迅速。因而，跨长距离的行动是残暴政府的一个有利条件。根据杠杆原理，借助于各地的战略要点作为杠杆的支点，它的力量随着距离的变远而增强①。

相反，人民的力量只有在集中起来的时候才是有效的；当它分散的时候，它就消失了，就像散在地上的火药只能星星点点地燃烧一样。因而人口最少的国家最适合于暴君制了，凶猛的野兽只是在荒漠地里称王称霸的。

---

① 这与我在本书第二卷第九章中所讲的大国的不利条件并不矛盾，因为在那里我是在讨论政府对于它的成员的权威，而这里却是一个政府对于臣民的权威问题。政府的分散的成员就像许多杠杆的支点服务于政府，对远方的人民施加压力，但政府却没有这样的支点对它自己的成员施加压力。因而，在一种情况下，杠杆的长度是它的弱点，而在另一种情况下，则是它的长处。

CHAPTER 9

The Signs Of A Good Government

When, therefore, one asks what in absolute terms is the best government, one is asking a question which is unanswerable because it is indeterminate; or alternatively one might say that there are as many good answers as there are possible combinations in the absolute and relative positions of peoples.

But if it is asked by what signs one can tell whether a given people is well or badly governed, that is another matter; and the question of fact can be answered.

Even so, it is not really answered, because everyone will want to answer it in his own way. Subjects prize public tranquillity; citizens the freedom of the individual— the former prefer security of possessions, the latter security of person; subjects think the best government is the most severe, citizens that it is the mildest; the former want crimes to be punished, the latter want them prevented; subjects think it is a good thing to be feared by their neighbours, citizens prefer to be ignored by them; the former are satisfied so long as money circulates, the latter demand that the people shall have bread. But even if there were agreement on these and suchlike points, should we be any more advanced? Moral dimensions have no precise standard of measurement; even if we could agree about signs, how should we agree in appraisal?

第九章　论一个好政府的标志

因此，当一个人询问什么是绝对意义上最好的政府时，他就是在提一个无法回答的问题，因为这是不确定的；或者我们可以这样回答：各民族的绝对处境和相对处境有多少种可能的组合，就有多少种最好的答案。

但是，如果有人问能否有一个标志可以判断某个特定的民族是否得到了良好的或者是不良的治理，那就是另一个问题了，对于这个事实上的问题是可以做出回答的。

即使如此，这个问题也并不能得到确实的回答，因为每个人都想按照自己的方式来回答这个问题。臣民们赞美公共的安宁，公民们则赞美个人的自由；前者更想要财产的安全，而后者宁愿要人身的安全；臣民们认为最好的政府是最严厉的政府，公民们则认为最好的政府是最温和的政府；前者希望犯罪得到惩罚，而后者则希望能防止犯罪；臣民们认为被周围的邻居所畏惧是一件好事，公民们则宁愿为周围的邻居所忽视；前者只要金钱能够周转就会感到满意，而后者则要求人们都能够丰衣足食。但是即使我们能在这些问题或者类似的问题上达成一致，我们是否就前进一步了呢？道德的维度是没有衡量的精确标准的，即使我们能在标志问题上达成一致，我们又怎么能在评判上也达成一致呢？

For myself, I am always astonished that people should fail to recognize so simple a sign, or be so insincere as not to agree about it. What is the object of any political association? It is the protection and the prosperity of its members. And what is the surest evidence that they are so protected and prosperous? The numbers of their population. Then do not look beyond this much debated evidence. All other things being equal, the government under which, without external aids like naturalization and immigration, the citizens increase and multiply most, is infallibly the best government. That under which the people diminishes and wastes away is the worst. Statisticians, this is your problem: count, measure, compare. ①

---

① One must judge on the same principle the centuries that merit preference in respect of the prosperity of the human race. People have too much admired those that have witnessed a flourishing of crafts and letters without penetrating the secret purpose of their culture, and without considering its fatal consequences, *idque apud imperitos humanitas vocabatur, cum pars servitutis esset*. Shall we never see behind the precepts of books the crude self-interest which prompts the authors to speak? No, whatever they may say, when, notwithstanding its brilliance, a country is depopulated, it is simply not true that all is going well; and it is not enough for a poet to have an income of 100,000 livres for his century to be the best of all. It is less important to consider the apparent repose and tranquillity of rulers than the wellbeing of whole nations and above all of the most populous states. A hailstorm may devastate a few cantons, but it rarely causes famine. Riots and civil wars may greatly alarm rulers, but they are not the true misfortunes of peoples, who can at least have a few months´respite during the quarrels as to who is to be the next tyrant. Their calamities and their happiness both arise from their permanent condition. When all remain supine under the yoke, it is then that everything decays, it is then that the rulers can destory them at their ease, ubi solitudinem faciunt pacem appellant. When the quarrels of the state disturbed the kingdom of France, and the Coadjutor of Paris attended the Parlement with a dagger in his pocket, this did not prevent the French people living happily and multiplying in a free and decent ease. In ancient times, Greece flourished at the height of the cruellest wars; blood flowed in torrents, but the whole country was thickly populated. ‘It appeared,’ says Machiavelli, ‘that in the midst of murder ,proscription and civil wars, our republic became stronger than ever; the civil virtue lf the citizens, theirmorals, and their independence, served more effectively to strengthen it than all theiv dissensions may nave done to weaken it.’ A little disturbance gives vigour to the soul, and what really makes the species prosper is not peace but freedom.

对于我自己来说，我总是会惊讶于人们不能够认识到如此简单的一个标志，或者他们是如此不真诚以至于不承认这个标志。政治联合的目标是什么呢？那就是对它的成员的保护和使之繁荣。而它的成员得到保护并且繁荣的最确定的证据是什么呢？那就是它们的人口数量。那么不必再到这个证据之外去寻找那些有争议的证据了。假定其他所有的情况都是相等的，如果在某个政府的治理下，不借助于诸如归化和移民等外在帮助，它的公民增长和繁衍最多，那么这个政府绝对无误地就是最好的政府。在其治理下人民减少并且逐渐衰弱的政府则是最坏的政府。统计学家们，这就是你们的问题了，请你们计算、测量、比较吧①。

---

① 我们必须根据同样的原则来判断，哪个世纪从有利于人类的繁荣这个方面讲更值得我们欣赏。人们对于那些见证了艺术、文学上的繁荣的世纪有太多尊崇了，而不能洞察到这些文化背后的目的，也不能想到它们不幸的后果，“无知者称之为‘人道’的，其实已是奴役的开始了。”〔1〕难道我们永远都不能从这书里的格言背后看到那些促使作者们夸夸其谈的粗鄙的自私自利吗？不，不管他们说了些什么，尽管一个国家声名显赫，但当它的人口减少的时候，还要说一切都运转良好就绝不是真实的了。一个诗人拥有十万里弗的收入并不足以证明他所处的世纪是所有世纪中最好的世纪。与顾虑统治者表面上的悠闲和安宁相比较，顾虑整个国家、特别是人口最多的国家的福利是更加重要的。一场冰雹可能会破坏几个行政区，但是却很少会导致饥馑。骚乱和内战可能会极大地震动统治者，但是对人民来说，它们并不是真正的不幸，因为在统治者们为谁会成为下一个暴君争论不休的时候，人民至少可以有几个月的喘息机会。人民的灾难和幸福都是来自于他们持久性的生存状态。当所有的人在枷锁之下都变得消极懒散的时候，正是这时，所有的东西才都毁灭了，也正是在这时，统治者才可以随意地摧残人民，“在他们造成废墟的地方，他们称之为和平。”〔2〕当国家内的争吵扰乱了法兰西王国的时候，当巴黎副主教口袋里藏着匕首去参加议会的时候，这并没有阻止法兰西人民在一种自由而体面的安逸中幸福地生活和繁衍。在古代，希腊在最残酷战争的高潮期间繁荣起来了；血流成了河，可是整个国家中却布满了密密的人口。马基雅弗利说：“看上去好像正是在谋杀、流放和内战中，我们的共和国变得比以前更加强大了；公民的德行、他们的精神、他们的独立对于共和国的加强，与他们的争执对共和国可能的削弱相比较更加有效。”小的震荡可以赋予人们的灵魂以活力，而真正使人类种族繁荣的，不是和平，而是自由。

〔1〕、〔2〕引自塔西佗（公元55～120年罗马历史家）的《历史·阿格瑞科拉传》

CHAPTER 10

The Abuse Of Government And Its Tendency To Degenerate

Just as the particular will acts unceasingly against the general will, so does the government continually exert itself against the sovereign. And the more this exertion increases, the more the constitution becomes corrupt, and, as in this case there is no distinct corporate will to resist the will of the prince and so to balance it, sooner or later it is inevitable that the prince will oppress the sovereign and break the social treaty. This is the inherent and inescapable defect which, from the birth of the political body, tends relentlessly to destroy it, just as old age and death destroy the body of a man.

There are two common ways by which a government degenerates— when it itself contracts and when the state dissolves.

The government contracts when its members pass from a greater to a smaller number, that is, from democracy to aristocracy, or from aristocracy to royal government. This is its natural tendency. ①If it were to move

① The slow formation and progress of the Republic of Venice in its lagoons provides a notable example of this progression; and it is really astonishing that after more than twelve hundred years, the Venetians seem still to be at the second stage, which began with the Serrar di Consiglio in 1198. As for the ancient

第十章　论政府的滥用权力和它退化的倾向

正像个别意志总是持续不断地反对公意一样，政府也在一刻不停地极力反对主权者。这种反对的努力越是增强，政府机构就越加腐败，而且由于在这种情况下没有一个截然独立的团体意志来对抗君主意志并平衡君主意志，所以君主意志迟早不可避免地要压抑主权者，并且破坏社会条约。这是一种与生俱来的、无法摆脱的缺陷，自从政治体诞生那时起，它就在无情地破坏政治体，正像衰老和死亡破坏人的身体一样。

一个政府的退化，有两种通常的方式：即政府自身的收缩和国家的解体。

当政府的成员数目由多转少的时候，就是说由民主制转为贵族制，或者由贵族制转为皇室政府的时候，政府就收缩了。这是一种自然的倾向①。如果政府沿着另外一个方向转

---

① 威尼斯共和国在其泻湖中的缓慢形成和发展，为这种变化进程提供了一个明显的例证。经过了一千二百多年之后，威尼斯人好像仍然处在 1198 年由塞拉尔·迪·康塞里奥所开启的第二个阶段上，这实在是令人感到惊讶。至

in the other direction from a smaller number to a greater, the government might be said to slacken; but such an inverse progression is impossible.

For indeed, a government never changes its form unless its exhausted energies are too feeble to maintain its original form.

Doges, for whom the Venetians are reproached, whatever may be said by the *squittinio della libertà veneta*, there is proof that the Doges were not their sovereigns.

People will not fail to quote against me the case of the Roman Republic, which is said to have followed a reverse sequence, from monarchy to aristocracy and from aristocracy to democracy. But I am very far from sharing this opinion.

The first constitution of Romulus was a mixed government, which promptly degenerated into a despotism. For special reasons, the state perished before its time, just as one sometimes sees an infant die before reaching the age of maturity. The expulsion of the Tarquins was the real moment of the birth of the Republic. But it did not at first assume a fixed form, because the failure to abolish the patriciate left the task half-finished. For the hereditary aristocracy, which is the worst of all legitimate administrations, remained in conflict with democracy, and the form of government, continuously uncertain and wavering, was not fixed (as Machiavelli has proved) until the establishment of the tribunes; only then was there a true government and a true democracy. For indeed the people then was not only sovereign, but also magistrate and judge; and the senate was no more than a subordinate commission to temper and concentrate the government, while the consuls themselves—in spite of their being patricians, chief magistrates and absolute commanders in war— were never more in Rome than presidents of the people.

From that time, the government was seen to follow its natural inclination, and tend strongly towards aristocracy. The patriciate having as it were abolished itself, the aristocracy was no longer seated in the body of the patricians, as in Venice and Genoa, but in the body of the senate composed of patricians and plebeians, even in the body of the tribunes, when they began to usurp the active power. For words do not alter things, and when the people have chiefs who govern on their behalf, this is still an aristocracy no matter what name those persons bear.

The abuse of aristocracy gave birth to civil war and the triumvirate. Sulla, Julius Caesar and Augustus became in fact as good as monarchs, and finally under the despotism of Tiberius the state was dissolved. Roman history, then, does not belie my principle: it confirms it.

变，即成员数目由少转多，那么可以说政府松弛了，但是这种反向的过程是不可能的。

因为事实上，一个政府除非它的能量过度消耗而变得太过于虚弱，以致不能维持自身原来的形式，否则它是永远也不会改变它的形式的。

于那些威尼斯人加以谴责的古代总督，不管《威尼斯自由论》一书中是如何评论他们的，有证据证明这些总督并不是他们的主权者。

人们一定会举出罗马共和国的例子来反驳我，据说罗马共和国是遵循着相反的次序发展的，即由君主制到贵族制，再由贵族制到民主制。但是我远不能赞同这种观点。

罗穆鲁斯建立的第一个政府是混和形式的政府，之后这个政府迅速地退化为专制政府。由于一个特别的原因，这个国家在其寿限之前就灭亡了，这就像我们有时会看到一个婴儿在达到它的成熟年龄之前就夭折了一样。塔尔干王朝的被驱逐才是罗马共和国诞生的真正时刻。但是一开始罗马共和国并没有采用一种固定的政府形式，因为罗马人没有能够废除贵族等级，因而使得这一事业半途而废了。由于世袭的贵族制，也就是所有合法的行政体制中最坏的那种体制，一直与民主制处在冲突当中，所以政府形式一直处于不确定和摇摆之中，直到保民官的设立，政府形式才确定下来（正如马基雅弗利所证实了的）；只有到了这时，罗马人才有真正的政府和真正的民主制。因为这时候，人民事实上就不仅仅是主权者，而且也是行政官员和法官；而元老院只不过是一个附属的代理机构，以缓和和集中政府的力量，执政官本人尽管是贵族、首席执行官以及战争中的绝对统帅，但在罗马也只不过是人民的主持人而已。

从那时开始，人们发现罗马政府便遵循了它的自然倾向并且强烈地趋向于贵族制。贵族等级好像自己消灭了自己一样，贵族制不再像威尼斯和热那亚那样存在于贵族的共同体之中，而是存在于贵族和平民共同构成的元老院共同体之中。由于名称并不能改变事物，所以当人民有了代表自己进行治理的首领的时候，不管这些人有什么样的名字，这实际上仍然是贵族制。

贵族制政府的滥用权力导致了内战和三头政治。苏拉、尤利乌斯·恺撒和奥古斯都事实上已经变得相当于君主了，而且最后在提贝留乌斯的专制之下，这个国家解体了。因而，罗马的历史并没有驳斥我的原则，它反而确证了我的原则。

If it slackened while expanding, its strength would be absolutely null, and it would be even less likely to survive. It must therefore wind up and tighten the mechanism as it begins to slacken, for otherwise the state which depends on it will fall into ruin.

The dissolution of the state may take place in two ways.

First it takes place when the prince ceases to administer the state according to the law and usurps the sovereign power. Then a remarkable change occurs; for it is not the government but the state which contracts— by which I mean that the state as a whole is dissolved and another is formed inside it, one composed only of members of the government and having no significance for the rest of the people except that of a master and a tyrant. Now, at the moment the government usurps sovereignty, the social pact is broken, and all the ordinary citizens, recovering by right their natural freedom, are compelled by force, but not morally obliged, to obey.

The same situation occurs when the members of the government separately usurp the power which they ought only to exercise as a body; for this is no less an infraction of the law, and it produces an even greater disorder. For then there are, so to speak, as many princes as there are magistrates, and the state being no less divided than the government, perishes or changes its form.

When the state is dissolved, the abuse of government, whatever it may be, takes the general name of *anarchy*. More precisely democracy degenerates into *ochlocracy*, aristocracy into *oligarchy*, and I would add that royal government degenerates into *tyranny*, except that this last word is ambiguous and requires explanation.

In the commonly understood sense, a tyrant is a king who governs violently and without regard to justice and the law. In the

如果一个政府随着扩张而松弛自身，那么它的力量将会归于绝对的零，而且它甚至不太可能继续生存。所以当一个政府开始松弛的时候，就必须为它上紧发条使它的机构紧张起来，否则的话，它所支撑的国家就会毁灭。

国家的解体可以通过两种方式发生。

首先，它发生在君主不再按照法律治理国家，并且篡夺了主权者权力的时候。这时，一个显著的变化发生了，因为这时收缩的就不是政府而是国家。这里我的意思是说，作为一个整体的国家解体了，而在它的内部却形成了另一个国家，这个国家仅仅是由政府的成员构成，而它对于其他所有的人民，除了是一个主人和暴君之外没有任何意义。因而，在政府篡夺了主权的那一刻，社会契约就被破坏了，所有的普通公民就正当地重新获得了他们天然的自由，他们的服从仅仅是由于武力的强迫，而非出于道德上的义务。

相同的情况还发生在当政府的成员分别地篡夺了他们本应该作为一个整体来行使的权力的时候，因为这同样是对法律的侵害，而这甚至会引起更大的混乱。可以说这时国家中就有了同行政官员数目相同的君主，国家像政府一样被分割了，它或者走向灭亡或者改变它的形式。

当国家解体的时候，政府对于权力的滥用，不管是什么样的滥用，都有了一个共同的名字——无政府状态。更加精确地讲，民主制退化成了暴民政治，贵族制退化成为寡头政治，而且我还要补充说皇室政府退化成为暴君制，只是后面的这个词语意思不甚明确，因而需要解释一下。

一般理解的意义上，一个暴君就是一个无视正义和法律而进行暴力统治的国王。在确切的意义上，一个暴君就是一个本没有

exact sense, a tyrant is an individual who arrogates to himself royal authority without having any right to it. It is thus that the Greeks understood the word 'tyrant'. They applied it indiscriminately to good and bad princes whenever their authority was not legitimate. ① Thus *tyrant* and *usurper* are perfectly synonymous words. To give different names to different things, I call a usurper of royal authority a 'tyrant' and the usurper of the sovereign power a 'despot'. The tyrant is one who intrudes, contrary to law, to govern according to the law; the despot is one who puts himself above the law. Thus the tyrant need not be a despot, but a despot is always a tyrant.

---

① '*Omnes enim et habentur et dicuntur Tyranni qui potestate utuntur perpetua, in ea Civitate quae libertate usa est.*' (Cornelius Nepos, *Life of Miltiades.*) It is true that Aristotle (*Nicomachean Ethics*, VIII, 10) distinguishes between a tyrant and a king, saying the former governs for his own advantage while the latter governs only for the advantage of his subjects; but in addition to the fact that in general all the Greek authors used the word 'tyrant' in another sense, as we see above all in the *Hiero* of Xenophon, it would follow from Aristotle's criterion, that there had never yet been a single king since the beginning of the world.

权利拥有皇权权威，但却把皇权权威强加于自己身上的个人。希腊人正是这样来理解“暴君”这个词的。如果君主的权威是不合法的[1]，不管他们是好是坏，希腊人都会不加选择地把这个词用到他们身上，因为暴君和篡位者是两个词义完全相同的词语。为了赋予不同的事物以不同的名称，我这里把皇权权威的篡夺者称为“暴君”，而把主权者权力的篡夺者称为“专制君主”。暴君是一个违背法律进入政权，但是却依照法律进行统治的人；而专制君主则是一个把自己置于法律之上的人。因此，暴君不一定是专制君主，但是一个专制君主总是一个暴君。

---

① “在一个习惯了自由的城邦中，那些永久地行使权力的人就会被认为是并称作暴君。”（考那留斯·尼波斯《米提阿底斯传》第八章）的确，亚里士多德《尼各马可伦理学》卷八，第十章）对暴君和国王做过区分，他说前者是为了他自己的利益而进行统治，而后者则是为了他的臣民的利益而进行统治；但是所有的希腊作家一般地都是在另一种意义上使用“暴君”这个词，就像我们在色诺芬尼的《希罗》一书中见到的那样；除此之外，我们从亚里士多德的标准可以得出结论，自从世界开始以来，还不曾有过一个国王。

CHAPTER 11

The Death Of The Body Politic

Such is the natural and inevitable inclination of the best constituted governments. If Sparta and Rome perished, what state can hope to last for ever? If we wish, then, to set up a lasting constitution, let us not dream of making it eternal. We can succeed only if we avoid attempting the impossible and flattering ourselves that we can give to the work of man a durability that does not belong to human things.

The body politic, no less than the body of a man, begins to die as soon as it is born, and bears within itself the causes of its own destruction. Either kind of body may have a constitution of greater or less robustness, fitted to preserve it for a longer or shorter time. The constitution of a man is the work of nature; that of the state is the work of artifice. It is not within the capacity of men to prolong their own lives, but it is within the capacity of men to prolong the life of the state as far as possible by giving it the best constitution it can have. And although even the best constitution will come to an end, it will do so later than any other, unless some unforeseen hazard fells it before its time.

The principle of political life dwells in the sovereign authority. The legislative power is the heart of the state, the executive power is the brain, which sets all the parts in motion. The brain may become paralysed and the individual still live. A man can be an imbecile and survive,

第十一章　论政治体的死亡

这就是政府自然的、不可避免的倾向，哪怕是最好的政府也是如此。如果斯巴达和罗马都灭亡了，那么我们还能希望什么样的国家能够永远存在呢？如果我们希望建立一种持久性的体制，那么我们就不要梦想着使它成为永恒的。只有当我们不去尝试那些不可能的事情的时候，当我们不自夸能够赋予人类的作品一种不属于人类的永恒性的时候，我们才可能成功。

政治体就像人体一样，从它一降生，它就开始走向死亡，而且它自身当中就含着使它走向死亡的原因。这两者[1]都可能拥有一种具备或多或少活力的体制，从而使它们在一个或长或短的时期内维持它们自身。人体的组织是大自然的产物，而国家的机制则是人工的作品。人们没有能力延长自己的寿命，但是他们却有能力通过赋予一个国家尽可能最好的体制，从而使一个国家的寿命尽可能地延长。尽管最好的体制也会有一个终结，但是与其他体制相比，它会终结得晚一些，除非有某种不可预知的危险使它在寿限到来之前就毁灭了。

政治生命的原则就在于主权权威。立法权力是国家的心脏，而行政权力是国家的大脑，大脑促使所有的部分运转起来。大脑可能会麻痹，但是这个人仍然会是活着的。一个人可能是白痴，

---

〔1〕 指政治体和人体。

but as soon as his heart stops functioning, the creature is dead.

It is not only through the law that the state keeps alive; it is through the legislative power. Yesterday's law is not binding today, but for the fact that silence gives a presumption of tacit consent and the sovereign is taken to confirm perpetually the laws it does not abrogate while it has power to abrogate them. Everything which it has once declared to be its will, it wills always— at least until it issues a revocation.

Why then do ancient laws command so much respect? Precisely because they are ancient. We must believe that it is only the excellence of such laws that has enabled them to last so long; if the sovereign had not continually recognized them as salutary, they would have been revoked a thousand times. This is why the laws, far from growing weaker, constantly gain new strength in every well-constituted state; the prejudice in favour of antiquity makes them every day more venerable; in those cases, on the other hand, where the laws become weaker with age, this shows that there is no longer any legislative power and that the state is dead.

但却活着，然而一旦他的心脏停止了跳动，这个人就死亡了。

使一个国家生存下去，不仅要通过法律，还要通过立法权力。过去的法律不能约束今天，但是基于我们可以假定沉默就是一种默认，在主权者有权力废除法律却没有废除它们的时候，我们就可以认为主权者是在持续确认着这些法律。主权者一旦宣布某事是它的意志，那它就永远是主权者的意志——至少在主权者发布一条撤回命令之前是。

那么为什么古老的法律会获得如此多的尊敬呢？这正是因为它们的古老。我们必须相信，正是由于这些法律的卓越才使得它们能够保存得这么久；如果不是主权者持续不断地确认它们是有益的，它们可能已经被废除过一千次了。这就是在一个体制良好的国家中，法律远不是越来越弱，而是持续不断地获得新的力量的原因了。人们对于古老的东西的偏爱使它们每天都能获得更多的尊敬；但是另一方面，在一些地方，随着年代的久远，法律变得越来越弱，这表明那里不再有立法权力了，而且国家死亡了。

CHAPTER 12

How The Sovereign Authority Maintains Itself

The sovereign, having no other force than the legislative power, acts only through the laws, and since the laws are nothing other than authentic acts of the general will, the sovereign can act only when the people is assembled. The people assembled, it will be said— what an illusion! It is indeed an illusion today; but two thousand years ago it was not. Has human nature so much changed?

The boundaries of the possible in the moral realm are less narrow than we think; it is our own weaknesses, our vices and our prejudices that limit them. Base minds do not believe in great men; low slaves smile in mockery at the word 'freedom'.

In the light of what has been done, let us consider what can be done. I shall not speak of the ancient republics of Greece; but the Roman Republic was, it seems to me, a large state and the town of Rome a large town: the last census gave four hundred thousand men in Rome carrying arms, and the last census calculation under the Empire more than four million citizens without counting subjects, foreigners, women, children or slaves.

One would suppose that it must have been difficult to bring together frequently the numerous people of the capital and its surroundings. In fact, very few weeks passed without the Roman people being assembled, even several times in one week. This people not

第十二章　论主权权威如何维持自身

主权者除了立法权力之外没有其他任何力量，所以他们只能通过法律起作用，但既然法律只不过是公意的正式表达，那么只有当人民集合在一起的时候，主权者才能起作用。人们可能会说，所有的人集合在一起，那是一个什么样的幻想啊！人类的本性如此大地改变了吗？

道德领域的事物可能性的界限，要比我们想象的宽广得多；正是由于我们的弱点、我们的恶行以及我们的偏见局限了它。卑鄙的心灵是不会信任一个伟大人物的；卑贱的奴隶总会嘲笑“自由”这个字眼。

以已经做过的事情为依据，我们可以考虑什么事情是可能做到的。我不想说古希腊共和国，但是罗马共和国在我看来是一个很大的国家，罗马城也是一个很大的城市。最近的普查显示：罗马城拥有武器的人达四十万之多。普查也显示：即使不计算属民、外邦人、女人、小孩和奴隶，整个罗马帝国的公民也有四百万以上。

有人可能会说，把首都及周围地区数量众多的人民经常地集合起来一定是很困难的。事实上，罗马人很少有一连几个星期不进行集会的，他们甚至一个星期中集会好几次。这些人民不仅

only exercised the rights of sovereignty, but also a part of the government. It dealt with certain business; it tried certain cases; and the entire people in the public assemblies enacted the role of magistrate almost as often as that of citizen.

Looking back to the earliest history of nations, we notice that the majority of ancient governments, even monarchical ones like those of the Macedonians and the Franks, had similar assemblies. In any case, the one indisputable fact I have cited answers our question; it seems to me good logic to reason from the actual to the possible.

行使主权权利，而且也行使一部分政府权利。他们处理某些事务，他们审判某些案件，而且在公共集会中，所有的人扮演行政官员的角色几乎和他们承担的公民角色一样地频繁。

反观各民族的早期历史，我们会注意到大多数古代政府，即使像马其顿人或者法兰克人的君主制政府，都曾有过类似的集会。无论如何，我所举的这个不可争辩的事实很好地回答了我们的问题；在我看来，从实际的推论是可能的，是很符合逻辑的。

CHAPTER 13

The Same: Continued

It is not enough that the assembled people should have once determined the constitution of the state by giving sanction to a body of laws; it is not enough that it should set up a perpetual government, or that it should have provided once and for all for the election of magistrates. In addition to the extraordinary assemblies that unforeseen events may necessitate, there must be fixed and periodic assemblies which nothing can abolish or prorogue, so that on the appointed day the people is rightfully summoned by the law itself without any further formal convocation being needed.

But apart from these assemblies which are lawful by their date alone, any assembly of the people which has not been summoned by the magistrate appointed for that duty and according to the prescribed form must be held to be unlawful, and everything it does must be void, for the order to assemble should itself emanate from the law.

As to whether legitimate assemblies should be more or less frequent, this depends on so many circumstances that one cannot lay down in advance any precise rules. One can only say that in general the more strength the government has, the more frequently the sovereign should reveal itself.

This, I shall be told, may be good for one single town, but what is to be done if the state consists of several towns? Is the sovereign

第十三章　论主权权威如何维持自身(续)

集合起来的人民通过批准一套法律体系而确定了国家的体制，这还是不够的；人民建立了永久性的政府，或者他们一劳永逸地提出了行政官员的选举办法，这也是不够的。除了那些由于不可预知的事件所必需的特别集会之外，国家中还必须要有固定的、定期举行的集会，而且什么事情都不能废除或者中止这些集会。这样，在那些指定的日期，人民便会依据法律本身合法地集合起来，而不再需要进一步的正式召集。

但是除了这些仅凭法定日期本身召集的合法集会之外，人民的其他的任何集会，如果不是由被指定的负有此种职责的行政官员根据法定形式召集的，就必须被认定是非法的，而且它所决定的任何事情都是无效的，因为集会的命令本身就应该是依据于法律的。

至于说这种合法集会应该举行的次数多少，这依赖于太多的环境因素，因而我们不能提前提出任何确切的规则。我们只能说政府拥有越强大的力量，主权者就应该越频繁地表达自己。

有人可能会告诉我，这对于一个单独的城镇可能是很好的，但是如果一个国家中包含了许多城镇，又该怎么办呢？是把主权

authority to be divided? Or should it be concentrated in one single town holding the others as subject? I answer that neither the one thing nor the other should be done. In the first place, the sovereign authority is simple and single; it cannot be divided without being destroyed. In the second place, a town cannot legitimately be subject to another any more than a nation may be, because the essence of the political body lies in the union of freedom and obedience so that the words 'subject' and 'sovereign' are identical correlatives, the meaning of which is brought together in the single word 'citizen'.

I should answer further that it is always an evil to unite several towns in one nation, and whoever wishes to form such a union should not flatter himself that the natural disadvantages can be avoided. It is no use complaining about the evils of a large state to someone who wants only small ones. But how are small states to be given enough strength to resist large states, as the Greek cities once resisted a great king and as, more recently, Holland and Switzerland resisted the House of Austria?

Nevertheless, if the state cannot be limited to reasonable boundaries, there remains one remedy, and that is to have no fixed capital, but to move the seat of government from one place to another and to assemble the estates of the country in each in turn.

People the territory evenly, extend the same rights to everyone, carry the same abundance and life into every quarter — it is by these means that the state will become at once the strongest and the best governed that is possible. Remember that the walls of towns are made only from the debris of rural houses. Every time I see a mansion being built in the capital I fancy I can see the whole countryside covered with hovels.

权威分割开来呢？还是把它集中在一个单独的城镇之上，并把其他城镇作为它的臣属呢？我的回答是，这两者都不可行。首先，主权权威是简单而且单一的，我们分割它，就一定会摧毁它。其次，正像一个国家一样，一个城镇不能合法地成为另一个城镇的臣属，因为政治体的本质就在于自由和服从的结合，所以“臣民”和“主权者”这两个词是有相同意义的相关语，它们的意义在“公民”这个词语上结合在了一起。

我还要进一步回答说，把几个城镇结合成为一个国家总是一件不好的事，任何一个希望建立这样一种结合的人都不能自诩说，这样就可以避免一些自然的不利了。对那些只希望有小国家的人诉说大国家的恶行是没有用的。但是怎样才能赋予小国家足够的力量以对抗大的国家呢？就像希腊的城市曾经抵抗大国王[1]一样，又像更晚近一些的荷兰和瑞士曾抵抗奥地利王室一样。

然而，如果不能把国家规模限定到一个合理的界限，这里也还有一个补救的办法，那就是不要有一个固定的首都，而是轮流把政府所在地从一个城镇转移到另外一个城镇，并且轮流在每个城镇召集国家的各个阶层。

人民均衡地遍布于领土之上，相同的权力扩展到每个人，给每个角落带去同样的富足和生机，正是通过这些方式，一个国家才可以立刻变得最为强壮，才能得到尽可能好的治理。请记住，城市的高墙都只能以乡间的房屋化为断壁残垣为代价。每次我在首都看到一座宫殿兴建起来，就好像可以看到整个乡村布满了废墟。

---

〔1〕 指波希战争时波斯王大流士第一和薛西斯。

CHAPTER 14

The Same: Continued

The moment the people is lawfully assembled as a sovereign body all jurisdiction of the government ceases; the executive power is suspended, and the person of the humblest citizen is as sacred and inviolable as that of the highest magistrate, for in the presence of the represented there is no longer any representation. Most of the disturbances which took place in the Roman assemblies were the result of this rule being either unknown or neglected. The consuls were no more than the presidents of the people; the tribunes were mere speakers;① the senate was nothing at all.

These intervals of suspension, when the prince recognizes— or ought to recognize— a real superior, are always alarming for princes; and the assemblies of the people, which are the shield of the body politic and the brake on the government, have always been the nightmare of magistrates; hence the latter spare no effort in raising objections, problems, promises to turn the citizens against assemblies. When the citizens are avaricious, cowardly, pusillanimous, and love repose more than freedom, they do not hold out against the redoubled efforts of the government. It is then that, as the opposing force increases continuously,

① The word is used here somewhat in the sense it has in the English parliament. The resemblance between these functions would have caused conflict between the Consuls and the Tribunes, even if all jurisdiction had been suspended.

第十四章　论主权权威如何维持自身（续）

一旦人民作为一个主权者共同体合法地集合起来，政府所有的权限就停止了，行政权力就暂时中止了，而且最卑贱的公民的人身也就和最高行政官员的人身一样神圣不可侵犯了。在罗马集会中发生的大多数骚乱都是规则不被了解或者被忽视的结果。执政官只不过是人民的主持人，保民官只是发言人①，而元老院则什么都不是了。

对于统治者来说，这些权力暂时中止的间歇期总是很可怕的，因为这时他们承认、而且也应该承认有一个真实的在上者；而且人民的集合作为政治共同体的保护者和政府的约束者，总是会成为行政官员的恶梦。因此，政府总是会不遗余力地提出种种反对、难题以及诺言以使公民转而反对集会。如果公民是贪婪的、胆怯的、懦弱的，或者热爱安逸超过于热爱自由，那么公民就不能长久反对政府的一再努力了。正是这时候，随着反抗〔1〕的力量增

---

① 这个词语在这里的用法有点类似于在英国的议院中的用法。即使所有的权限都被暂时中止了，这些职能之间类同之处也还导致了执政官和保民官之间的冲突。

〔1〕 指政府反抗主权者。

the sovereign authority atrophies in the end and the majority of republics fall and perish before their time.

But between the sovereign authority and arbitrary government there sometimes appears an intermediate power of which we must now speak.

强，最后主权权威萎缩了，大多数共和政体也过早地衰落、毁灭了。

但是在主权权威和专断的政府之间有时会出现一种中间力量，对这种中间力量我们接下来必须要谈一谈了。

CHAPTER 15

Deputies Or Representatives

As soon as public service ceases to be the main concern of the citizens and they come to prefer to serve the state with their purse rather than their person, the state is already close to ruin. Are troops needed to march to war? They pay mercenaries and stay at home. Is it time to go to an assembly? They pay deputies and stay at home. Thanks to laziness and money, they end up with soldiers to enslave the country and deputies to sell it.

It is the bustle of commerce and the crafts, it is the avid thirst for profit, it is effeminacy and the love of comfort that commute personal service for money. Men give up a part of their profits so as to increase the rest at their ease. Use money thus, and you will soon have chains. The word 'finance' is the word of a slave; it is unknown in the true republic. In a genuinely free state, the citizens do everything with their own hands and nothing by means of money; far from paying for exemption from their duties, they would pay to discharge them in person. I am very far from sharing received ideas: I believe that compulsory service is less contrary to liberty than is taxation.

The better the state is constituted, the more does public business take precedence over private in the minds of the citizens. There is indeed much less private business, because the sum of the public happiness furnishes a larger proportion of each individual's happiness,

第十五章　论议员或者代表

一旦公共服务不再是公民的主要关注点，一旦他们变得宁可用他们的钱包为国家服务，也不愿意亲自为国家服务，那么这个国家就已经接近毁灭了。国家需要军队开赴战场吗？那他们就花钱雇佣军队而自己待在家里。到日期该参加集会了吗？那他们就花钱雇用代表而自己待在家里。由于懒惰和金钱的缘故，他们最终让士兵来奴役这个国家，让代表来出卖这个国家。

正是商业和工艺业的驱逐，由于对于利益的热切渴望，以及由于柔弱和贪图舒适，才使得可以用金钱交换亲身的服务。人们放弃了他们的一部分利益，这样一来他们就可以无拘无束地增加其他的利益。出钱吧，你们不久就会得到锁链的。因为“钱财”这个词是属于奴隶的词语，在一个真正的共和国之中，人们是不知道这个词语的。在一个真正自由的国家中，公民亲身做一切事情，而不用金钱做任何一件事；他们远不是花钱以免除义务，他们宁可为了亲自履行义务而付钱。这里我与人们普遍接受的观点相去甚远了：我相信义务性服务与征税相比更不违背自由。

一个国家的体制越好，在公民的心目中，公共事务就越是优先于私人事务。事实上，这里很少有私人事务了，因为公共幸福的总和便为每个人提供了绝大部分的私人幸福，所以为个人留下

so there remains less for him to seek on his own. In a well-regulated nation, every man hastens to the assemblies; under a bad government, no one wants to take a step to go to them, because no one feels the least interest in what is done there, since it is predictable that the general will will not be dominant, and, in short, because domestic concerns absorb all the individual's attention. Good laws lead men to make better ones; bad laws lead to worse. As soon as someone says of the business of the state — 'What does it matter to me?' — then the state must be reckoned lost.

The cooling-off of patriotism, the activity of private interest, the vastness of states, conquests, the abuse of government — all these have suggested the expedient of having deputies or representatives of the people in the assemblies of the nation. This is what in certain countries they dare to call the third estate — the private interest of two classes being there given first and second place, and the public interest only third place.

Sovereignty cannot be represented, for the same reason that it cannot be alienated; its essence is the general will, and will cannot be represented — either it is the general will or it is something else; there is no intermediate possibility. Thus the people's deputies are not, and could not be, its representatives; they are merely its agents; and they cannot decide anything finally. Any law which the people has not ratified in person is void; it is not law at all. The English people believes itself to be free; it is gravely mistaken; it is free only during the election of Members of Parliament; as soon as the Members are elected, the people is enslaved; it is nothing. In the brief moments of its freedom, the English people makes such a use of that freedom that it deserves to lose it.

The idea of representation is a modern one. It comes to us from feudal government, from that iniquitous and absurd system under which the human race is degraded and which dishonours the name of man.

来的、需要他亲自去追求的幸福就很少了。在一个治理良好的国家中，每个人都踊跃参加集会，但在一个坏政府之下，任何人都懒得动一步去参加集会，因为既然人们可以预知在那里公意是不会占主导地位的，而且家务私事又吸引了所有人的注意，于是便没有一个人对集会所做的事情有一点兴趣了。好法律可以引导人们制订更好的法律，而坏法律却只能引导人们制订更坏的法律。一旦一个人对国家事务说出："这与我有什么关系呢？"这个国家肯定就完蛋了。

爱国热情的冷却、私人利益的活跃、国家的辽阔、四处征服以及政府的滥用权力，所有这些都暗示着在国家的集会中人民的议员或者代表的出现。这便是在某些国家公然号称的第三等级。在那里，两个阶级的私人利益被赋予了第一第二的位置，而公共的利益却只是第三位的。

主权是不能被转让的，基于同样的原因，它也是不能被代表的；主权的本质就是公意，而意志是不能代表的。意志或者是公意或者是别的什么意志，而根本不会有中间的可能。因此人民议员就不是而且也不能是人民的代表，他们仅仅是人民的代理人，而且他们不能最终决定任何事情。任何一条不是由人民亲自批准的法律都是无效的，它根本就不是法律。英国人认为他们是自由的，这是一个严重的错误；他们只有在选举国会议员的时候才是自由的，一旦国会议员选举出来之后，他们就被奴役了，他们就什么都不是了。在自由的短瞬时间中，英国人对自由的使用方式，使他们注定要失去自由。

代表的观念是一个近代的观念。它是从封建政府那里来的，是从使人类蒙受屈辱并且羞辱了“人”这个称号的那种不公正的、荒

In the republics and even in the monarchies of the ancient world, the people never had representatives; the very word was unknown. It is remarkable in the case of Rome, where the tribunes were so sacred, that no one ever imagined that they might usurp the functions of the people; and in the midst of such a great multitude, they never attempted to pass on their own authority a single *Plebiscitium*. One can judge, however, the embarrassment the crowd sometimes caused from what happened at the time of the Gracchi, when a great part of the citizens voted from the rooftops.

Where rights and freedom are everything, inconveniences are nothing. Among these wise people, everything was given its just measure; the lictors were allowed to do what the tribunes would not have dared to do; the people were not afraid that their lictors would wish to represent them.

To explain how, even so, the tribunes did represent the people, it is enough to consider how the government represents the sovereign. Since the law is nothing other than a declaration of the general will, it is clear that there cannot be representation of the people in the legislative power; but there may and should be such representation in the executive power, which is only the instrument for applying the law. This indicates that if we look carefully, we shall find that very few nations have laws. However that may be, it is certain that the tribunes, having no part of the executive power, could never represent the Roman people by the rights of their own office, but only by usurping those of the senate.

Among the Greeks, all that the people had to do, it did itself; it was continuously assembled in the market place. The Greek people lived in a mild climate; it was not at all avaricious; slaves did the work; its chief concern was its freedom. Without the same advantages, how can the same rights be preserved? Your harsher climate creates more necessities; ①six months of the

---

① To adopt in cold countries the luxury and softness of the orientals is to ask to have their chains, to make submission even more inevitable than theirs.

谬的制度那里来的。在古代共和政体中，甚至是在古代君主制中，人民都不曾有过代表，他们不知道这样一个词语。罗马便是一个很明显的例子。在罗马，保民官是如此的神圣，以至于没有人能想象他们会篡夺人民的职能；保民官在如此盛大的群众集会中也未曾试图对他们的权威进行一次全民投票表决。然而，从格拉古时代所发生的事情我们可以得知人口众多有时会带来不方便，那时候曾经有很大一部分人要在屋顶上进行投票。

在权利和自由就是一切的地方，不方便也就不算什么了。在那些贤明的人民那里，任何事情都会有恰当的处理方式；他们会让他们的扈从去做那些保民官从来都不敢去做的事情，人民不必害怕他们的扈从会想要代表他们。

要解释保民官是如何代表人民的，只要我们考虑一下政府是如何代表主权者的就足够了。既然法律只不过是公意的宣告，那么很明显，在立法权力上，人民是不能有代表的；但是在行政权力上，人民可以有而且应该有这样的代表，因为行政权力只是应用法律的工具。这就表明如果我们仔细观察的话，我们就会发现很少国家是真有法律的。无论如何，可以确定，保民官一点都没有行政权力，根据他们职位的权限，除非他们通过篡夺元老院的权利，他们是永远不能代表罗马人民的。

在希腊，所有人民必须要做的事情，他们都是亲自去做；他们坚持不断地在市场上集会。希腊人生活在一种温和的气候之中，他们都不贪婪，工作都是由奴隶来做，他们首要关注的就是他们的自由。没有了这样的便利条件，现在的人们又怎么能保有相同的权利呢？你们的严寒气候使你们产生更多的需求①，一年中

① 在寒冷的国家，要采纳东方人的奢侈与温和，就是要求带上他们的枷锁，就会比东方人更加不可避免地屈服于二者。

year the public places are uninhabitable; your muted tongues cannot make themselves heard in the open air; you care more for your profits than your freedom; and you fear slavery less than you fear poverty.

What? Is freedom to be maintained only with the support of slavery? Perhaps. The two extremes meet. Everything outside nature has its disadvantages, civil society more than all the rest. There are some situations so unfortunate that one can preserve one's freedom only at the expense of the freedom of someone else; and the citizen can be perfectly free only if the slave is absolutely a slave. Such was the situation of Sparta. You peoples of the modern world, you have no slaves, but you are slaves yourselves; you pay for their liberty with your own. It is in vain that you boast of this preference; I see more cowardice than humanity in it.

I do not mean by all this to suggest that slaves are necessary or that the right of slavery is legitimate, for I have proved the contrary. I simply state the reasons why peoples of the modern world, believing themselves to be free, have representatives, and why peoples of the ancient world did not. However that may be, the moment a people adopts representatives it is no longer free; it no longer exists.

All things carefully considered, I do not see how it will be possible henceforth among people like us for the sovereign to maintain the exercise of its rights unless the republic is very small. But if it is very small, will it not be subjugated? No. I shall show later① how the external strength of a large people can be combined with the free government and good order of a small state.

---

① This is what I intended to do in the remaining part of this work, when, in dealing with foreign relations, I should have come to the subject of confederations. This subject is entirely new, and its principles have yet to be established.

有六个月在公共场所不适合久留，在露天的场合中你们微弱的声音根本不能让人们听得到，你们关心你们的利益超过了关心你们的自由，而且你们害怕被奴役远不如你们害怕贫穷。

什么？难道自由只能借助于奴隶制度的支持才能维持吗？或许是的。这两个极端相遇在一起了。任何非自然的东西都有其缺点，公民社会与其他非自然物相比有更多的缺点。有些情况是很不幸的，以至于一个人只能以牺牲别人的自由为代价才能保持自己的自由；只有在奴隶是绝对的奴隶的时候，公民才能是完全自由的。斯巴达的情况就是如此。你们这些近代世界的人，你们没有奴隶，但是你们自身就是奴隶；你们用你们自己的自由偿还了奴隶的自由。你们在此吹嘘你们的这种选择是无益的；我在其中看到的懦弱远比人道要多。

通过所有这些，我并不是想说奴隶是必须的，或者奴役的权利是合法的，因为我已经证明了相反的观点。我只是陈述为什么近代世界中认为自己是自由的人们会有代表，而古代世界的人们却没有。不管怎么样，一旦人民接受了代表，他们就不再自由了；自由就不再存在了。

仔细地考虑了所有的情况之后，我在像我们一样的人民当中，看不到任何主权者可以继续行使其权利的可能性，除非这个国家是非常小的。但是如果它是很小的，难道它不会被征服吗？不会。以后[①]我将说明，人民如何能够把一个大的民族的对外力量同一个小的国家的自由的政府与良好的秩序结合起来。

---

① 这是我在本书的剩余部分中想要做的，在探讨对外关系时，我本应该想到联邦这个主题的。这个主题是全新的，它的原则还未被确立起来。

CHAPTER 16

That The Institution Of The Government Is Not A Contract

Once the legislative power is well established, it remains to establish similarly the executive power; for the latter, which operates only by particular acts, is essentially different from the former, and is naturally separate from it. If it were possible for the sovereign, considered as such, to have the executive power, then the *de jure* and the *de facto* would be so confused that people would no longer know what was law and what was not; and the body politic, thus perverted, would soon fall prey to that very violence it was instituted to prevent.

The citizens being all equal by the social contract, all may prescribe what all must do, instead of nobody having a right to demand that another shall do what he does not do himself. For it is precisely this right, indispensable for giving life and movement to the body politic, that the sovereign gives to the prince in instituting the government.

Several theorists have claimed that this act of institution is a contract between the people and the magistrates it sets over itself, a contract which stipulates between the two parties the conditions under which the one undertakes to command and the other to obey. It will be admitted, I am sure, that this is a strange way of contracting. But let us see if the theory is tenable.

First, the supreme authority can no more be modified than it can be alienated; to limit it is to destroy it. It is absurd and self-contradictory that the sovereign should give itself a superior;

第十六章　论政府的创制不是一项契约

一旦立法权力确立之后，行政权力同样也要被确立起来；对于后者，它只能通过个别行为来行使，所以它就与前者有着本质的区别，也就自然地与前者是相分离的。如果主权者就其作为主权者而言，也能拥有行政权力，那么权力和事实就会严重混淆，以至于人们再也分不清什么是法律，什么不是法律；政治共同体因而也就是不正当的了，它不久将会成为暴力的牺牲品，而政府建立起来本来是要防止这种暴力的。

根据社会契约，所有的公民都是平等的，所有的人都可以规定哪些事情是所有的人都必须做的，但是任何一个人都无权命令另外一个人做他自己都不去做的事情。在政府创制的时候，主权者授予统治者的，正是这种赋予政治体以生命并维持其运转所必不可少的权利。有些理论家曾经宣称，这种政府的创制行为是人民和他们设立的统治者之间的一项契约，这个契约规定了这两者的地位，即一方发布命令，而另一方服从命令。我确信，人们会承认这是一种莫名其妙的缔约方式。让我们看看这种理论是否站得住脚吧。

首先，最高的权威是不能改动的，正如它不能转让一样，限制它就是毁坏它。主权者给自己设立一个在上者是荒谬的、自相矛

to undertake to obey a master would be to return to absolute freedom.

Furthermore, it is clear that this contract of the people with such or such persons would be a particular act. From this it follows that this contract could not be a law, or an act of sovereignty, and hence that it would be illegitimate.

We see further that the contracting parties would, between themselves, be subject only to natural law, and so without any guarantee of their reciprocal commitments— and this is wholly repugnant to the civil state. Since the man who has force in his hand is always the master of what shall be done, this is like giving the name of ‘contract’ to the act of a man who says to another: ‘I give you all my property on condition that you give me back what you please.’

There is only one contract in the state: that of the association itself, and this excludes all others. One cannot imagine any public contract that would not be a violation of the original contract.

盾的；承诺服从于一个主人，那就是人们又恢复了绝对的自由。此外，很明显，人们和某些人订立的契约是一个个别的行为。由此可以得出结论，这种契约不是一个法律，不是一种主权行为，因此它就是不合法的。

我们可以进一步看到契约的双方只是受自然律的支配，而他们之间的相互承诺得不到任何保证，因而这与社会状态是完全不一致的。既然一个手中拥有强力的人总会作为主人决定人们应该做什么，那么如果一个人对另外一个人说，“我把我所有的财产都给你，条件是你想回赠我多少就多少”，这种行为也可以被赋予以“契约”的名号了。

国家中只有一个契约，即结成共同体的契约，这个契约本身就排斥了其他所有的契约。我们不能想象有任何一个公共契约会不违背最初的契约。

CHAPTER 17

The Institution Of The Government

In what conceptual terms then should we think of the act by which the government is instituted? I shall explain first that this act is complex, or composed of two others, namely the establishment of the law and the execution of the law.

By the first, the sovereign enacts that there shall be a body of government established with such or such form; and it is clear that this act is a law.

By the second, the people names the magistrates who are to be invested with the government thus established. Since this nomination is a particular act, it is not a second law, but simply a sequel to the first and a function of government.

The difficulty is to understand how there can be an act of government before the government exists, and how the people, which is only sovereign or subject, can in certain circumstances become prince or magistrate.

Now it is here once more that the body politic reveals one of those astonishing properties by which it reconciles operations that seem to be contradictory. For this operation is accomplished by the sudden transformation of the sovereignty into democracy in such a way that without undergoing any visible change, and simply through a new relation of all to all, the citizens become magistrates and pass from general acts to particular acts, and from the law to its execution.

This change of relation is not a refinement of speculative theory

第十七章　论政府的创制

那么，我们应该以何种观念来思考政府创制这一行为呢？我首先要解释的是，这种行为是合成的，或者说是由另外两者构成的，即法律的制订和法律的执行。

首先，主权者以法律规定，必须有一个以这种或者那种形式建立起来的政府实体；很明显，这种行为就是一项法律。

其次，人民任命行政官员，并把如上建立起来的政府授予他们。既然这种任命只是一个个别行为，那么它就不是第二个法律，它只是第一个法律的结果，是政府的一项职能。

困难就在于理解，在政府存在之前怎么就能有了一种政府的行为呢？只是作为主权者或者臣民的人民怎么又能在某种情况下成为统治者或行政官员呢？

正是在这里，政治体显示了它令人惊讶的一个特性，通过这一特性，政治体使看上去相互矛盾的行为协调起来了。因为这种行为是通过一种由主权到民主的迅速转变完成的，这种转变方式使转变几乎是不可见的，而且只是通过一种全体对全体的新联系，公民成为行政官员，普遍的行为转变为个别的行为，法律转变成为对法律的执行了。

这种联系上的改变并非是一种在实践中没有任何例证的玄

without example in practice; it happens every day in the English parliament, where the lower House on certain occasions transforms itself into a committee of the whole House the better to discuss affairs, and so becomes a simple committee of that sovereign court which it was itself a moment before; then later it reports to itself, in its capacity of House of Commons, on what it has just settled as a committee of the whole House, and again debates under one name what it has already decided under another.

It is the advantage peculiar to democratic government that it can be established in fact by a simple act of the general will. After this, the provisional government remains in office if such is the form adopted, or there is established in the name of the sovereign whatever government is prescribed by the law; and everything is then in order. It is not possible to institute the government in any other legitimate manner, without abandoning the principles established in earlier chapters.

虚的思辨理论，它每天都在英国的议院中发生着。在那里，为了更好地处理事务，在某些特定的情况下下议院把自身转变成为全院委员会，因而，刚才它自身还是一个主权者的会场，现在它却变成了主权者的一个简单的委员会；之后，它要以全院委员会的身份就刚才已经解决的问题向作为下议院的它本身做出汇报，而且又要以其中一方的名义对以另一方的名义已经做出决定的事情进行争辩。

民主制政府的优点就在于这种政府事实上只要通过公意的一次简单行为就可以确立起来。这之后，如果这种政府形式被采纳了，那么这种临时政府就可以继续执政，否则就以主权者的名义建立任何一种由法律所规定的政府形式，这样任何事情就都是合乎规定的了。除此之外，我们就不可能以合法的形式创立政府，同时又不会抛弃以上各章所确立的原则。

CHAPTER 18

Means Of Preventing The Usurpation Of Government

From these explanations, it follows, in confirmation of Chapter 16, that the act which institutes the government is not a contract but a law, and that the holders of the executive power are not the people's masters but its officers; and that the people can appoint them and dismiss them as it pleases; and that there is no question of their contracting, but of obeying; and that in discharging the functions which the state imposes on them, they are only doing their duty as citizens, without having any sort of right to argue terms.

Thus when it happens that the people institutes a hereditary government, whether monarchical in one family, or aristocratic in a class of citizens, it does not enter into any undertaking; hereditary government is simply a provisional form that it gives to the administration until such time as it pleases to arrange it differently.

It is true that such changes are always dangerous, and that one should never touch an established government unless it has become incompatible with the public welfare; but such circumspection is a precept of politics and not a rule of law; and the state is no more bound to leave civil authority to its magistrates than military authority to its generals.

It is true again that in such cases one cannot observe with too

第十八章　论防止政府篡权的方式

由这些解释可以得出的证实第十六章观点的结论，即创制政府的行为并不是一项契约行为，而是一种法律的行为。行政权力的掌握者并不是人民的主人，而只是人民的职员；人民可以随其所愿地任命他们或者解雇他们；这里没有一个与他们缔约的问题，而是一个服从的问题；他们在履行国家赋予他们的职能的时候，只是作为公民在承担他们的义务，而没有任何权利对条件进行讨价还价。

因而，如果人民创制了一个世袭的政府，不管它是在一个家庭内部继承的君主制，或者是在一个阶级的公民中世袭的贵族制，人民在此并没有做出任何承诺；世袭政府只是人民赋予行政机构的一种临时形式，直到人民愿意用不同方式来组织它的那个时候为止。

确实，这种改变总是很危险的，而且人民永远都不应该触动一个已经建立的政府，除非它已经变得和公共福利不相调和了。但是这种谨慎是一项政治的规则，却不是一项法律的准则；国家并不是必须要把公共权威授予它的行政官员，正像它不必把军队的权威授予它的将军们一样。

同样确实的是，在这样的情况下，人民不能过多地拘泥于规

great care all the formalities required to distinguish a regular and legitimate act from a seditious tumult, and the will of a whole people from the clamour of a faction. It is here above all that one must avoid yielding to socially harmful claims any more than is required by the strict application of the law; and it is from this obligation too that the prince derives a great opportunity of holding his power in defiance of the people, without it being possible to say that he has usurped it. For while appearing to exercise only his rights it is very easy for him to enlarge those rights and to prevent, on the pretext of public tranquillity, assemblies designed to re-establish good government; thus he exploits the silence which he prevents men breaking, and the irregularities which he makes them commit, to assume in his own favour the tacit consent of those whose mouths are closed by fear and to punish those who dare to speak. It was thus that the decemvirs, having been first elected for one year, and then continued for another, tried to retain their power in perpetuity, by no longer allowing the *comitia* to assemble. And it is by this simple means that all the governments of the world, once armed with the public force, sooner or later usurp the public authority.

The periodic assemblies of which I have already spoken are the right means to prevent or postpone this evil, above all those assemblies where no formal convocation is needed; for then the prince cannot prevent their meeting without openly proclaiming himself a violator of the laws and an enemy of the state.

At the opening of these assemblies, of which the only purpose is the maintenance of the social treaty, two motions should be put, motions which may never be annulled and which must be voted separately:

The first: 'Does it please the sovereign to maintain the present form of government?'

定的程序，以至于不能把一个正常的、合法的行为同一个煽动性的骚乱区分开来，不能把全体人民的意志同派系的叫嚣区分开来。尤其重要的是，在此，人们对于那些对社会有害的要求的屈服，不应该超过法律的严格应用所许可的范围。正是通过这种屈服的义务，使得统治者获得了极好的机会可以不顾人民意愿地维护他们的权力，而且又不会被说成是他们篡夺了权力。因为在表面上看来他们仅仅是在行使他们自己权利的时候，他们很容易地就可以扩大这些权利，并且以公共安全为借口，阻止人们计划重建一个好政府的集会；这样他便利用他禁止人们打破的沉默，利用他使人们造成的不正常状态，来随其所好地假定那些因害怕而不敢开口的人是对他的默许，并且又惩罚那些胆敢说话的人。罗马十人会议就是这么做的，他们最初被选举出来执政一年，接下来又继续执政一年，他们力图通过不再允许召集人民大会的方法，永久地保留他们的权力。正是通过这种简单的方式，世界上所有的政府一旦以公共力量武装起来，它们迟早会篡夺公共权威的。

我前面已经说过的定期集会是阻止和推迟这种恶行的恰当方法，特别是那些不需要正式召集的集会；因为这样一来，统治者就不能阻止人民集会，否则，他们就是公开地宣布自己是法律的违反者和国家的敌人了。

在这些以维护社会条约为唯一目的的集会上，一开始就必须提出两个议题，这两个议题永远都不能被废除，而且必须单独进行投票。

第一个议题是：“保持目前的这种政府形式会使主权者感到满意吗?”

The second: 'Does it please the people to leave the administration to those at present charged with it?'

I assume here what I believe I have demonstrated, namely, that there is not in the state any fundamental law which may not be revoked, not even the social pact; for if all the citizens assemble to end this pact by a common accord, one cannot doubt that it is very legitimately ended. Grotius indeed thinks that each citizen may renounce his membership of the state, and recover his natural liberty and his goods on withdrawing from the country. [①] And it would be absurd if all the citizens united could not do what each of them separately can do.

---

① It being understood that none may leave the country to evade his duty, or avoid saving his country when it needs him. In such a case, flight would be criminal and punishable; it would not be withdrawal but desertion.

第二个议题是："让目前执掌行政的那些人继续执政会使得主权者感到满意吗?"

这里我假定我已经证明了我所相信的东西，那就是，在一个国家中没有任何根本法律，甚至社会契约是不可以被否决的；因为如果所有的公民举行集会一致同意结束一个契约，那么没有人能够怀疑这是一种合法的终结行为。事实上，格劳秀斯就认为每个公民都可以宣布放弃自己国家成员的身份，并且通过离开这个国家①而重新获得他天然的自由和财富。如果联合起来的所有公民反而不能做他们独自一人时所能够做的事情，那是荒谬的。

① 人们都明白，任何人都不能为了逃避义务而离开他的国家，也不能在国家需要他的时候不去挽救他的国家。在这种情况下，逃避就将是有罪的，而且应该得到惩罚；这就不是退出，而是背弃了。

BOOK Ⅳ

CHAPTER 1

That The General Will Is Indestructible

So long as several men joined together consider themselves a single body, they have only one will, which is directed towards their common preservation and general well-being. Then all the animating forces of the state are vigorous and simple; its principles are clear and luminous; it has no incompatible or conflicting interests; the common good makes itself so manifestly evident that only common sense is needed to discern it. Peace, unity, equality are enemies of political sophistication. Upright and simple men are difficult to deceive precisely because of their simplicity; strategems and clever arguments do not prevail upon them; they are not indeed subtle enough to be dupes. When we see among the happiest people in the world bands of peasants regulating the affairs of state under an oak tree, and always acting wisely, can we help feeling a certain contempt for the refinements of other nations, which employ so much skill and mystery to make themselves at once illustrious and wretched?

A state thus governed needs very few laws, and whenever there is a need to promulgate new ones, that need is universally seen. The first man to propose such a law is only giving voice to what everyone already feels, and there is no question either of intrigues or of eloquence to secure the enactment of what each has already resolved to do as soon as he is sure that all the others will do likewise.

第四卷

第一章　论公意是不可破坏的

只要有一些人结合在一起并自认为是一个整体，那么他们就只有一个意志，这个意志是指向他们的共同生存和公共福利的。于是，这个国家全部的力量就是强大充沛而且单一的，它的原则就是清晰而且光辉的，它没有不相调和的、互相矛盾的利益，共同的利益变得如此地明显可见，以至于只需要常识就可以发现它。和平、团结、平等与政治上的尔虞我诈是为敌的。正直和纯朴的人是难以欺骗的，原因恰恰就在于他们的纯朴；诡计和花言巧语在他们身上根本无用；事实上，他们还没有精明到足以上当受骗。当我们在世界上那些最幸福的民族中看到成群的农民在橡树底下处理国家事务，而且总是会处理得非常明智，我们能忍得住对那些使用种种技巧和玄虚从而使他们变得既杰出又悲惨的民族有一些轻蔑的感觉吗？

一个被如此治理着的国家只需要很少的法律，而且一旦需要颁布一个新法律的时候，人们会普遍地看到这种需要。所以提议这样一项法律的第一个人只不过是把所有人都感觉到的东西表达出来而已。只要这个人能确定其他所有的人同样都会这么做，那么把所有的人都已经决定要做的事情制定为法律就绝不是阴谋的问题，也不是雄辩的问题。

What misleads theorists is that, as a result of looking only at states which are badly constituted from the beginning, they are struck by the impossibility of maintaining such a régime there. They laugh at the thought of all the follies that a clever knave or a sly orator could persuade the people of Paris or London to commit. They do not realize that Cromwell would have been put to forced labour by the people of Berne, and the Duc de Beaufort imprisoned by the Genevese.

However, when the social tie begins to slacken and the state to weaken, when particular interests begin to make themselves felt and sectional societies begin to exert an influence over the greater society, the common interest becomes corrupted and meets opponents; voting is no longer unanimous; the general will is no longer the will of all; contradictions and disputes arise; and even the best opinion is not allowed to prevail unchallenged.

In the end, when the state, on the brink of ruin, can maintain itself only in an empty and illusory form, when the social bond is broken in every heart, when the meanest interest impudently flaunts the sacred name of the public good, then the general will is silenced: everyone, animated by secret motives, ceases to speak as a citizen any more than as if the state had never existed; and the people enacts in the guise of laws iniquitous decrees which have private interests as their only end.

Does it follow from this that the general will is annihilated or corrupted? No, that is always unchanging, incorruptible and pure, but it is subordinated to other wills which prevail over it. Each man, in detaching his interest from the common interest, sees clearly that he cannot separate it entirely, but his share of the public good seems to him to be nothing compared to the exclusive good he seeks to make his own. Where his private good is not concerned,

误导了一些理论家的是，由于他们只看到了那些一开始就建制不好的国家，所以他们就认为在那些国家维持这样一种政权体制是不可能的。一想到一个精明的流氓或者一个狡猾的雄辩家能够说服巴黎人民或者伦敦人民去做的所有蠢事，他们就发笑。他们没有认识到克伦威尔是曾经被伯尔尼人民判处过强制劳动的，波弗特公爵也曾被日内瓦人民囚禁过。

然而，当社会的纽带开始松弛、国家开始削弱的时候，当特殊利益开始为人们感受到、小的集团开始尽力对大社会施加影响的时候，共同利益便开始受到腐蚀并且遇上反对者。投票不再是全体一致的了，公意不再是所有人的意志了，矛盾和争论出现了，而且即使是最好的建议也不会不遇到丝毫挑战就获得成功。

最后，当国家濒于毁灭，并只能维持它空洞、虚幻的形式的时候，当社会联系在每个人的心中破裂的时候，当最卑鄙的利益也厚颜无耻地以公共利益的神圣名义招摇过市的时候，公意就沉默了：每个人在其不可告人的动机鼓动之下，就不再是作为公民而发表意见了，就好像国家从来都不存在一样；而且人民会假借法律的名义制定那些以个人利益为唯一目标的不公正法令。

是否由此便可以得出结论，即公意被消灭了或者被腐蚀了呢？不能，公意总是不变的、不会被腐蚀的、纯洁的，但是它却屈从于其他那些胜过它的意志。每个人在把他的利益同公共利益分开的时候，他清楚地看到它们是不能完全分开的，但是他分得的那一部分公共利益与他努力为自己争取的那些非我莫属的利益相比，就不算什么了。在不关涉个别利益的地方，他为了自己的

he wills the general good in his own interest as eagerly as anyone else. Even in selling his vote for money, he does not extinguish the general will in himself; he evades it. The fault he commits is to change the form of the question, and to answer something different from what is asked him; so that instead of saying, with his vote, 'It is advantageous to the state', he says, 'It is advantageous to this man or to that party that such or such a proposal should be adopted.' For this reason the sensible rule for regulating public assemblies is one intended not so much to uphold the general will there as to ensure that it is always questioned and always responds.

I might say a great deal here about the simple right of voting in every act of sovereignty, a right of which nothing can deprive citizens, and also about the right of speaking, proposing, dividing and debating — a right which the government always takes great care to assign only to its own members — but this important subject would require a separate treatise, and I cannot put everything in this one.

利益也会像其他任何人一样热切地渴望普遍的利益。甚至是在为了金钱而出卖他的选票的时候，他也没有消灭他心中的公意，他只是躲避了它而已。他所犯的错误是改变了问题的形式，他做出的回答与对他的提问是不一致的，所以通过他的选票，他不是在说，“这对于国家是有益的”，他是在说：“如果这种或者那种建议能够被采纳，那么这对这个人或者那个团体是有益的。”由于这个原因，调整公共集会的贤明法则的目标，就并非主要是在集会中维持公意，而是要确保公意总是会被提问到，而它也总是会做出回应。

关于在每一个主权行为中的简单的投票权（这是公民不能被剥夺的权利），还有关于发言的权利、建议的权利、分配的权利和争论的权利（这是政府费尽心思要使之仅在政府成员内部分配的权利），我这里可以说得非常多，但是这个重要的主题需用单独的一篇文章论述，我就不能把所有的观点都在这一章中说清楚了。

CHAPTER 2
The Suffrage

It will be evident from what has been said in the preceding chapter that the manner in which public affairs are conducted gives a sufficiently accurate indication of the moral character and the state of health of the body politic. The greater harmony that reigns in the public assemblies, the more, in other words, that public opinion approaches unanimity, the more the general will is dominant; whereas long debates, dissensions and disturbances bespeak the ascendance of particular interests and the decline of the state.

This will seem less evident when two or several orders enter into the constitution, as in Rome with its patricians and plebeians, whose quarrels often disturbed the *comitia* even in the finest days of the Republic; but this exception to the rule is more apparent than real, for in Rome, as a result of an inherent defect in the body politic, there were, in a manner of speaking, two states in one, and what is not true of both together is true of each separately. And, indeed, even in the most tumultuous times, the plebiscites of the people always proceeded peacefully when the senate did not interfere, and votes were given with large majorities. The citizens having only one interest, the people had only one will.

At the other extreme of the cycle, unanimity reappears. This is when the citizens, lapsed into servitude, have no longer either freedom or will.

第二章　论投票

从前面章节的论述我们可以清楚地看到，处理公共事务的方式是一个政治共同体的道德特征和健康状态十分准确的标志。在公共集会中越是能够达到和谐一致，换句话说，公众的观点越是能够接近于全体一致，那么公意就越能占据主导地位；而持久的争论、意见的分歧和骚乱则预示着个别利益占据了上风，国家走向衰落。

但当一个国家的体制中有两个或者几个等级的时候，这一规则就不甚明显了。就像在罗马有贵族和平民，即使在共和国的黄金时期，他们的争吵也经常会扰乱人民大会；但是这个例外，与其说是实际上的，不如说是表面上的，因为在罗马，由于这个政治共同体的内在缺陷，所以从某种意义上说，罗马这个国家内部又有了两个国家，以上的规则对于这两者结合在一起来说是不正确的，但是对它们分别来说却是正确的。而且事实上，如果元老院不进行干预的话，即使是在最动荡的时代，公民的投票也会和平地进行，并且是根据多数票来表决的。由于公民只有一个利益，所以人民就只有一个意志。

在这个循环的另一个极端，全体一致同样也会出现，那就是当公民完全堕入奴隶状态，不再具有自由和意志的时候。这时，

Then fear and flattery change voting into acclamation; people no longer deliberate, they worship or they curse. Such was the shameful manner in which the senate gave voice to its opinions under the emperors. Sometimes it did so with absurd precautions. Tacitus mentions that under Otho, the senators covered Vitellius with execrations, but took care at the same time to make a deafening noise, so that Vitellius would not be able to distinguish what each one of them had said, lest he should ever by any chance become master.

These various considerations suggest the principles by which the counting of votes and the comparing of opinions should be arranged, depending on whether the general will is more or less easy to recognize, and on whether the state is more or less in decline.

There is only one law which by its nature requires unanimous assent. This is the social pact: for the civil association is the most voluntary act in the world; every man having been born free and master of himself, no one else may under any pretext whatever subject him without his consent. To assert that the son of a slave is born a slave is to assert that he is not born a man.

If, then, there are opposing voices at the time when the social pact is made, this opposition does not invalidate the contract; it merely excludes the dissentients; they are foreigners among the citizens. After the state is instituted, residence implies consent: to inhabit the territory is to submit to the sovereign. ①

Apart from this original contract, the votes of the greatest number

---

① This should always be understood to refer only to free states, for elsewhere family, property, lack of asylum, necessity or violence may keep an inhabitant in the country unwillingly, and then his mere residence no longer implies consent either to the contract or to the violation of the contract.

恐惧和奉承把投票变成了附和；人们不再有深思熟虑，他们要么是崇拜，要么是咒骂。这便是在罗马皇帝的统治下，元老院表达他们的观点的可耻方式。有些时候他们做这些事情时谨慎得可笑。塔西佗曾提及在奥东的治下，元老院中充满了对维提留斯的咒骂，但是同时又小心地制造一种震耳欲聋的喧闹声，这样，一旦维提留斯有机会成为了主人，他也不能辨别出他们中的每个人都说了什么。

这种种的考虑都提示了要有一些规则，人们应该依据这些规则，视公意是否更容易被认识以及国家是否会衰落的情况，来安排计算票数的方式和比较各种意见的方式。

只有一种法律，从其本性上讲是需要全体一致同意的，这就是社会契约，因为公民的结合是世界上最自愿的行为。每个人都天生是自由的，都天生是自己的主人，任何人没有经过他的同意，都不能以任何借口使他屈从。断言奴隶的儿子天生就是奴隶，就是断言他生来就不是一个人。

因而，如果在缔结社会契约的时候有反对的声音，则这些反对并不能使社会契约变得无效；它只是把反对者排除在社会契约之外而已，这些反对者就是公民当中的外邦人。国家一旦建立之后，居住就意味着同意：居住在一块领土之上就是服从于这个主权①。

除了这个原始的契约之外，多数人的投票总是可以约束其他

① 我们应该理解：这仅仅是指在自由的国家中，因为在别的地方，家庭、财产、无容身之处、生活之所需或者暴力等因素都可能会使一个居民不情愿地居住在一个国家中，这时，他这种单纯的居住就不再意味着他认可社会契约或者破坏社会契约了。

always bind the rest; and this is a consequence of the contract itself. Yet it may be asked how a man can be at once free and forced to conform to wills which are not his own. How can the opposing minority be both free and subject to laws to which they have not consented?

I answer that the question is badly formulated. The citizen consents to all the laws, even to those that are passed against his will, and even to those which punish him when he dares to break any one of them. The constant will of all the members of the state is the general will; it is through it that they are citizens and free. ① When a law is proposed in the people's assembly, what is asked of them is not precisely whether they approve of the proposition or reject it, but whether it is in conformity with the general will which is theirs; each by giving his vote gives his opinion on this question, and the counting of votes yields a declaration of the general will. When, therefore, the opinion contrary to my own prevails, this proves only that I have made a mistake, and that what I believed to be the general will was not so. If my particular opinion had prevailed against the general will, I should have done something other than what I had willed, and then I should not have been free.

This presupposes, it is true, that all the characterisics of the general will are still to be found in the majority; when these cease to be there, no matter what position men adopt, there is no longer any freedom.

When I showed earlier in this essay how particular wills come to take the place of the general will inpublic deliberations, I made sufficiently clear what practical means may prevent that abuse,

---

① In Genoa the word *Libertas* may be seen on the doors of all the prisons and on the fetters of the galleys. This use of the motto is excellent and just. In fact, it is only the malefactors of all states who prevent the citizens from being free. In a country where all such people were in the galleys, the most perfect liberty would be enjoyed.

少数人的投票的；而且这也是契约本身的结果。然而有人可能会问，一个人怎么可能既是自由的，同时又要遵从那些并非他自己的意志呢？那些反对的少数人怎么能够既是自由的，又要服从于那些他们并不同意的法律呢？

我的回答是，这个问题的提出就是错误的。公民赞同了所有的法律，即使是那些违背他的意志而通过的法律，甚至还有那些如果公民胆敢违反其中一条的话，就会对他进行惩罚的法律。国家所有成员永恒的意志就是公意，正是通过这一点，他们才是公民，才是自由的①。在人民的集会上提议一个法律的时候，人们被提问的问题并不是他们赞同还是反对这个提议，而是问这个提议是否与属于他们自己的公意相符合。每个公民通过投票在这个问题上表达了他们的观点，而对投票进行计算就产生了公意的宣告。因此，当与我自己的观点相反的观点胜出的时候，这只是证明我犯错误了，即我认为是公意的那个东西并不是公意。如果我的个别观点竟然胜过了公意，那么我就将是在做一些本非是我所愿做的事情，我便将会是不自由的了。

当然，这里的先决条件是在按大多数表决的投票中仍然可以找到公意的所有特征；而当公意的所有特征不再存在于按大多数表决的投票中的时候，不管人们采用何种立场，都将不再有自由了。

早些时候我在说明公众的讨论中个别意志如何取代公意的时候，已经充分地指明了什么样的实际方法可以防止这种弊

---

① 在热那亚，人们可以在监狱的门上和囚犯的脚镣上看到“自由”这个词。这个格言的用法是极好而且公正的。事实上，在所有国家中，唯有犯罪分子才妨碍了公民获得自由。如果在一个国家中，所有这样的人都被关进罪犯船，那么人们就会享受到最完美的自由。

and I shall return to this subject later. As for the proportional number of votes required to declare the general will, I have also set forth the principles by which that number can be determined. A difference of a single vote destroys an equal division; a single opposing voice destroys unanimity; but between unanimity and an equal division there are numerous unequal divisions, and the desired proportion can be fixed at any of these points in accordance with the condition and on the needs of the body politic.

Two general maxims may serve to determine these ratios: the first, that the more important and serious the matter to be decided, the closer should the opinion which is to prevail approach unanimity; the second, the swifter the decision the question demands, the smaller the prescribed majority may be allowed to become; and in decisions which have to be given immediately, a majority of one must suffice. The first of these maxims might seem to be more suited to the enactment of laws, the second to the dispatch of administrative business. At all events, it is by a combination of the two maxims that we can determine the right size for the majority that is to decide on any question.

端，后面我会回到这个题目上的。至于宣告公意所必需的投票的比例数目，我已经指出了一些原则，根据这些原则，这个比例数就可以确定。一票之差就可以打破双方的票数均衡；一个反对票就可以破坏全体一致；但是在全体一致和双方平均分配之间，还有数量众多的双方不等的票数分配，根据政治体的状况和政治体的需要，人们可以在任何一个点上确定宣告公意所需的票数比例。

有两个普遍的准则可以帮助我们决定这些比率：第一个是，要决定的事情越是重要、越是严重，那么占上风的观点就越是应该接近于全体一致；第二个是，一个问题越是需要迅速地做出决定，规定的多数就被允许可以越小，在那些必须立刻做出的决定上，一票的多数就足够了。这两个准则中的第一个可能看上去更适合于颁布法律，而第二个则更适合于行政事务的迅速完成。无论如何，正是通过这两条准则的结合，我们才可以确定在某个问题上做出决定时所要求的多数的恰当尺度。

CHAPTER 3
Elections

Elections of the prince and magistrates, which are, as I have said, complex acts, can be arranged in two ways, by choice or by lot. Both means have been employed in different republics, and a very complicated mixture of the two can still be seen in the election of the Doge of Venice. 'Election by lot,' says Montesquieu, 'is natural to democracy.' I agree. But why is this so? 'Drawing lots,' he continues, 'is a method of election that wounds no one and gives every citizen a reasonable hope of serving his country.' But these are not good reasons.

If we remember that the election of chiefs is a function of government and not of sovereignty, we shall see why the method of lot is natural to democracy, where the administration is all the better in proportion as its acts are fewer.

In every true democracy, magistrature is not a privilege but a heavy responsibility, so that it cannot justly be imposed on one man rather than another. The law alone can impose this burden on the man to whom the lot falls. For in this case, since the conditions are equal for all and the choice does not depend on any human will, the universality of the law is not distorted by any particular application.

第三章　论选举

对于统治者和行政官员的选举，正如我曾说过的，是一种复合的行为，它可以通过两种方式来进行，即推选和抽签。在不同的共和政体中这两种方式都曾经被采用过。在威尼斯的总督选举中，我们甚至可以看到这两种方式的复杂混合。“通过抽签进行选举，”孟德斯鸠说，“对民主制来说是很自然的。”我赞同这一点。但是为什么会是这样呢？“抽签，”他继续说到，“是一种选举的方式，这种方式不会伤害任何人，而且又赋予了每个公民为他的国家服务的合理希望。”但是这并不是一个好的理由。

如果我们还记得首领的选举是政府的一项职能，而不是主权的一项职能，那么我们就会明白为什么抽签这种方式对民主制来说是自然的了，因为在民主制中，行政行为越是少，行政就会成比例地变得越好。

在真正的民主制中，行政官职并非是一项特权，而是一项沉重的责任，所以人们就不能把它公正地强加于某一个人，而不是加于另一个人。唯有法律才可以把这项负担加在那个抽中签的人的身上。因为在这种情况下，既然对于所有的人来说条件都是相等的，而且这个选举也不是取决于任何人的意志的，所以法律的普遍性就不会被它的个别应用所歪曲了。

In an aristocracy the prince chooses the prince, the government perpetuates itself by its own actions; and then election by choice is appropriate.

The example of the election of the Doge of Venice, far from undermining this distinction, confirms it: such a mixed form suits a mixed government. It is a mistake to regard the government of Venice as a genuine aristocracy. For while the Venetian people has no part in the government, the Venetian nobility is itself a people. A multitude of poor Barnabites never comes near any magistrature, and its nobility rests on the empty title of Excellency and the right to attend the Great Council. And since this Great Council is as numerous as our General Council in Geneva, its illustrious members have no more privileges than our plain citizens. Hence there is no doubt that, apart from the extreme disparity between the two republics, the bourgeoisie of Geneva corresponds precisely to the patriciate of Venice; our natives and inhabitants correspond to the townsmen and the people of Venice, and our peasants to their subjects on the mainland; to sum up, from whatever point of view the Venetian Republic is considered, apart from its size, its government is no more aristocratic than our own. The whole difference lies in the fact that we have no head of state who holds office for life, and so we have not the same need for the method of election by lot.

Election by lot would have few disadvantages in a true democracy, for where all men were equal in character and talent as well as in

在贵族制中，是君主选举君主，是政府通过自己的行为使自己永久统治，于是通过投票选择的选举方式就是最恰当的了。

威尼斯总督选举的例子，远不是取消了这两种选举方式的差别，它恰恰确证了两者的差别：那样一种混合的形式适合于一个混合政府。把威尼斯的政府看作是真正的贵族制是一个错误。因为既然威尼斯的人民不能分享政府的任何权力，那么威尼斯贵族本身就是人民了。大量贫穷的巴拿波特[1]从来都不会接近于任何行政职权，他们的高贵仅仅停留在拥有“阁下”的空洞头衔以及参加大议会的权利。而且既然这种大议会就像我们日内瓦的全民会议一样人数众多，那么它的显赫成员并不会比我们的普通公民拥有更多的特权。所以毫无疑问，除了这两个共和国的极端不一致之处而外，日内瓦的有产者阶层[2]恰恰对应于威尼斯的贵族阶层，我们的土著和居民对应于威尼斯的市民和人民，而我们的农民则对应于威尼斯大陆上的臣民。总而言之，不管以什么样的观点来考察威尼斯共和国，除了它的面积大小之外，这个政府绝不比我们日内瓦政府更加是贵族制的。两者的全部不同就在于，我们没有一个终身掌握职权的国家首领，所以我们就不需要通过抽签的选举方式。

在真正的民主制中，通过抽签选举并没有什么不方便，因为在那里，所有的人不但在品质和才能上，而且在节操和

---

〔1〕 威尼斯贵族分为贵爵和巴拿波特，巴拿波特是贫穷的贵族。

〔2〕 十六世纪以来，日内瓦人分为五个等级：公民、市民、居民、土著和臣民，这里的有产者阶层指市民阶层。

principles and fortune, it would hardly matter who was chosen. But as I have already said, no true democracy exists.

When election by choice and election by lot are both employed, choice should be used to fill places that call for special skills, such as military commands, and lot for those where common sense, justice and integrity are enough, as in the case of political offices, for in a well constituted state, such qualities are found among all the citizens.

Under monarchical government, neither election by lot nor election by choice has any place. Since the monarch is by right the sole prince and only magistrate, the choice of his lieutenants belongs to him alone. When the Abbé de St Pierre proposed to increase the Councils of the King of France and have their members elected by ballot, he did not realize that he was proposing to change the form of government!

I have yet to speak of the method of voting and collecting votes in the people's assembly, but perhaps the history of the Roman system would serve to demonstrate more forcefully all the principles that I might myself set forth. It will not be beneath the dignity of a thoughtful reader to consider in some detail how public and private business was conducted in an assembly of two hundred thousand men.

财富上也都是相等的，所以不管谁当选，几乎都没什么关系。但是正如我曾说过的，真正的民主制是不存在的。

如果通过投票进行选举和通过抽签进行选举同时被采用，那么投票选举应该被应用于填充那些需要特殊才能的职位，比如军事指挥；而抽签选举则适用于那些只需要常识、正义和诚实就足够了的职位，比如行政职位，因为在一个建制良好的国家中，这些品质是从所有公民身上都能找到的。

在君主制下，不管是抽签选举还是投票选举都是不存在的。既然君主是法定的、唯一的统治者和唯一的行政官员，所以对附属官员的选举权就仅仅属于君主自己。当圣皮埃尔神甫建议增加法兰西国王的顾问班子，并且通过投票选举其成员的时候，他并没有意识到他是在建议改变政府的形式。

我还要说到人民集会中的投票以及收集投票的方式，但是也许罗马体制的历史可以更强有力地论证我所要确立的原则。稍加详细地看一下在一个由二十万人构成的集会中人们是如何处理公共事务或私人事务的，这对一个有思想的读者来说不为屈尊吧。

CHAPTER 4
The Roman Comitia

We have no trustworthy records of the early history of Rome, and there is every likelihood that most of the tales we are told are fables;① indeed, in general, that most instructive part of the annals of peoples, which is the history of their institution, is the part we most lack. Experience teaches us daily the causes of revolutions in empires, but as peoples are no longer instituted, we have nothing better than conjecture to explain how they were once instituted.

The customs that we find established show at least that such customs must have had an origin. Traditions that recall these origins, that are supported by the best authorities, and confirmed by the best reasons, should pass for the most certain. Such are the principles I have tried to follow in enquiring how the freest and strongest people of the world exercised its supreme power.

After the foundation of Rome, the new-born Republic— that is, the founder's army, made up of Albans, Sabines and foreigners— was divided into three classes, which acquired by this division the name of *tribes*. Each of these tribes was further divided into ten *curiae*,

---

① The name 'Rome', which is said to derive from *Romulus* is really Greek, and it means *force*; the name 'Numa' is also Greek, and it means *law*. Is it very probable that the first two kings of that city should have borne before they reigned names so clearly related to what they did?

第四章　论罗马的人民大会

对于罗马的早期历史并没有值得信赖的记载，而且很有可能我们听说到的大部分罗马故事都只是寓言①。事实上，一般而言，各民族的编年史中最有教育意义的部分，就是它们的形成史，也是我们所最缺乏的部分。经验虽然每天都在告诉我们各帝国产生革命的原因，但是由于不再有民族形成了，所以我们只能凭借推测来解释它们是如何形成的。

我们已经发现的各种已经确立的习俗至少可以说明这些习俗一定是有一个起源的。能追溯这个起源的传统，能得到最大的权威支持和最好的理性确证的传统应该被看成是最可靠的。这便是我在探索世界上最自由、最强大的民族如何行使它们的最高权力的时候，所力图遵循的原则。

罗马建国之后，这个新生的共和国——也就是由奥尔本人、萨宾人和外邦人构成的建国者的军队——被划分成了三个种类，由于这种划分，他们便有了部族这个名称。这些部族中的每一

---

① 罗马这个名字，据说是源自于罗穆鲁斯，实际上它是希腊文，它的意思是力量；“努玛”这个名字也是希腊文，它的意思是法律。罗马城最早的两位国王极有可能在他们统治之前就采用了这些与他们后来所做的事情明显相联的名字，不是吗？

and each *curia* subdivided into *decuriae*, with chiefs named *curiones* and *decuriones* placed at their head.

In addition to this, there was drawn from each tribe a body of a hundred equites or knights, called a *century*, which indicates that these divisions, hardly necessary in a city, were in the first place purely military. But it seems that an instinct for greatness led this little town of Rome to provide itself from the outset with a system well suited to the capital of the world.

However, this original division soon had one disadvantageous consequence. The tribes of Albans① and Sabines② remained constant, while the tribe of foreigners③ Luceres. grew continuously as more foreigners were recruited, and it soon contained more members than the other two tribes combined. The remedy that Servius found for this dangerous fault was to alter the basis of the division, and in place of the racial distinction, which he abolished, he introduced one based on the district of the town occupied by each of the tribes. Instead of three tribes, he set up four, each occupying one of the hills of Rome and bearing its name. Thus he both corrected an existing inequality and forestalled any future inequality; and to ensure that the division should be one of men and not of places, he forbade the inhabitants of one district to move to another, and so prevented the races from merging together.

He also doubled the three original centuries of equites and added

---

① Ramnenses.

② Tatientes.

③ Luceres.

个又被进一步划分为十个库里亚，而且每个库里亚又被划分成一些德库里亚，其中的首领便叫做库里昂或者德库里昂。

除此之外，还从每个部族中抽出一个由一百个骑兵或者武士组成的团体，称作百人团。这说明这种划分最初是纯军事性的，因而在城市中几乎没有必要性。但是，看上去似乎有一种追求伟大的天分引导着罗马这个小城在一开始就为自己提供了一套适合成为世界的首都的体制。

然而，这种最初的划分不久就有了一个不利的结果。奥尔本人①的部族和萨宾人②的部族保持不变，但是外邦人③的部族则随着越来越多的外邦人补充进来，因而持续增长，不久它所包含的成员数就超过了其他两个部族合在一起的成员数。塞尔维乌斯所找到的对这个危险缺陷的补救办法，就是改变划分的基础。为了取代并废除原先的种族划分，他引入了一种以每个部族在城中所占有的地区为基础的划分方式。他建立了四个部族，以取代原先的三个，每个部族都占有罗马的一座小山，并由此而得其名。这样，他不仅修正了现存的不平等，而且又预先防止了未来可能的不平等；为了保证这种划分是对人的划分，而不是对地区的划分，他禁止一个区中的居民迁移到另一个区中去，这样便防止了各种族的人混合在一起。

他还把原先的三个骑兵百人团增加了一倍，并且又增加了

---

① 拉姆内斯人。
② 塔提埃斯人。
③ 鲁塞尔人。

twelve new ones, but he let them keep their former names— a shrewd and simple means by which he succeeded in distinguishing the body of knights from that of the people without making the latter complain.

To these four urban tribes, Servius added fifteen others which were called rustic tribes, because they were formed of inhabitants of the country, arranged in so many cantons. Afterwards as many new tribes were formed, and the Roman people found itself divided into thirty-five tribes, a number which remained unchanged until the end of the Republic.

This distinction between tribes of the town and tribes of the country had one consequence worth noting since there is no other instance of it, and since Rome was indebted to it both for the preservation of her morals and for the growth of her empire. It might have been thought that the urban tribes would have soon monopolized the power and the honours and have been quick to diminish the standing of the rustic tribes. What happened was the contrary. The taste of the early Romans for a country life is well known. This taste came from their wise founder, who made freedom go together with rural labour and military service and, in a manner of speaking, relegated crafts, trades, intrigue, wealth and slavery to the city.

Since all the illustrious men in Rome thus lived in the country and cultivated the land, it became customary to look to the country for the mainstays of the Republic. And as this way of life was that of the most noble patricians, it was honoured by everyone; the simple and laborious life of villagers was preferred to the loose and idle life of the Roman bourgeois, and a man who would have been nothing but a miserable proletarian in the town became as a tiller of the soil a respected citizen. It was not without reason, says Varro, that our magnanimous ancestors established in the village the nursery of those robust and valiant men who defended them in time of war and nourished them in time of peace.

十二个新的百人团，但是他却让它们维持原来的名称。这是一个精明而且简单的方法，通过这种方法他成功地把骑士团体和人民团体区分开来，同时又没有使人民团体产生抱怨。

在这四个城市部族之外，塞尔维乌斯又增加了另外十五个部族，它们被称为乡村部族，因为它们是由分布在十五个行政区域内的乡村居民构成的。之后，又有相同数量的新部族建立起来，罗马人民最后发现他们被划分成三十五个部族，这个数目后来一直没有改变，直到罗马共和国的终结。

城市部族和乡村部族之间的区别所产生的一个结果是值得注意的，因为以前还从未有过这样的例子，也因为罗马人道德的保持和罗马帝国的成长都要归功于此。人们可能会认为城市部族不久就会垄断所有的权力和荣誉，并且会迅速地削弱乡村部族的声望。事实上完全相反，古代罗马人对乡村生活的品味是众所周知的。这种品味来自于他们贤明的奠基者，这些奠基者把自由和乡村劳动、军事服务结合在一起，并且在某种意义上又是把工艺、贸易、阴谋、财富和奴隶制度都转移到城市中去了。

这样，既然杰出的人物都居住在乡村并且耕种土地，所以到乡村中去寻找共和国的中流砥柱就成为一个惯例。而且由于这种生活方式是大多数贵族的生活方式，所以它受到所有人的尊崇。乡村人的这种简朴而勤劳的生活与罗马市民的那种放纵、懒散的生活相比更受到人们的喜爱，而且一个在城市中只不过将会成为悲惨的无产者的人，若是作为一个耕地的农夫，那么他就会变成一个受人尊敬的公民了。瓦罗说，我们高尚的先辈在乡村中建立了培养那些健壮而且英勇的人的基地，这些人在战争时保卫他们，在和平时供养他们，这些话不是没有道理的。

Pliny states positively that the rustic tribes were honoured because of the men who belonged to them, and that whenever it was intended to degrade a coward, he was transferred in disgrace to one of the urban tribes. When Appius Claudius, the Sabine, came to set himself up in Rome, he was loaded with honours and inscribed as a member of a rustic tribe which afterwards took the name of his family. Finally, all the freed men joined the urban and never the rustic tribes, and throughout the Republic there was not a single example of any one of these freed men acceding to any magistrature, even though he had become a citizen.

This principle was excellent; but it was pushed so far that it finally produced an alteration, and certainly an abuse in the political system.

First, the censors, having long arrogated to themselves the right arbitrarily to transfer citizens from one tribe to another, allowed most men to enrol in the tribe of their choice, a concession which certainly did no good and which deprived the censorship of one of its great advantages. Moreover, the exalted and powerful men all had themselves enrolled in the rustic tribes, and the freed men remained with the common people in the urban tribes, so that the tribes generally ceased to have any local or territorial bases, and all were so muddled together that it was no longer possible to identify anyone without consulting the register; and this is why the word *tribe* came to have a personal instead of a territorial meaning, or rather came to be virtually fictitious.

It also came about that the urban tribes, being closer to the centre, often found themselves the strongest group in the *comitia*, and sold the state to such as deigned to buy the votes of the rabble who composed that assembly.

As for the *curiae*, since the founder had created ten in each tribe, the whole of the Roman people, at that time enclosed within the walls of the city, was composed of thirty *curiae*,

普林尼也肯定说，乡村部族之所以受到尊崇，就是因为有那些属于乡村部族的人的原故，也由于一旦乡村部族想要羞辱一个懦夫，就会把这个人很不光彩地转移到一个城市部族中去。当萨宾人阿皮乌斯·克劳狄乌斯来到罗马居住的时候，他是满载着荣誉的，所以他成为一个乡村部族的成员，以后，这个乡村部族就以他的姓氏命名。最后，所有获得自由的奴隶都加入了城市部族，但从没有一个加入乡村部族，而且整个罗马共和国也没有任何一个获得自由的奴隶就任一种行政职务的例子，即使他们已经成为公民了。

这个原则是极好的，但是它被推行得过了头，最后产生了改变，的确也导致了政治系统中的滥用权力。

首先，监察官长期强占着可以任意把一个公民从一个部族转移到另一个部族的权利，并且允许大多数人根据他们自己的选择而编入一个部族，这种让步当然是无益的，而且也剥夺了监察官一个重要的有利条件。此外，所有那些高贵而强力的人都会把自己编入乡村部族，而那些获得自由的奴隶和普通人则只能一起留在城市部族中。这样一般来讲，部族就不再具有任何地方的或者领土上的基础，所有的部族都混合在一起，如果不查阅登记簿，就再也不可能识别出任何一个部族成员的身份了。这就是为什么“部族”这个词语逐渐具有了人格上的含义，而不再具有领土的意义，或者说它变得名不副实了。

还有一个转变，即城市部族由于接近大会中心，所以经常会发现他们自己是人民大会中力量最强大的群体，而且他们会把国家出卖给那些不惜屈尊从组成集会的乌合之众手中购买选票的人。

至于库里亚，既然建国者曾经在每个部族中划分了十个库里亚，那么那个时候被围入罗马城城墙之内的全体罗马人

each with its own temples, its Gods, its officials, its priests and its festivals called *compitalia*, which resembled the *Paganalia* later held by the rustic tribes.

When Servius introduced his new division, this number of thirty could not be divided equally between his four tribes, and he did not wish to alter it; in consequence, the *curiae*, becoming independent of the tribes, formed another category of inhabitants of Rome. But there was no question of *curiae* in the rustic tribes or among the people who belonged to them; for after the tribes had become a purely civil institution, and another system introduced for the levying of troops, the military divisions of Romulus proved superfluous. Thus, although each citizen was enrolled in a tribe, there were many who were not members of a *curia*.

Servius made yet a third division, which had nothing to do with the first two, and which became by reason of its consequences the most important of all. He distributed the whole Roman people into six classes, arranged neither on a personal nor on a residential basis, but according to wealth; so that the first classes were filled with the rich, the last with the poor, and the intermediate classes with men of moderate fortunes. These six classes were subdivided into 193 other bodies called centuries, and these bodies were so distributed that the first class accounted for more than half of them, and the last class for a single one only. Thus it came about that the class with the fewest number of men had the greatest number of centuries, while the last whole class counted only as one single subdivision, although it contained more than half the inhabitants of Rome.

In order that the people should less well perceive the consequences of this division, Servius disguised it in a military form; he put into the second class two centuries of armourers and into the fourth class two centuries of weaponmakers. In each class, except the last,

民就构成了三十个库里亚，每个库里亚都有它自己的庙宇、它的神明、它的官员、它的祭司和它称为大陆节的节日，这种节日类似于后来乡村部落举行的乡村节。

当塞尔维乌斯引入新的划分方式的时候，三十这个数目不能在他的四个部族之间平均分配，而他又不想改变这个数目，结果“库里亚”就成为独立于部族的了，并形成了对罗马居民的另外一种划分。但是在乡村部族，或者属于乡村部族的那些人民中间就没有一个库里亚的问题。后来部族变成纯粹的民事机构之后，另外一种征集军队的制度已经引入，罗穆鲁斯的这种军事性的划分就被证明是多余的了。因而，虽然每个公民都会被编入一个部族中，但是却有很多人不是库里亚的成员。

塞尔维乌斯甚至还做了第三种划分，这种划分与前面的那两种划分没有任何关系，但是由于它的后果，它却成为所有划分中最重要的一种。他把整个罗马人民划分为六个等级，这既不是根据人的身份，也不是根据居住地区，而是根据财富划分的，所以第一等级中全部是富人，而最后一个等级中则全部是穷人，中间的阶级则是由中等富裕的人构成。这六个等级又被细分为一百九十三个团体，称为百人团，这些团体是这样分配的：即第一等级占据了其中的半数以上，而最后一个等级则只是其中的一个团。这样就导致了人数最少的等级却拥有数量最多的百人团，而最末的整个等级却只算作一个团，虽然它包含了罗马居民的半数以上。

为了使人民不能很好地认识到这种划分的后果，塞尔维乌斯把它伪装成一种军事的形式：他在第二等级中安插了两个军械士百人团，又在第四等级中安插了两个兵器制造者百人团。除了最

he differentiated between young and old, that is to say, between those liable to bear arms and those legally exempt on grounds of age; and this distinction, more than that of wealth, made it necessary to hold frequent censuses. Finally he prescribed that the assembly should be held in the Campus Martius, and that all those of military age should attend bearing arms.

The reason he did not make the same differentiation between young and old in the last class is simply that the common people who belonged to it did not have the honour of bearing arms in the service of their country; only those who owned hearths had the right to defend them. Among the countless hordes of beggars who ornament the armies of kings today there is perhaps none who would not have been expelled with disdain from a Roman cohort in the days when soldiers were the defenders of liberty.

In the last class, however, a distinction was made between *proletarians* and those who were called *capite censi*. The former, not wholly reduced to nothing, at least gave citizens to the state, even sometimes soldiers in times of pressing need. But those who possessed nothing whatever, and could be reckoned only by the counting of heads, were considered altogether null, and Marius was the first who condescended to enrol them.

Without deciding here whether this third classification was good or bad in itself, one can, I think, safely say that it was practicable only because of the simple habits of the early Romans, their taste for agriculture, and their contempt alike for commerce and for the pursuit of profit. Where is the modern people, whose devouring greed, unsettled hearts, intrigue, continual movement and constant reversals of fortune would have allowed such a system to last for twenty years without overturning the whole state? It should also be remembered that the morals of the Roman people and the office of censorship had the strength to correct the evils of this system, and that a rich man could find himself relegated to the class of the poor for making too ostentatious a display of his wealth.

末一个等级，他还在每个等级中对年轻人和老年人做出了区分，就是说，对那些有义务服兵役的人和那些因为年龄的缘故合法地免除了义务的人做出了区分；这种区分与基于财富的区分相比较，使得举行经常性的人口普查变得更加有必要。最后他又规定集会要在玛尔提乌斯校场举行，而且所有那些达到了服兵役年龄的人都必须携带武器参加。

塞尔维乌斯没有在最后一个等级中对年轻人和老年人做出同样区分的原因，只是在于要使属于这一等级的普通人没有拿起武器为他的国家服务的荣誉；只有那些拥有自己的家的人才有权力保卫家啊！今天点缀在国王军队中的数不清的乞丐队伍，若在那个士兵是自由的捍卫者的时代，大概没有一个不会被满怀鄙视地从罗马军队中排斥出去吧。

在最后的一个等级中，人们还是对无产者和被称作是按人头计数的人做出了区分的。前者尚没有变得一无所有，至少他们可以为国家提供公民，甚至在紧急需要之时还为国家提供士兵。但是那些一无所有而且只能通过数人头来计数的人，则完全被视为无物了，马留乌斯是第一个肯屈尊招募他们的人。

这里我姑且不判断这第三种划分就其本身而言是好是坏，我认为我们可以确定地说这种划分之所以是行得通的，只是因为早期罗马人的纯朴风俗，他们对农业的情趣，以及他们对于诸如商业和追逐利润的轻蔑。由于无厌的贪欲、浮躁的心灵、阴谋诡计、持续不断的浮沉，以及永久的祸福变换，所以没有一个近代民族能够保证这种划分制度维持二十年时间，而不至于颠覆这个国家。我们也应该记住罗马人民的道德和监察机构的职权有力量纠正这种制度的弊病，而且一个富人会因为过分地炫耀他的财富，而被贬斥到穷人阶级中去。

From all this it is easy to understand why more than five Roman classes are hardly ever mentioned, even though there were actually six. The sixth, which provided neither soldiers for the army nor voters for the Campus Martius① and had therefore virtually no function in the Republic, was seldom given any thought.

Such were the different divisions of the Roman people. Let us now consider the effect the divisions had in the assemblies. The assemblies which were lawfully convened were called *comitia*, and generally met in the Roman forum or in the Campus Martius; they were distinguished as *comitia curiata*, *comitia centuriata* and *comitia tributa*, according to which form was employed. The *comitia curiata* was founded by Romulus, the *comitia centuriata* by Servius, and the *comitia tributa* originated in the tribunes of the people. No law was sanctioned and no magistrate elected except in the *comitia*, and as there was no citizen who was not enrolled in a *curia*, century or tribe, it follows that no citizen was excluded from the right to vote, and that the Roman people was truly sovereign, both in law and in fact.

For the *comitia* to be legally convened and for its decisions to have the force of law, three conditions had to be observed: first, the body or the magistrate convening the assembly had to be vested with the necessary authority; secondly, the assembly had to be held on one of the days permitted by law; thirdly, the auguries had to be favourable.

---

① I say 'Campus Martius' because this was where the *comitia centuriata* met. In the other two forms of assembly, the people met in the forum or elsewhere, and then the *capite censi* had as much influence and authority as the leading citizens.

由这一切便可以很容易明白为什么人们所提到的罗马等级几乎不会超过五个，虽然实际上罗马有六个等级。第六个等级既不能向军队提供士兵，也不能在玛尔提乌斯校场上投票①，因此，实际上他们在共和国中没有任何职权，因而也就很少得到人们的关注。

这就是罗马人民的各种不同的划分。现在就让我们考虑一下这些划分在集会中的作用吧。合法召集的集会被称作是人民大会，而且人民大会通常是在罗马广场或者玛尔提乌斯校场上召集的。根据以何种形式召集人民大会，可以把它们分为库里亚大会、百人团大会和部族大会。库里亚大会是由罗穆鲁斯创立的，百人团大会是由塞尔维乌斯创立的，而部族大会则是起源于保民官的。除非是在人民大会上，否则便不能批准任何法律，不能选举任何行政官员，而且由于所有的公民都是被编入“库里亚”、百人团或者是部族的，所以任何公民都没有被排斥在投票权之外，罗马人民是法律上和事实上的真正主权者。

为了使人民大会可以合法地召集，为了使人民大会的决定具有法律的效力，那就必须具备三个条件：首先，召集大会的团体或者行政官员必须具有召集大会所必需的权限；其次，集会必须在法律所许可的日期举行；第三，占卜所得必须为吉兆。

---

① 我说“玛尔提乌斯校场”，是因为这是百人团大会召集的地方。在其他两种形式的集会中，人民在广场上或者其他地方集会，那时那些按人头计数的人就和最重要的公民一样有相同的影响和权威了。

The reason for the first of these rules needs no explanation. The second was a matter of policy; the assembly was not allowed to meet on holidays or market days, because the country people, who came to Rome to do business, did not have time to spend the day in the forum. The third rule enabled the Senate to keep a restraining hand on a proud and restless people and temper the ardour of seditious tribunes— although the latter found more than one way of evading this check.

Laws and the election of chiefs were not the only matters submitted to the judgement of the *comitia*. Since the Roman people had usurped the most important functions of government, one could say that the fate of Europe was determined in those assemblies. The variety of public business explains the several forms which the *comitia* took, according to the matters which had to be decided.

To judge these various forms it is necessary only to compare them. Romulus, in establishing the *curiae* aimed to balance the Senate against the people and balance the people against the Senate, while himself dominating both alike. Under this arrangement he gave the people all the authority of numbers to balance the authority of power and wealth which he left to the patricians. But true to the spirit of monarchy, he nevertheless gave the great advantage to the patricians, in that they could buy clients to influence numerical majorities. This admirable institution of patrons and clients was a masterpiece of politics and humanity, without which the patriciate, so contrary to the spirit of the Republic, could not have survived. To Rome alone belongs the honour of giving the world this noble example, from which no abuse has ever come, but which has never been followed elsewhere.

This same form of *curiae* continued under the kings up to Servius, and as the reign of the last of the Tarquins was not held to be legitimate, the royal laws were generally known by the name of *leges curiatae*.

第一条规则的原因就不需要解释了。第二条规则是一项政策；集会是不允许在假日或者是集市日举行的，因为那时乡村的人民要到罗马城去办事，因而不能在会议上耗费整天的时间。第三条规则使元老院能够制约一个骄傲而且不安宁的民族，并且可以调节具有煽动性的保民官的狂热，虽然保民官会找到种种办法来逃避这种约束。

法律和选举首领并不是提交人民大会决议的唯一的事情。既然罗马人民篡取了政府最重要的职能，那么我们可以说欧洲的命运就是在那些集会上决定的。公共事务的种种不同说明了为什么人民大会要根据它所要决定的事情而采用种种不同的形式。

要评判这种种的大会形式，只要比较一下它们就可以了。罗穆鲁斯创立库里亚的目的是要借助于元老院以制衡人民，同时又借助于人民以制衡元老院，而他自己则可以支配这两者。在这种安排之下，他赋予了人民数量上的权威，以平衡他留给贵族的权力和财富的权威。但是与君主制的精神相符合，他仍然给了贵族等级更多的有利条件，即贵族可以通过贿买他们的被保护者以影响多数票的表决。这种令人钦佩的保护者和被保护者的制度实在是政治上和人道上的一个杰作，没有这种制度的话，与共和国精神是如此背离的贵族统治就不会存在了。

给世界做出如此好的榜样的荣誉只属于罗马，这一制度从未产生过任何弊病，但是在其他的地方却也从来没有被效仿过。

库里亚这种形式在王政时期到塞尔维乌斯的时代为止一直存在着，而且又由于塔尔干王朝末期的统治被认为是不合法的，所以王政时期的法律就又被称作是库里亚法。

Under the Republic, the *curiae*, which were still limited to the four urban tribes, and still included only the population of Rome, pleased neither the Senate, which led the patricians, nor the tribunes who, in spite of being plebeian, led the more moneyed citizens. Thus the *curiae* fell into discredit, fell so low indeed that their thirty lictors met to do what the *comitia curiae* should have done.

The division into centuries was so favourable to the aristocracy that it is not at first easy to see why the Senate did not always carry the day in the *comitia* which bore that name, and by which the consuls, censors and other cural magistrates were elected. For indeed, of the 193 centuries which formed the six classes of the entire Roman people, the first class contained 98, and since votes were counted by centuries only, this first class had a majority over all the others. When all these centuries were in agreement, the rest of the votes were not even counted; and what had been decided by a minority passed for a decision of the multitude; so it can be said that in the centuriate assemblies matters were decided by majorities of money rather than of votes.

But this excessive power was tempered in two ways. First, the tribunes ordinarily, and a large number of plebeians always, were in a class with the rich, and balanced the influence of the patricians in the first class.

Secondly, the centuries were not always summoned to vote in their order or rank, which would have meant beginning with the first class; instead, a century was chosen by lot[①] and that century alone

---

① The century thus drawn was called *praerogativa* because it was the first required to cast its vote; and this is the origin of our word ‘prerogative’.

在共和国时期，库里亚由于仍然只局限在四个城市部族当中，仍然仅仅包括罗马城中的居民，所以它就既不能令领导着贵族阶层的元老院感到满意，也不能令那些虽然自己身为平民但却领导着更多有钱的公民的保民官感到满意。这样库里亚就失去了信用，以至于事实上只要他们的三十个扈从集合在一起就可以做那些本来是库里亚大会所应该做的事情了。

百人团的划分方法对贵族制是如此有利，以至于一开始我们都很难看明白：为什么元老院在那个被称为是百人团大会并且选举了执政官、监察官和其他高级行政官员的人民大会之中总是不能占主导地位呢？因为事实上，在那个构成了全部罗马人民的六个等级的一百九十三个百人团之中，第一等级就包含了九十八个；而既然投票只是按百人团的数目来计算的，那么第一等级就拥有超过其他所有等级投票数的多数。如果第一等级所有百人团意见一致的话，其他的投票数就不需要再计算了，由少数人所做出的决定就被看作是大多数人的决定；所以可以说在百人团大会中事务是按照财富的多数来表决的，而不是按投票的多数来表决的。

这种过度的权力是通过两种方式来缓和的。首先，保民官通常会、而且大部分的平民总是会和富人一起处在一个等级之中，并在第一等级中制衡了贵族等级的影响。

其次，百人团并不总是按照它们的次序或者是等级进行投票，因为按次序和级别进行投票就意味着从第一等级开始；相反，先通过抽签的方式选出一个百人团[①]，由这个百人团单独进行

① 这样被抽出的百人团被称作是“优先者”，因为它是被要求第一个进行投票的；而且这也是“特权”这个词的来源。

went on to elect, after which the other centuries were convened on a different day by order of rank to repeat the election, and generally they confirmed it. Thus the authority of example was taken away from rank and given to chance, according to the principle of democracy.

This custom had yet another advantage; it meant that the citizens from the country had time between the elections to inform themselves of the merits of the candidates provisionally nominated, and therefore did not vote in ignorance. But under the pretext of speeding up procedure this custom was finally abolished, and both elections were held on the same day.

The *comitia tributa* was, strictly speaking, the council of the Roman people. It could be convened only by the tribunes; it was the assembly where the tribunes were elected and it was there that they passed their plebiscites. Not only had the Senate no status in the assembly, but no senator had even the right to attend, and being thus forced to submit to laws in the enactment of which they had no voice, the senators were to that extent less free than the humblest citizen. This injustice was altogether ill conceived, and alone sufficed to invalidate the decrees of a body to which all its members were not admitted. Had all the patricians attended the *comitia*, according to their rights as citizens, they would not, as simple individuals, have had any great influence on a vote taken by enumerating heads, and in which the humblest proletarian would count for as much as the prince of the Senate.

Thus, it will be seen that besides the order which emerged from the various systems of collecting the votes of so vast a people, these several methods were not in themselves insignificant, but that each had effects connected with the opinions that led to its being chosen.

Without going further into long details, it emerges from the explanation already given, that the *comitia tributa* was the assembly most favourable to popular government and the *comitia centuriata* to aristocracy.

选举，之后在另外的一天，再召集其他的百人团按照级别次序进行同一个选举，这通常会确认前面的选举结果。这样，根据民主制的原则，示范的权威便由级别转到了偶然的抽签上。

这种选举习惯还有另外一个优点，那就是从乡村来的公民在两次选举期间就可以有时间使自己了解那些临时被提名的候选人的优点，因而就不会盲目地投票了。但是在加快选举进程的借口之下，这个办法最后被废除了，两次选举就在同一天内举行了。

严格来讲，部族大会是罗马人民的议会。它只能由保民官来召集；正是在这种集会上才选举出了保民官，也正是在这些集会上通过了平民们制定的法律。元老院在这种集会中不仅没有任何地位，元老们甚至都没有权利参加这种集会，而且由于元老们被迫要服从于那些他们在制定过程中根本没有发言权的法律，所以元老们以至于比最卑微的公民还没有自由。这种不公正的规定完全是拙劣的设计，仅凭这一点就足以使一个不能包容其所有成员的团体制定的法令变得无效。如果所有的贵族根据他们作为一个公民的权利参加“人民大会”，他们作为单纯的个人，在这样一种以人头计算的投票中就不能有任何大的影响，因为在这种投票方式中最卑微的无产者和首席元老完全是等价的。

因而，我们可以看到除了由如此广大的一个民族收集选票的种种不同制度而产生的次序之外，这些收集选票的办法本身也不是无关紧要的，而是每种办法都会有与其意图相联系的效果，而这种意图恰是导致这一办法之所以被选中的原因。

不需要进一步阐述更多的细节，由前面的解释就可以看到，部族大会是最适合于人民政府的一种集会，而百人团大会则

In the case of the *comitia curiata*, where the populace of Rome alone formed the majority, their tendency to favour tyranny and evil designs led them to fall into disrepute, so that even the seditious elements avoided these assemblies lest their presence should arouse suspicion concerning their conspiracies. There is no doubt that the whole majesty of the Roman people was to be seen only in the *comitia centuriata*; this alone was a full assembly, for the *comitia curiata* excluded the rustic tribes and the *comitia tribute* excluded the Senate and patricians.

The system of voting used by the Romans was as simple as were their manners and morals, if less simple than that of Sparta. Each man gave his vote by word of mouth, and a clerk recorded it; the majority of individual votes in each tribe determined the decision of that tribe, the majority of tribal votes the decision of the people; and the same thing was done in the *curiae* and *centuriae*. This was a good method so long as honesty prevailed among the citizens and everyone was ashamed to give his vote to an unjust cause or an unworthy candidate. But when the people grew corrupt and votes were bought, it became expedient for the ballot to be cast in secret, so that the buyers of votes might be restrained by mistrust of the sellers, and scoundrels given the chance of not being traitors also.

I am aware that Cicero condemns this change of method, and holds it partly responsible for the ruin of the Republic. But while I am mindful of the weight which the authority of Cicero ought to bear, I do not agree with him. On the contrary, I think that it was by having too few such changes that the ruin of the state was accelerated. For just as the diet of healthy people is unsuited to the sick, so one should not try to give to a corrupt people the same laws as those which suit a virtuous people. Nothing does more to bear out this principle than the long life of the Republic of Venice, which still retains a simulacrum of existence solely because its laws are uniquely suited to wicked men.

是最适合于贵族制的。就库里亚大会而言，在这种大会中罗马的平民自己就构成了其中的大多数，由于它有一种有利于暴政和邪恶阴谋的倾向，这使它名誉扫地，以至于那些叛乱分子也避免利用这种集会方式，以防止人民产生对他们的阴谋的怀疑。毫无疑问，罗马人民的全部尊严只有在百人团大会中才能看到；只有这种大会才是全民的集会，因为库里亚大会是把乡村部族排斥在外的，而部族大会则又把元老院和贵族排斥在外。

罗马人所使用的投票制度就像他们的习俗和道德一样简单，虽然可能还比不上斯巴达人的投票方式那么简单。每个人都口头地给出他的投票，有一个职员把它们记录下来，每个部族中个人投票的大多数就产生了那个部族的决定；在库里亚和百人团当中也是这样做的。只要诚实能够在公民中占据上风，只要每个人都耻于投票给一项不公正的事业或者一个卑劣的候选人，那么这种方式便是一种很好的方式。但是当人民变得腐败而且选票可以被贿买的时候，秘密地进行投票就成为有利的了，因为这样一来，贿买选票的人就会因为对出卖选票的人不信任而受到限制，而且也给了恶棍一个不至于变成叛国者的机会。

我知道西塞罗谴责这种方法上的改变，他认为这种改变要为共和国的毁灭负部分的责任。虽然我没有忘记西塞罗的权威可能具有的分量，但是我还是不赞同他的观点。相反，我认为正是由于这种改变太少了，所以才加速了国家的毁灭。因为正像一个健康的人的食谱并不适合于一个生病的人一样，人们不能试图把那些适合于有道德的民族的法律赋予一个腐化了的民族。没有什么能比威尼斯共和国的悠久历史更能证实这个原则了，威尼斯共和国现在还影子般存在着，完全是因为它的法律仅仅是适合于不道德的人的。

Now the Roman citizens had tablets distributed among them, so that each might cast his vote without anyone's knowing his opinion. New arrangements were also devised for the collection of tablets, the counting of votes, the comparison of numbers, and so forth. This did not prevent the officers[1] entrusted with these functions from being suspected of dishonesty. Finally, edicts designed to prevent intrigue and the buying and selling of votes were passed in such numbers that their very multiplicity proclaims their ineffectiveness.

Towards the last years of the Republic, the Romans were often forced to resort to extraordinary expedients to make up for the inadequacy of the law. Sometimes miracles were invoked, but this device, if it could impose on the people, did not impose on those who ruled them. Sometimes assemblies were hurriedly convened, before candidates had time to pay out their bribes; sometimes a whole session was taken up with filibustering, when it was seen that the people had been seduced and was about to make a wrong decision. But ambition in the end overcame all obstacles; and the most incredible fact of all is that so numerous a people, in the midst of so many abuses, still continued, thanks to its ancient rules of order, to elect magistrates, to enact laws, to judge cases and to conduct private and public business with almost as much facility as the Senate itself might have commanded.

---

① *Custodes, Diribitores, Rogatores suffragiorum.*

填票单被分发给了罗马公民，这样每个公民就可以做出自己的投票而又不让任何人知道自己的观点。人们同样也为填票单的收集、投票的计数、票数的比较等设计了新的办法，但是这些并不能防止担负这些职能[①]的官员被人们怀疑为不诚实。最后，人们又通过了为防止舞弊和贿买、出卖选票而设计的法令，这些法令数量是如此之多，而这种数量之多就显示了这些法令是无效的。

到了罗马共和国的最后时期，罗马人被迫求助于特别的权宜之计以弥补法律的不足。有些时候他们借用神迹，但是这种策略只能欺骗人民，却不能欺骗统治人民的人。有时候在候选人有时间进行贿赂之前就匆忙召集大会；有时候因为看到人民已经被引诱并且准备做出错误的决定了，所以就在整个会议上尽力阻止议案通过。但是野心家最终还是冲破了所有的障碍；而最令人难以置信的是，如此众多的人民，在如此众多的弊病之中，依赖于它古老的规则，竟然持续地进行着选举行政官员、颁布法律、审判案件以及处理私人和公共的事务，而且做起来和元老院自己所能做的一样相当熟练。

① 选票的监督、分配、查询。

CHAPTER 5
The Tribunate

When it is impossible to settle an exact balance between the constitutive parts of the state, or when causes beyond control go on altering the relations between them, then a special magistrate is established, as a body separate from the other magistrates, to put every element in its right balance and to serve as a link or middle term, either between the prince and the people or between the prince and the sovereign, or alternatively, between both at the same time if that is necessary.

This body, which I shall call the *tribunate*, is the guardian of the laws and of the legislative power. It serves sometimes to protect the sovereign against the government, as did the tribunes of the people in Rome, sometimes to uphold the government against the people, as does the Council of Ten today in Venice, and sometimes to keep a balance between the two, as did the Ephors of Sparta.

The tribunate is not a constitutive part of the republic, and it ought to have no share of either the legislative or executive power, but for this very reason its own power is all the greater, for although it can do nothing, it can prevent anything from being done. As the defender of the laws, it is more sacred and more venerated than the prince who executes laws or the sovereign which legislates. This is very clearly shown in the case of Rome, where the proud patricians, who always despised the people as a whole, were forced to bow before an ordinary officer of the people who wielded neither sacred nor legal authority.

第五章　论保民官制

当人们不能在国家各个构成部分之间设定一个确切的比例的时候，或者当不可控制的原因持续地改变着它们之间的关系的时候，人们就建立了一个独立于其他行政机构的特殊行政团体，它使国家的各组成部分处于其恰当的比例上，并且在统治者和人民之间，或者在君主和主权者之间，如果需要的话，或者同时在这两者之间起到一种联系的作用或者说比例中项的作用。

这种我称之为保民官的团体，是法律和立法权力的护卫者。有时候它会起到保护主权者以反对政府的作用，就像在罗马，人民的保民官所做的那样；有时候它起到支持政府以反对人民的作用，就像今天威尼斯的十人会议所做的那样；而有时候又在这两者之间保持一种平衡，正如斯巴达的五人监察院所做的那样。

保民官制度并不是共和国的一个构成部分，它也不应该分享立法权力或者行政权力，但正是由于这个原因，它拥有的权力又是最大的，因为尽管它不能做出任何事情，但它却可以禁止任何事情的进行。作为法律的保卫者，它比执行法律的统治者和制定法律的立法者更加神圣、更受到尊崇。在罗马，我们可以很清楚地看到这一点，在那里那些总是看不起所有人民的高傲的贵族，却不得不在一个既无神性的权力，又无法定权威的人民官员面前卑躬屈膝。

A wisely tempered tribunate is the strongest buttress of a good constitution, but if it has the least degree of power beyond what is necessary, it will overthrow everything. It is not by its nature prone to weakness, and if it is anything at all, it will never be less than it ought to be.

It degenerates into tyranny when it usurps the executive power of which it is only the moderator, and when it tries to make the laws it ought only to protect. The enormous power of the Ephors, which represented no danger so long as Sparta preserved its morale, sped corruption once corruption began. The blood of Agis shed by the tyrants was avenged by his successor; the crimes and the punishments of the Ephors equally hastened the collapse of the Republic, and after Cleomenes, Sparta was nothing. Rome perished in the same way, and the excessive power which the tribunes usurped by degrees finally served, with the aid of laws made to defend liberty, to protect the very emperors who destroyed liberty. As for the Council of Ten in Venice, it is a tribunal of blood, which is baneful as much to the patricians as to the people, and which, far from giving supreme protection to the law, serves only, now that the law has been debased, for the striking of stealthy blows that none dare look upon.

A tribunate, like a government, is weakened by the multiplication of its members. When the tribunes of the Roman people, originally two, then five, sought to double their number, the Senate gave its consent, confident of using one part to check the others; and this it did not fail to effect.

The best method of preventing the usurpations of such a formidable body— though it is a method which no government has ever yet employed— would be not to make the tribunate permanent but to prescribe the intervals diuring which it should remain suspended.

一个得到明智的调节的保民官制度是一个良好体制的最强大支柱，但是一旦它拥有了超出它所必需的哪怕是一丁点的权力，它就会颠覆一切。保民官就其本性来讲是不会趋向于软弱的，只要它成了气候，它就永远不会适可而止。

当保民官篡夺了那些它本是作为其调节者的行政权力的时候，当保民官试图去制定那些它本只应保护的法律的时候，它就堕落成暴君了。只要斯巴达能够保持它的民风，监督官庞大的权力就不会是危险的，但一旦他们开始腐化，这个腐化就会加速进行。被这些暴君杀害的阿基斯，他的后继者替他复了仇；这些监督官们所犯的罪行和所受到的惩罚同样加速了共和国的崩溃，到了克里奥门尼斯之后，斯巴达就不值一提了。罗马也是以同样的方式毁灭的，保民官逐步篡夺了过分的权力，并在为了保护自由而制定的法律的保护之下，最终竟然起到了保护那些破坏自由的皇帝的作用。至于威尼斯的十人会议，它是一个血腥的裁判所，它对于人民和对于贵族一样是有害的，它远不是给予法律以至高的保护，相反法律被贬低了，它只是在鬼鬼祟祟地施放一些见不得人的冷枪暗箭。

保民官制度正像政府一样，随着它的成员的增加而削弱。罗马人民的保民官最初是两个，后来是五个，当他们试图把这个数目增加一倍的时候，元老院予以了支持，元老院自信可以利用其中的一部分人控制另外一部分人，而后来真的达到了这种效果。

防止这样一个强大的团体篡权的最好办法（虽然这是任何政府都未曾采用过的一种办法）就是不要让保民官成为永久性的，而是规定一些间歇期，在这些间歇期中保民官制度暂停存在。

These intervals, which should not be so great as to give abuses time to take root, could be specified by law in such a manner that in case of need they might be shortened by an extraordinary commission.

This method appears to me to have no disadvantages, for since, as I have said, the tribunate is in no sense a part of the constitution, it can be removed without detriment to it; this also seems to me an efficacious method, since a newly established magistrate would not enter office with the power that his predecessors had, but only with that given him by law.

这些间歇期不能太长，以避免权力的滥用有时间生根发芽。这些间歇期应该由法律按一种方式做出规定，以便于一旦需要，这些间歇期可以根据特别的命令而被缩短。

这种方法在我看没有什么不利，因为既然正如我所说的，保民官制绝不是国家体制的一部分，所以撤销它也不会对体制有损害；而且在我看来这还是一种有效的方法，因为一个新任命的行政官员，不是秉持他前任手中的权力，而只是秉持法律赋予他的权力上任的。

CHAPTER 6
Dictatorship

The inflexibility of the laws, which prevents them from bending to circumstances, may in certain cases make them injurious, and bring about in a time of crisis the ruin of the state. The ordered and slow procedures of legal formalities require a measure of time that circumstances do not always afford. There may be a thousand eventualities which the lawgiver has not foreseen, and it is a very necessary part of foresight to know that one cannot foresee everything.

For this reason, one should not seek to make political institutions so rigid that one is deprived of the power to suspend their operation. Even Sparta allowed its laws at times to lie dormant.

But it is only the greatest emergency that can counterweigh the dangers of tampering with the public order; and the sacred power of the laws should never be suspended except when the safety of the fatherland is at stake. In these rare and obvious cases, the public security is provided for by a special act making that security the responsibility of the person who is most worthy. This responsibility may be assigned in two ways, according to the nature of the emergency.

If increasing the activity of the government is adequate to counteract the danger, then this activity should be concentrated in the hands of one or two members of the government. In this case, it is not the authority of the laws which is being diminished, but only the form of the administration.

第六章　论独裁制

法律的缺乏弹性使它们不能根据环境做出变通，以致在一些情况下使法律本身成为有害的，并且在危机的关头会导致国家的毁灭。法定形式的种种规定以及拖沓的程序，往往都会耗费一定的时间，而这种时间并不总是为局势所允许的。很可能会出现成千种立法者所不能预见的偶然事件，因而能够认识到人们并不能预见所有的事情，这本身就是一种必要的先见之明。

因为这个原因，所以人们就不应该试图去把政治体制变得如此僵硬，以至于竟然剥夺了人们暂时中止它的执行的权力。即使是斯巴达有时也允许它的法律暂时失效。

但是只有最大的紧急事件的危险才能与改变公共秩序带来的危险同日而语；而且除非祖国已经危如累卵，否则人们就永远都不能暂停法律神圣的权力。在这些罕见但又显而易见的情况下，人们通过一种特别的行为把维护国家安全的责任赋予一个最值得信任的人。根据紧急事件的性质，对这一责任的指派可以通过两种方式进行。

如果增加政府的能动性就足以应付危险，那么就应该把政府集中在政府的一个或者两个成员手中。在这种情况下，并不是法律的权威被削弱了，只是执行法律的形式改变了。但如果面临

But if the danger is such that the apparatus of law is itself an obstacle to safety, then a supreme head must be nominated with power to silence all the laws and temporarily suspend the sovereign authority. In such a case the general will is indubitable; for it is clear that the prime concern of the people is that the state shall not perish. Thus the suspension of the legislative authority does not abolish it; the magistrate who silences it cannot make it speak; he dominates it, without having the power to represent it; he can do everything, except make laws.

The first of these two methods was used by the Roman Senate when, according to a hallowed formula, it entrusted the consuls with the safety of the Republic; the second was used when one of the two consuls nominated a dictator[①]—a device that Rome had learned from Alba.

At the beginning of the Republic, the Romans often resorted to dictatorship, because conditions were not yet sufficiently settled for the state to maintain itself by the strength of its constitution. The people's moral character made unnecessary at that time many of the precautions which might have been needed at other times, so men did not fear that a dictator would abuse his position or that he would attempt to prolong his office beyond its term. It seemed, on the contrary, that so much power was a burden to those who wielded it; for they hastened to divest themselves of it, as if standing in the place of the laws made it altogether too onerous and perilous an office.

So it is not because there was a danger of its being abused, but because there was a danger of its being degraded that one condemns the imprudent employment of this supreme magistrature in

---

① This nomination took place by night and in secret, as if they were ashamed to put a man above the law.

这样一种危险，即法律的规定本身已经成为国家安全的障碍，那么就必须任命一个至高无上的首领，使他有权力让法律沉默下来，并且暂时中止立法者的权威。在这种情况下，公意仍然是不容置疑的；因为很明显，这时人们首要关心的乃是国家不能毁灭。因而立法权威暂时中止并不是要废除它，这个行政官能使立法权威闭口不言，但是却无权让它开口说话；他能控制立法权威，但却没有权力代表它；他可以做任何事情，只是不能制定法律。

在罗马的元老院根据一种神圣的仪式把维护国家安全的责任赋予它的执政官的时候，他们便采用了这两种方法中的第一种；而当罗马的两个执政官中一个被任命为独裁者[①]的时候，便是采用了第二种方法。这种方法是罗马从阿尔巴那里学来的。

在罗马共和国的初期，罗马人经常求助于独裁制，因为对国家而言，要仅凭其体制的力量以保存自身，这样的条件还没有充分地建立起来。罗马人民的道德品格使得那些在别的时代中很有必要的防范措施在这个时代中成为多余的，所以人们并不害怕一个独裁者会滥用他的职权，也不担心他会把自己的任期延长得超过了规定的期限。相反，看上去好像如此多的权力对于那些拥有它的人来说是一个重负，因为他们会急匆匆地要摆脱这种权力，好像站在法律的位置上使他们的职位变得非常繁重而且危险一样。

所以本人指责在罗马共和国早期这种最高行政官制度的草率应用，其原因倒不在于有权力的危险，而在于这种权力

---

① 这种任命是在夜间秘密进行的，好像他们为把一个人置于法律之上而感到羞耻似的。

the early days of the Republic. For while it was wasted on elections, dedications and purely formal things, there was reason to fear that it would become less forceful when it was really needed, and that the people would come to regard dictatorship as an empty title used only to give dignity to idle ceremonies.

Towards the end of the Republic, the Romans, becoming more circumspect, were as sparing in their use of dictatorship as they had once been prodigal, and with as little reason. It was easy to see that their fears were ill founded, and that the weakness of the capital was at that time its protection against the magistrates it had in its midst, that a dictator could in certain cases defend the public freedom without ever being able to invade it, and that the fetters of Rome were not forged in Rome itself, but in the Roman armies; the weak resistance that Marius offered Sulla, and Pompey Caesar, showed plainly what could be expected of internal authority faced with external force.

This mistake led the Romans to commit great wrongs. There was, for example, their failure to nominate a dictator in the Catilina affair; for since this was a matter which concerned only the city itself, or at most a few Italian provinces, the unlimited authority which the law gave a dictator would have facilitated the ready crushing of that conspiracy, which was in fact suppressed only by a concurrence of lucky accidents, such as human prudence could never have expected.

Instead of naming a dictator, the Senate was content to transmit all its powers to the consuls, as a result of which Cicero, in order to act effectively, was obliged to exceed his powers on a crucial point; and though, in a first transport of joy, the Romans approved of his conduct, it was not without justice that he was afterwards asked to account for the blood of citizens shed in violation of the laws — a reproach which could not have been addressed to a dictator.

有被贬低的危险。因为当这种制度滥用于选举、飨祭以及种种纯粹形式化的事务上的时候，我们完全有理由担心，当我们真的需要这些权力时，它已经变得不够强大了，而且也有理由担心人们会逐渐把独裁者的职位看成一种仅仅适用于无价值的仪式上的空洞头衔。

在罗马共和国的晚期，罗马人变得更加谨慎了，他们在运用这种独裁制上的保守，就像他们曾经在运用这种制度上的浪费同样的毫无道理。我们可以很容易地看到他们的担心是没有根据的，那时候首都力量的薄弱保护了它以防范它内部的行政官员。在某些情况下，一个独裁者可以保卫公共的自由，却永远不能够侵犯这种自由。罗马的枷锁并非是在罗马自身铸成的，而是在罗马军队中铸成的；马留乌斯对苏拉、庞贝对恺撒的软弱抵抗，很明白地显示了当内部的权威面对外部的力量时，我们能期待什么样的结果。

这种过失使罗马人犯了一些重大的错误。比如，在卡提里那事件中，他们没有能够任命一个独裁者；因为既然这个事件仅仅涉及罗马城本身，至多也只是涉及意大利的几个省份，那么法律赋予一个独裁者的无限权威本可以使得对这一阴谋的粉碎变得非常便利，而事实上只是靠着人类的审慎所不能预期的机缘巧合，这一阴谋才被平息了。

元老院并没有任命一个独裁者，而只是满足于把所有的权力转移给执政官们。结果，西塞罗为了更有效地行动，被迫在一个至关重要的问题上超越了他的权限；虽然一开始，在喜悦的激动情绪当中，罗马人支持了他的行为，但是后来人们便要求他为公民们在这一破坏法律的行为中所流的血负责了，这也不是不公正的（这

But the consul's eloquence carried everything before him, and he himself, though a Roman, loved his own glory better than his country; and instead of seeking a lawful and certain means of serving the state, he sought all the honour of the affair for himself.① Thus he was justly honoured as the liberator of Rome, and no less justly punished as the violator of Roman laws. However splendid his recall from exile may have been, it was undoubtedly an act of pardon.

For the rest, in whatever manner this important commission of dictatorship is conferred, it is imperative to limit its duration to one short term that can never be prolonged; in the emergencies which call for its institution, the state is soon lost or saved, and once the urgent need is over, dictatorship becomes either tyrannical or useless. In Rome, where the term was of six months, most of the dictators abdicated before that time had expired. If the term had been longer, they might have been tempted to prolong it still further, like the decemvirs, who held office for a year. The dictator, having only the time to meet the need which had prompted his appointment, had none in which to meditate on further projects.

---

① He could not have been sure of this if he had proposed appointing a dictator, for he did not dare to name himself, and he could not be sure that his colleagues would name him.

种指责就不会被加在一个独裁者身上)。但是这位执政官的雄辩战胜了所有反对的声音，而他自己虽然作为一个罗马人，但是他热爱自己的荣誉远过于热爱他的国家；他并不是去寻求一种为国家服务的合法的、妥当的方法，相反他力求为自己从这一事件中获得所有的荣誉①。因而，作为罗马的解放者他公正地得到人们的尊敬，而作为罗马法律的破坏者，他同样公正地受到了惩罚。不管后来对他的流放的撤销是多么的光彩，毫无疑问那只是一种宽恕的行为。

此外，独裁制这种重要的任命不管是以何种方式授予的，必要的一点是，要把它的任期限制在一个短的时间之内，而且这一任期永远都不能延长。在需要建立独裁制的紧急时刻，国家不是很快地陷落，就是很快地得到挽救，而一旦这种紧急需要结束了，独裁制会变得或者残暴，或者无用。在罗马，这个任期是六个月，大多数独裁者在任期届满之前就退位了。如果这个期限再长一些的话，独裁者会试图把它延长得更长，就像任期为一年的十人会议一样。独裁者只应有时间来应付那些使他们得以被任命的紧急需要，而不应有时间来筹谋更进一步的计划。

---

① 如果他提议任命一个独裁者的话，他就不能确保这一点了，因为他既不敢任命他自己，而且他又不能确定他的同僚会任命他。

CHAPTER 7
The Censorial Tribunal

Just as the general will is declared by the law, so is the public judgement declared by the censorial office; public opinion is that form of law of which the censor is the minister, and which he, on the model of the prince, merely applies to particular cases.

Far, then, from the censorial tribunal being the arbiter of the people's opinion, it is only the spokesman; and as soon as it departs from this, its decisions are void and without effect.

It is useless to separate the morals of a nation from the objects of its esteem; for both spring from the same principle and both necessarily merge together. Among all the peoples of the world, it is not nature but opinion which governs the choice of their pleasures. Reform the opinions of men, and their morals will be purified of themselves. Men always love what is good or what they think is good, but it is in their judgement that they err; hence it is their judgement that has to be regulated. To judge morals is to judge what is honoured; to judge what is honoured, is to look to opinion as law.

The opinions of a people spring from its constitution; although the law does not regulate morals, it is legislation that gives birth to morals;

第七章　论监察官制

正像公意是通过法律来宣布的一样，公众的判断是由监督机关来宣布的；舆论是一种法律，监察官则是这种法律的执行者，而且依照君主的模式，监察官也只能把这一法律应用于个别事件。

因此，监察官的法庭就远不是人民的观点的仲裁者，而仅仅是其宣告者；一旦离开了这一点，它的决定就是无效的、没有任何作用的。

要把一个民族的道德和他们尊崇的对象区分开来是徒劳无功的；因为这两者是源自于同样的原则的，而且两者必然地要融合在一起。在世界上所有的民族之中，支配着他们的喜怒选择的并不是天性，而是他们的观点。端正了他们的观点，他们的道德自然地就会纯正起来。人们总是热爱好的东西，或者说热爱他们认为是好的东西，但是正是在这个判断中，他们就会犯错误了，因此正是他们的判断才是需要被调整的。对道德进行评判就是对他们所尊崇的东西进行评判，而要对他们所尊崇的东西做出评判，则是要把公众的观点作为其法则。

一个民族的种种观点源自于它的体制。虽然法律并没有规范道德，但正是立法才产生了道德；当立法削弱的时候，道德

when legislation weakens, morals degenerate; and then the rulings of the censors will not accomplish what the law has failed to achieve.

From this it follows that the censorial office may be useful in preserving morals, but never in restoring morals. Set up censors while the laws are still vigorous; for as soon as the vigour is lost, everything is hopeless; nothing legitimate has any force once the laws have force no longer.

The censorial office sustains morals by preventing opinions from being corrupted, by preserving their integrity with wise rulings, and sometimes even by settling points on which opinion is uncertain. The use of seconds in duels, carried to an impassioned extreme in the kingdom of France, was abolished by a single edict of the King: 'as for those who are cowardly enough to name seconds'. This judgement anticipated that of the public, and settled it with one stroke. But when the same edicts sought to declare that it was cowardice also to fight duels— which is very true, but at variance with popular opinion— the public scoffed at this decision on a matter about which its mind was made up.

I have said elsewhere① that since public opinion is not subject to constraint, there should be no vestige of constraint in the tribunal established to represent it. We cannot too greatly admire the skill with which this device, entirely alien to the moderns, was put into effect by the Romans and even by the Lacedaemonians.

---

① In this chapter I have only indicated what I have already discussed at great length in my *Lettre à d' Alembert*.

也就退化了；那时候，监察官的裁决也不能做成法律所不能做成的事情。

由此可以得出结论，监察机关在维护道德上可能是有用的，但是在重建道德上则永远都不会起到什么作用。要在法律还充满活力的时候设立监察官，因为一旦这种活力消失了，任何事情就都没有希望了；一旦法律不再有力量了，那么任何合法的东西也就不再有力量了。

监察机关通过防止舆论被腐蚀的办法来维持道德，也通过以贤明的裁决保持舆论的正直性的办法来维持道德，甚至有时候还会通过把不确定的舆论确定下来的办法来维持道德。决斗中带副手的习俗在法兰西王国曾风靡至极，但是却由于国王的一纸敕令而被废除了："至于那些懦弱到需要任命一个副手的人。"这种判断预见了公共的判断，并且一下子就把公众的判断确定了下来。但是如果试图用同样的法令宣布决斗同样是懦弱胆小的（虽然这是事实，但是却与流行的观点不相符合），公众就会嘲笑这个决定，因为对此事公众的看法早已形成了。

我在别的地方①已经说过，既然舆论是不会屈从于任何强制力量，那么在为了代表舆论而设立的监察官的法庭中就不应该有丝毫的强制。对于罗马人，甚至是对于拉西第蒙人在把这种现代人已经完全失掉了的制度付诸实施时所运用的技巧，我们怎么赞美都不过分。

---

① 在这一章中，我只不过是简单地阐述了我在我的《致达朗贝先生书》中所详细论述过的观点而已。

Once when a man of bad character put forward a good idea in the council of Sparta, the Ephors, ignoring him, had the same thing proposed by a virtuous citizen. What an honour for the one, what a disgrace for the other; yet neither praise nor blame was given to either. Certain drunkards from Samos' ① once defiled the tribunal of the Ephors; the following day the Samians were given permission by public edict to be filthy. An actual punishment would have been less severe than such a form of impunity. When Sparta has pronounced on what is and what is not decent, Greece does not dispute its judgements.

① They were actually from another island, but delicacy of language forbids me to name it here.

·

一个道德败坏的人曾在斯巴达的议会中提出一个好想法，五人监察院对他不予理睬，而是把这个同样的想法让一个有道德的公民来提出。这对于其中的一个是多么大的荣誉，而对于另一个来说则是多么大的耻辱啊！虽然对这两者中的任何一个都既没有表扬也没有谴责。萨摩斯岛[①]的几个醉汉曾经弄脏了五人监察院的法庭；第二天五人监察院就通过公开的法令允许萨摩斯人可以是肮脏的。一个实际的惩罚也不会比这样一种不加惩罚来得更加严厉了。当斯巴达已经明确地宣布了什么是正派的以及什么是不正派的时候，希腊对此判断未加争辩。

① 他们实际上是来自另外一个岛的，只是我们语言的微妙不允许我在这里指出它的名字。

CHAPTER 8

The Civil Religion

At first men had no kings but the Gods, and their only government was theocratic. They reasoned like Caligula, and in the circumstances they reasoned rightly. A prolonged debasement of feelings and ideas was needed before man could make up his mind to accept one of his own kind as master, and to persuade himself that in doing so he had done well.

From this single fact, that a God was placed at the head of every political society, it follows that there were as many Gods as peoples. Two peoples alien to one another, and nearly always enemies, could not long recognize the same master: two armies going into battle could not obey the same commander. Thus national divisions produced polytheism, and this in turn produced religious and civil intolerance, which are naturally the same, as I shall explain later.

The fanciful idea of the Greeks that they had rediscovered their own Gods being worshipped by barbarian peoples originated in the Greek habit of regarding themselves as the natural sovereigns of those same peoples. But in our own times, it is a ludicrous parody of learning which studies the identity of the Gods of different nations, as if Moloch, Saturn and Chronos could be the same God, as if the Baal of the Phoenicians, the Zeus of the Greeks, and the Jupiter of the Romans could be identical;

第八章　论公民宗教

一开始人类并没有国王，有的只是神明，而且他们的政府也只是神权政治的政府。他们像卡里古拉一样思考问题，而在那个时代他们这样思考也是正当的。在人类下定决心接受他们同类中的某一个作为自己的主人，并且说服自己这样做会对他们有好处之前，他们是需要经过感情上和思想上长时间的改造的。

由一个简单的事实，即每个政治社会的上面都供奉着一个神明，可以得出结论：神灵的数目会和民族的数目一样多。两个迥异的并且几乎总是敌对的民族是不能长时期地认可同一个主人的：正如投入战斗的两支军队是不可能服从同一个指挥官的。因此，民族的区分产生了多神制，而多神制进而产生了宗教上和政治上的不宽容，而这两种不宽容本质上是一回事，这一点我在后面会解释到。

希腊人认为他们发现了自己的神明在野蛮民族中也受到崇拜，这种稀奇的想法，源自于希腊人常常把他们自己看成是这些野蛮民族的天然主人。但是在今天这个时代，如果我们再去研究不同民族的神明的一致性，那就是一种荒谬的模仿了：好像莫洛克、萨土林、科洛诺斯可能是同一个神，好像腓尼基人的巴力、希腊人的宙斯以及罗马人的朱比特之间具有一致性，好像在这些有

as if there could be anything in common between chimerical beings with different names!

But if it is asked why under paganism, when each state had its own religious cult and its own Gods, there were no wars of religion, I answer that it was due to this very fact that each state, having its own faith as well as its own government, did not distinguish between its Gods and its laws. Political war was just as much theological war; the provinces of the Gods were determined, so to speak, by the frontiers of nations. The God of one people had no rights over other peoples. The Gods of the Pagans were in no sense jealous Gods; they divided the empire of the world between them; even Moses and the Hebrew people sometimes countenanced this idea by speaking of the God of Israel. It is true that they did not recognize the Gods of the Canaanites, a proscribed people who were doomed to destruction, and whose country they were to occupy; but consider how they spoke of the divinities of neighbouring peoples, whom they were forbidden to attack: 'Is not the possession of that which belongs to Chamos your God lawfully your due?' says Jephthah to the Ammonites. 'By the same title we possess the lands which our conquering God has taken.'①

But when the Jews, subject to the Kings of Babylon, and afterwards to the Kings of Syria, stubbornly sought to recognize no

---

① *Nonne ea quae possidet Chamos deus tuus, tibi jure debentur*? Such is the text of the Vulgate. Father de Carrières translates it thus: 'Do you not believe that you have a right to possess that which belongs to your God Chamos?' I do not know the bearing of the Hebrew text, but I notice that in the Vulgate, Jephthah positively recognizes the rights of the God Chamos, and that the French translation weakens this recognition by adding an 'according to you' which is not in the Latin.

着不同名字的虚构者之间有一些共同之处似的！

但是如果有人问，为什么在异教信仰之下，即当每个国家都有它自己的宗教祭仪和它自己的神明的时候，却不曾有过宗教战争呢？我的答案是，正是由于这样的一个事实，即每个国家由于都有它自己的信仰以及自己的政府，所以就不曾在它的神灵和法律之间做出划分。政治的战争恰恰就是神学上的战争，可以说国家的边境就限定了神灵的管辖范围。一个民族的神明对于另外的其他民族没有任何的权利。异教徒的神灵绝不是嫉妒的神灵，这些神灵把整个世界大帝国在它们之间进行了划分；即使是摩西和希伯来人在谈到以色列人的上帝的时候，有时也会赞成这种观点。的确，他们根本不承认迦南人的神灵，迦南人是一个被放逐的、而且命中注定是要毁灭的民族，而希伯来将会占领他们的国土；但是请想一下他们是如何谈论邻近民族的神明的吧，他们是被禁止进攻这些民族的，因为正如耶弗他对亚扪所说："那些属于你们的神基抹的财产难道不也是你们的合法所有物吗？""基于同样的名义，我们也拥有我们的神灵由于征服而占有的土地。"①

但是当犹太人先臣服于巴比伦，后来又臣服于叙利亚，并且倔强地坚持拒不承认除了他们自己的上帝之外的其他任何神明

① *Nonne ea quae possidet Chamos deus tuus, tibi jure debentur?* 拉丁文圣经的原文是这样的。伽利埃神甫这样来翻译这段话："难道你们不认为你们有权利拥有那些属于你们的神明基抹的东西吗？"我不知道这段希伯来原文的语气，但是我注意到在拉丁文圣经中，耶弗它积极地肯定了基抹神的权利，但法文翻译却因为增加了"照你们看来"，而把这种肯定削弱了，而这几个字在拉丁文原文中是没有的。

other God but their own, this refusal was regarded as a rebellion against their conquerors, and it brought on the Jews those persecutions of which we read in their history, and of which we find no other example before the coming of Christianity. ①

Since each religion was thus attached exclusively to the laws of the state which prescribed it, and since there was no means of converting people except by subduing them, the only missionaries were conquerors; and since the obligation to change faith was part of the law of conquest, it was necessary to conquer before preaching conversion. Far from men fighting for the Gods, it was, as in Homer, the Gods who fought for men; each people asked its own God for victory, and paid for it with new altars. The Romans, before taking a town, called upon its Gods to abandon it; when they allowed the Tarentines to keep their angry Gods, it was in the belief that those Gods were subject to their own and obliged to pay them homage. They let the vanquished keep their own Gods just as they let them keep their own laws. A crown dedicated to Jupiter of the Capitol was often the only tribute they exacted.

In the end, when the Romans had spread their faith and their Gods with their empire, and often themselves adopted those of the vanquished in giving one or the other the rights of citizenship, the peoples of this vast empire gradually found themselves with a multitude of Gods and faiths, which were everywhere almost the same; and this is how paganism became one and the same religion throughout the known world.

---

① It is clear beyond dispute that the Phocian war, called the Holy War, was not a war of religion. Its object was to punish sacrilege, and not to make unbelievers submit.

的时候，这种拒绝便被看作是对他们的征服者的一种反抗，而且这种拒绝给犹太人带来了我们可以从他们的历史中读到的种种迫害，对这种迫害，我们在基督教之前是从来没有找到过先例的[①]。

既然每种宗教都是这样完全依附于规范着它的一个国家的法律，既然除了征服之外没有别的办法使一个民族改变信仰，那么征服者便是唯一的传教士；既然改变宗教信仰的义务是被征服者的法律的一部分，那么在传道来改变他们的信仰之前，就必须先进行征服。所以，远不是人在为神明而战，相反，正如荷马史诗中所说的，却是神明在为人类而战；每个民族都向自己的神明祈求胜利，并且设立新的祭坛来酬答他们的神明。罗马人在占领一个城镇之前，都是首先召请这个城镇的神明放弃这个城镇；当他们允许塔伦坦人保留他们愤怒的神的时候，那是因为他们相信那些神明已经臣服于他们自己的神明，并且向他们的神明表示敬意了。他们让被征服者保留他们自己的神明，就像让他们保留他们自己的法律一样。向罗马主神殿中的朱比特进献一顶王冠，常常是罗马人索要的唯一供品。

最后，当罗马人随着帝国的扩张而四处传播了他们的信仰和他们的神明的时候，当他们自己也通过赋予这个或者那个民族以公民的身份而采用了他们的信仰和神明的时候，这个广阔的帝国的人民逐渐发现他们自己拥有了大量的神明和信仰，而且几乎在每个地方都是完全一样的；异教信仰在整个已知世界中就是这样成为唯一一个宗教信仰的。

---

① 无疑地，那场被称为是圣战的福西人的战争，并非是一场宗教战争。它的目的是惩罚亵渎神明者，而不是要让不信教的人信教。

It was in these circumstances that Jesus came to establish a spiritual kingdom on earth; this kingdom, by separating the theological system from the political, meant that the state ceased to be a unity, and it caused those intestine divisions which have never ceased to disturb Christian peoples. Now as this new idea of a kingdom of another world could never have entered the minds of pagans, they always regarded the Christians as true rebels who, under the cloak of hypocritical submission, only awaited the moment to make themselves independent and supreme, and cunningly to usurp that authority which they made a show of respecting while they were weak. Such was the cause of the persecutions.

What the pagans feared did indeed happen; then everything altered its countenance; the humble Christians changed their tune and soon the so-called kingdom of the other world was seen to become, under a visible ruler, the most violent despotism of this world.

However, since princes and civil laws have always existed, the consequence of this dual power has been an endless conflict of jurisdiction, which has made any kind of good polity impossible in Christian states, where men have never known whether they ought to obey the civil ruler or the priest.

Many peoples, even in Europe or nearby, have tried to preserve or re-establish the ancient system, but without success: the spirit of Christianity has won completely. The religious cult has always kept, or recovered, its independence of the sovereign, and has lacked its necessary connexion with the state. Mahomet had very sound opinions, taking care to give unity to his political system,

正是在这种情形下，耶稣出来在世上建立了一个精神的王国。这个王国区分了神学体系和政治体系，因而便意味着国家不再是一个统一的整体，而且这也导致了国家内部的分裂，这些分裂永不停息地扰乱着基督教各民族。由于另外一个世界的王国这种新的观念永远都不能进入异教徒的心灵，所以他们总是会把基督徒看成是真正的反叛者，这些反叛者只是在伪善的顺从的掩饰之下，等待着时机以使他们变得独立而且至高无上，并且狡猾地伺机篡夺那些在他们软弱的时候表面上非常尊重的权力，这就是宗教迫害的原因了。

异教徒所担心的事情真的发生了；接下来，所有的东西都换了一副面孔：谦逊的基督徒改变了他们的语调，而且人们不久就发现那个所谓的另外一个世界的王国在一个看得见的首领[1]的掌控之下，竟然变成了世界上最残暴的专制。

然而，既然君主和世俗的法律总是会存在的，那么这种双重权力的后果便是无穷无尽的权限上的冲突，这使得在一个基督教国家中根本不可能有好的政治，因为在那里人们永远都不会知道他们该服从于世俗的统治者还是一个牧师。

许多民族，甚至是在欧洲或者欧洲邻近的民族，都曾试图保存或者重建那种古老的制度[2]，但是没有成功，因为基督教精神获得了彻底的胜利。宗教祭仪总是会保持或者重新获得对于主权的独立性，并且已经失去了跟国家政权的必然联系。穆罕默德有很健全的观点，以赋予它的政治体系一种一体性，而且只要在

〔1〕 指教皇。

〔2〕 是指政权和教权未曾分离的制度。

and for as long as the form of his government endured under the caliphs who succeeded him, the government was undivided and, to that extent, good. But the Arabs, in becoming prosperous, cultured, polished, effeminate and soft, were subjugated by the barbarians; then the division between the two powers was started afresh, and even though the division is less apparent among the Moslems than among the Christians, it nevertheless exists, above all in the sect of Ali and in states like Persia where it has never ceased to make itself felt.

Among us, the Kings of England have established themselves as heads of the church and the Czars have done the same. But with this title they have made themselves not so much masters as ministers, and have acquired not so much the right to change the church as the power to preserve it; they are not legislators, they are only princes. Wherever the clergy constitutes a body,[①] it is master and legislator in its own house. Thus there are two powers, two sovereigns, in England and in Russia, just as there are elsewhere.

Of all Christian authors, the philosopher Hobbes is the only one who saw clearly both the evil and the remedy, and who dared to propose reuniting the two heads of the eagle and fully restoring that political unity without which neither the state nor the government will ever

---

① It should be noted that it is not so much the formal assemblies, like those of France, which bind the clergy together in a body, but rather the communion of churches. Communion and excommunication are the social compact of the clergy, one through which they will always be masters of both peoples and kings. All the priests who communicate together are fellow citizens, even though they are at opposite ends of the earth. This invention is a masterpiece of politics. There was nothing like it among the pagan priests; hence they never constituted a body of clergy.

他的继任者哈里发那里，他的这种政府形式能够存留下去，那么这个政府就不会分裂，而且可以达到良好的程度。但是阿拉伯人由于后来变得繁荣了，有教养了，文明了，娇气而且柔弱了，所以就被野蛮民族征服了。接下来，两种权力的分裂又开始重新出现，虽然这种分裂在穆斯林国家中不如在基督教国家中那么明显，然而它确实是存在的，特别是在阿里的教派中；而且在有些国家，比如波斯，我们一直都能感受到这种分裂的存在。

在我们中间，英格兰的国王已经把自己确立为教会的首领，沙皇也是这么做的。但是通过这个头衔，他们与其说是把自己变成了主人，不如说是变成了大臣。他们没有取得改变教会的权力，而只是取得了维持教会的权力；他们不是立法者，而只是统治者。在神职人员构成一个共同体①的任何地方，他们就是自己领域之内的主人和立法者。因此，在英国、在俄国，正像在其他地方一样，就有两种权力，有两个立法者。

在所有的基督教作家中，哲学家霍布斯是唯一一个能够清楚地看到其弊端并有挽救办法的人，也是唯一一个敢于建议把鹰的两只头[1]重新合在一起并且彻底重建政治上的统一体的人，因为如果没有这种一体性，无论是国家还是政府就都不能得到良好

① 必须指出，把神职人员联结成一个共同体的，并不是像法兰西的集会那样的正式集会，而是教会的圣餐仪式。圣餐仪式和逐出教会是神职人员的社会契约，通过这一契约，他们便总是人民和国王的主人了。所有共同参加圣餐仪式的教士就都是同胞公民，虽然他们可能处在地球的两极。这一发明实在是政治上的一大杰作。在异教的教士中间就没有这样的事情，因此他们永远都不会形成一个神职人员的共同体。

〔1〕 指政权和教权两者。

be well constituted. But he should have seen that the dominant spirit of Christianity was incompatible with his system, and that the interest of the prince will always be stronger than that of the state. It is not so much the horrible and false parts of Hobbes's system that have made it hated, but the parts which are just and true.①

I believe that if the historical facts were analysed from this point of view, we could easily refute the opposing beliefs of both Bayle and Warburton, the one holding that no religion is useful to the body politic, the other that Christianity is its best support. We could refute the first by showing that no state has ever been founded without religion as its base; and we could refute the second by showing that the Christian law is at bottom more injurious than serviceable to a robust constitution of the state. For this to be clearly understood, I think I have only to give a little more precision to the exceedingly vague idea of religion, as it bears upon my subject.

Religion, considered in connexion with societies, whether general or particular, can be divided into two categories, the religion of the man and the religion of the citizen. The first, without temples, altars or rituals, and limited to inward devotion to the supreme God and the eternal obligations of morality, is the pure and simple religion of the Gospel, the true theism, and might be called the divine natural law. The religion of the citizen is the religion established in a single country; it gives that country its Gods and its special tutelary deities; it has its dogmas, its rituals, its external forms of worship laid down by law;

---

① See, among other things, in a letter of Grotius to his brother dated 11 April 1643, what that learned man approved of and what he disapproved of in Hobbes's *De Cive*. It is true that, being inclined to indulgence, he forgives that author the bad for the sake of the good, but not everyone is so merciful.

的建制。但是他本应该看到基督教的支配精神是与他的体系不能相容的，而且统治者的利益总是会比国家的利益更为强大。霍布斯的体系之所以被人憎恨，与其说是因为这一体系的可怕和错误的部分，不如说是因为其正确和真实的部分①。

我相信，如果我们能以这样的观点来分析历史事实，我们就可以很容易地反驳贝尔和华尔伯登两人针锋相对的信念了。他们中的一位坚持任何宗教对于政治体都是没有用的，而另一位则坚持基督教是对政治体最有力的支持。我们可以通过证明任何国家都要以宗教为其基础而建立起来以反驳前者，而且又可以通过证明实际上基督教的法律对于建立一个强有力的国家体制与其说是有利的，不如说是有害的以反驳后者。为了让人们更清楚地理解这一点，也因为这是与我的主题相关的，所以我想我必须赋予极为含糊的宗教概念多一点的精确性。

就宗教与社会的关系而言，即这一关系是普遍或还是个别的，可以把宗教分为两种：人类性的宗教和市民性的宗教。前者没有庙宇、没有祭坛、没有仪式，仅仅限于一种对于至高无上的神灵发自内心的虔诚以及对于道德永恒的义务感，这种宗教是纯粹的、简朴的福音的宗教，是真正的有神论，而且可以被称作是自然的神圣法律。市民性的宗教则是在个别国家中建立起来的宗教，这种宗教指定了这个国家的神灵，规定了这个国家的守护神；它有它的教条、它的仪式、它的由法律加以规定的崇拜形式；而

① 有关的其他材料，请参看格劳秀斯于 1643 年 4 月 11 日写给他兄弟的一封信，你就可以看到这位学识渊博的人对霍布斯的《论公民》一书赞同什么，又反对什么。的确，由于他倾向于宽容，所以他因为这本书的好处而原谅了这本书的坏处，但是并不是所有的人都能够如此仁慈的。

and to the one nation which practises this religion, everything outside is infidel, alien, barbarous; and it extends the rights and duties of man only so far as it extends its altars. Such were the religions of all the early peoples; and we might give it the name of civil or positive divine law.

There is a third and more curious kind of religion, which gives men two legislative orders, two rulers, two homelands, puts them under two contradictory obligations, and prevents their being at the same time both churchmen and citizens. Such is the religion of the Lamas, such is that of the Japanese, and such is Catholic Christianity. One might call this the religion of the priest. It produces a kind of mixed and antisocial system of law which has no name.

From the political point of view, each of these three kinds of religion has its defects. The third kind is so manifestly bad that the pleasure of demonstrating its badness would be a waste of time. Everything that destroys social unity is worthless; and all institutions that set man at odds with himself are worthless.

The second kind of religion is good in that it joins divine worship to a love of the law, and that in making the homeland the object of the citizens' adoration, it teaches them that the service of the state is the service of the tutelary God. This is a kind of theocracy, in which there can be no pontiff other than the prince, and no priests except the magistrates. Then to die for one's country is to become a martyr, to break the law to be impious, and to subject a guilty man to public execration is to hand him over to the wrath of God: *sacer esto*.

But this kind of religion is also bad; since it is based on error and lies, it deceives men, and makes them credulous and superstitious; it buries the true worship of God in empty ceremonials. It is bad, again, when it becomes exclusive and tyrannical, and makes a people bloodthirsty and intolerant, so that men breathe

且对于奉行这种宗教的一个国家来说，国家之外的一切就都是背逆的、异端的和野蛮的；而且它使人民的权利和义务所及的范围总不会超过祭坛所涉及的领域。所有早期民族的宗教都是这样的宗教，而且我们可以把它称为公民的神圣法律或者积极的神圣法律。

还有第三种更加奇特的宗教，因为它给予了人类两种立法秩序、两个统治者、两个祖国，所以把人类置于相互矛盾的义务之中，并且使他们不能同时既是牧师又是公民。喇嘛教就是这样的，日本的宗教是这样的，罗马公教也是这样的。我们或可称为牧师的宗教。它产生了一种混合的、反社会的法律体系，对这种法律体系我们无以名之。

从政治的观点来看，这三种宗教中的每一种都有其缺陷。第三种宗教的坏处是如此明显，以至于再对它的坏处进行论证只是浪费时间。任何破坏统一的东西都是没有价值的，而且任何使人陷于自相矛盾的体制也都是没有价值的。

第二种宗教的好处在于它把对于神明崇拜和对于法律的热爱结合在了一起，在于它把祖国变成公民崇拜的对象，它教导人民为国家服务就是为保护他们的神灵服务。这是一种神权政治，在这里除了君主之外没有教皇，除了行政官员之外并无牧师。那么为国家献出生命就成为一个殉教者，而违反法律就是不敬神明，使一个有罪的人受公众的诅咒就是把他交给了神谴：让他受到谴责吧。

但是这种宗教也是有坏处的：因为它是建立在错误和谎言的基础上的，它欺骗人们，并且使他们变得轻信而且迷信；它又使对于神明的真正崇拜变得流于空洞的形式。它的坏处还在于，当它变得唯我独尊而且残暴的时候，它使得一个民族变得嗜杀而且

only murder and massacre, and believe they are doing a holy deed in killing those who do not accept their Gods. This puts the people concerned into a natural state of war with all others, and this is something destructive of its own security.

There remains the religion of the private person, or Christianity, not the Christianity of today, but that of the Gospel, which is altogether different. Under this holy, sublime and true religion, men, as children of the same God, look on all others as brothers, and the society which unites them is not even dissolved by death.

But this religion, having no specific connexion with the body politic, leaves the law with only the force the law itself possesses, adding nothing to it; and hence one of the chief bonds necessary for holding any particular society together is lacking. Nor is this all: for far from attaching the hearts of the citizens to the state, this religion detaches them from it as from all other things of this world; and I know of nothing more contrary to the social spirit.

It is said that a people of true Christians would form the most perfect society imaginable. I see but one great flaw in this hypothesis, namely that a society of true Christians would not be a society of men.

I would say, too, that this imagined society, for all its perfection, would be neither the strongest nor the most durable, Being perfect, it would be without bonds of union; its ruinous defect would lie in its very perfection.

Everyone would do his duty; the people would obey the law; the rulers would be just and moderate; the magistrates would be honest and incorruptible; the soldiers would scorn death; there would

不宽容，以至于人们面对的只有谋杀和屠戮，而且让人们相信当他们杀死那些不接受他们的神灵的人的时候，他们是在做一件神圣的事情。这便会把这个民族同其他所有的民族置于一种天然的战争状态之中，这对于这个民族自身的安全也是很有破坏性的。

剩下的便是个人的宗教了，或者说基督教，这并不是指今天的基督教，而是福音的基督教，这两者是完全不同的。在这种神圣的、庄严的、真正的宗教中，人们作为同一个上帝的儿女，把其他所有的人都看成是兄弟，这样即使是死亡也不能使把他们结合在一起的社会解体。

但是这种宗教由于与政治体没有特别的联系，所以只给法律留下法律自身所具有的力量，而不能给它增加任何力量，因此维持一个特殊社会所必须的最重要的一项联系就失去了。这还不是全部的坏处，因为这种宗教远不是使公民的心都凝聚到国家之上，相反它使得公民远离了国家，就像远离了俗世上其他所有的东西一样，我不知道还有什么东西能比这个更背离社会精神了。

有人说一个真正的基督教的民族将会构成能够想象到的最完美的社会。我在这种假设中看到的只是一个巨大的缺陷，那就是一个真正的基督徒的社会将不会是人类的社会。

我还要说，正是因为它的完美性，这个理想的社会才既不是最强大的，也不是最持久的。由于它的完美性，它就会缺乏联系的纽带；它的招致毁灭的缺陷恰恰就存在于它的完美性之中。

每个人都会履行他的义务；人们都会遵守法律；统治者会是公正而且有节制的；行政官员会是诚实而廉洁的；士兵会蔑视

be neither vanity nor luxury. But let us look further.

Christianity is a wholly spiritual religion, concerned solely with the things of heaven; the Christian's homeland is not of this world. The Christian does his duty, it is true, but he does it with profound indifference towards the good or ill success of his deeds. Provided that he has nothing to reproach himself for, it does not matter to him whether all goes well or badly here on earth. If the state prospers, he hardly dares to enjoy the public happiness; he fears lest he become proud of his country's glory; if the state perishes, he blesses the hand of God that weighs heavily on His people.

For such a society to be peaceful and for harmony to prevail, every citizen without exception would have to be an equally good Christian. If, unhappily, there should appear one ambitious man, one hypocrite, one Catilina, for example, or one Cromwell among them, that man would readily trample over his pious compatriots. Christian charity does not allow us readily to think ill of our neighbours. When a man is cunning enough to master the art of imposing on others, and gains a part of the public authority, there, behold, is a man of established dignity; and God wills that he be respected; soon, we see a man of power, and God wills that he be obeyed. Suppose he abuses the power of which he is the depositary? Then he is the scourge with which God chastises his children. Christians would have scruples about expelling the usurper; for that would mean disturbing the public peace, using violence, shedding blood, and all this accords ill with Christian mildness. And after all what does it matter whether one is free or a slave in this vale of tears? The essential thing is to go to paradise,

死亡；这里将既没有空虚，也没有奢侈。但是让我们更进一步地观察一下吧。

基督教是纯粹精神上的宗教，它只关心天国的事务，基督徒的祖国并不属于这个世界。基督徒履行他们的义务，这是事实，但是他们履行义务时总是会带着一种对于他们的行为的成功与否漠不关心的态度。假若他们对于自身没有什么可以指责的，那么这个世界上所有的事情到底是好是坏都与他毫不相干。如果国家繁荣了，他几乎不敢享受公众的幸福，他唯恐因为国家的荣耀而变得骄傲；如果国家毁灭了，他就会祝福上帝之手惩罚了他的子民。

为了使这个社会太平，也为了使和谐之风盛行，每个公民毫无例外地都应该成为同样优秀的基督徒。如果很不幸在他们中间出现了一个野心勃勃的人，一个伪君子，比如一个卡提里那或者一个克伦威尔，那么那个人很容易就可以蹂躏他虔诚的同胞们。因为基督徒的仁慈不允许我们轻易地就认为我们的邻居是不好的。如果一个足够狡猾的人掌握了欺骗别人的伎俩，并且获取了部分的公共权力，那么这里就会冒出一个被人们认为是高贵的人，上帝都希望他能够得到人们的尊敬；不久，我们就会看到一个强权的人物，好像上帝也希望人们都能服从于他。想象一下：如果他滥用了他受托保管的权力会怎样呢？那时他便俨然成为上帝惩罚他的子民的鞭子了；基督徒在驱逐这样的篡权者的问题上就会犹豫不决了。因为驱逐他们便意味着要破坏公共的和平，要使用暴力，要流血，而所有这些都是与基督徒的温和不相符合的。再说，在这个烦恼的人世间，一个人是自由的抑或是个奴隶，究竟又有什么关系呢？最重要的事情就是要升上天堂，而顺

and resignation is but one more means to that end.

Suppose a foreign war breaks out. The citizens will march without reluctance to war; no one among them will think of flight; all will do their duty— but they will do it without passion for victory; they know better how to die than to conquer. It does not matter to them whether they are victors or vanquished. Does not providence know better than they what is needful? One can imagine what advantage a proud, impetuous and passionate enemy would draw from their stoicism. Set them at war against a generous people whose hearts are devoured by an ardent love of glory and their country; imagine your Christian republic confronted by Sparta or Rome, and your pious Christians will be beaten, crushed, destroyed before they have time to collect their wits, or they will owe their salvation only to the contempt which their enemy feels for them.

I myself think it was an excellent oath that was taken by the soldiers of Fabius; they did not swear to conquer or die, but to return as conquerors, and they kept their word. Christians would never have dared to do this; they would have felt that it was tempting God.

But I err in speaking of a Christian republic; for each of these terms contradicts the other. Christianity preaches only servitude and submission. Its spirit is too favourable to tyranny for tyranny not to take advantage of it. True Christians are made to be slaves; they know it and they hardly care; this short life has too little value in their eyes.

It is said that Christian troops are excellent. I deny it. Show me these Christian troops. Personally I know of none. You may mention the crusades. But without disputing the valour of the crusaders,

从只是达到这个目标的又一种方法罢了。

假设一场对外战争爆发了，公民们会心甘情愿地投入战争，他们当中没有人会想要逃跑，所有的人都会履行他们的义务——但是他们在履行这一义务时是没有对胜利的热情的；他们更知道如何去效死，而不是如何去征服。他们是胜利者或者是被征服者对他们来说是无关紧要的。上帝不是比他们更清楚他们需要什么吗？人们可以想象一个自豪的、精神焕发的、充满激情的敌人会从他们这种斯多葛主义中获得多么大的好处。如果把他们置于一场反抗一个心中充满着对荣耀以及对祖国热情洋溢的爱戴的勇敢民族的战争之中，设想一下如果你们的基督教共和国对抗的是斯巴达或者是罗马，那么你们虔诚的基督徒还来不及运用他们的智慧就已经被击败、被粉碎、被毁灭了，或者仅仅是由于他们的敌人对他们的蔑视，他们才得以保全。

我自认为法比乌斯的士兵所发的誓言是极好的誓言，他们并没有发誓去征服或者去效死，他们只是发誓要作为征服者凯旋，而且他们信守了他们的诺言。基督徒是永远都不敢这么做的，他们会感觉这是在试探上帝了。

但是我在说“基督教共和国”的时候，就已经犯了一个错误，因为这两个词语是互相矛盾的。基督教只是鼓吹奴役和服从，它的精神太有利于暴政，所以暴政不能不利用它。真正的基督徒是被培养出来做奴隶的，他们了解这一点，但是他们对此几乎毫不在乎，因为在他们眼中，人短暂的一生是几乎没有什么价值的。

有人说，基督徒的军队是极好的军队，我反对这一点。请举出这样的基督徒军队来给我看。就我个人而言，我不知道有这样的军队。你可能会举出十字军，但是这里我不去争辩十字军

I shall say that they were far from being Christians. They were soldiers of the priests. They were citizens of the Church; they were fighting for its spiritual homeland, which it had in some strange way made temporal. Strictly speaking, this comes under the heading of paganism; for since the Gospel never sets up any national religion, holy war is impossible among Christians.

Under the pagan Emperors, Christian soldiers were brave. All the Christian authors tell us this, and I believe them; but those soldiers were competing for honour against pagan troops. Once the Emperors became Christian, this emulation ceased; and once the cross had driven out the eagle, all Roman valour disappeared.

But leaving aside considerations of politics, let us return to those of right; and settle the principles which govern this important question. The right which the social pact gives the sovereign over the subjects does not, as I have said, go beyond the boundaries of public utility. ①Subjects have no duty to account to the sovereign for their beliefs except when those beliefs are important to the community. Now it is very important to the state that each citizen should have a religion which makes him love his duty, but the dogmas of that religion are of interest neither to the state nor its members, except in so far as those dogmas concern morals and the duties which everyone who professes that religion is bound to perform towards others. Moreover, everyone may hold whatever opinions he pleases, without the sovereign having any business to take cognizance of them.

---

① 'In the republic,' says the M d'A, 'everyone is perfectly free to do what does not injure others.' Here is the invariable boundary; one could not express it more exactly. I have not been able to deny myself the pleasure of quoting sometimes from this manuscript, although it is not known to the public, in order to pay homage to the memory of an illustrious and honourable man, who, even as a Minister of State, kept the heart of a true citizen, together with just and sound opinions on the government of his country.

的勇敢与否，我要说他们远不是基督徒，他们是牧师的士兵，他们是教会的公民；他们是在为他们精神上的祖国而战，但是这个祖国通过一种奇怪的方式竟变成世俗的了。严格地讲，他们可以归入异教的标题之下，因为既然福音从来都没有设定任何一种国家的宗教，所以在基督徒中就不可能有圣战。

在异教皇帝的统治之下，基督徒士兵是很勇敢的。所有的基督教作家都告诉我们这一点，我相信他们，但那些士兵只是在与异教军队为荣誉而竞争。一旦皇帝成为基督徒了，这种竞争也就停止了。而且一旦十字架驱逐了鹰，所有罗马人的勇敢就消失了。

但是先把政治的考虑放在一边，让我们回到权利问题上来，并且确立那些支配着这个重大问题的原则。正如我所说的，社会契约赋予主权者统治其臣民的权利不能超出公共用途的界限①。臣民没有义务向主权者说明他们的信仰，除非是在这些信仰对共同体来说是非常重要的时候。每个公民都应该有一种可以使他热爱自己的义务的宗教，这对于国家来说是非常重要的，但是这个宗教的教条，除非是它涉及了每个信仰这种宗教的人都应该对其他的人应履行的道德和义务的时候，才是与国家或国家的成员有关的。此外，每个人都可以坚持任何他所喜欢的观点，而主权者

---

① 阿冉松爵士说："在共和国中，每个人都可以自由地做那些不会伤害到别人的事情。"这是一个不可更改的界限；没有人能够把它表述得更准确一点了。我总是会禁不住要引用这篇还不为公众所熟知的手稿，以表示我对于这个杰出而可敬的人物的怀念。这个人即使在成了国家的大臣的时候，仍然保持着一颗真正的公民的心，并且持有对其国家的政府的公正而且合理的见解。

For the sovereign has no competence in the other world; whatever may be the fate of the subjects in the life to come, it is nothing to do with the sovereign, so long as they are good citizens in this life.

There is thus a profession of faith which is purely civil and of which it is the sovereign's function to determine the articles, not strictly as religious dogmas, but as sentiments of sociability, without which it is impossible to be either a good citizen or a loyal subject. ① Without being able to oblige anyone to believe these articles, the sovereign can banish from the state anyone who does not believe them; banish him not for impiety but as an antisocial being, as one unable sincerely to love law and justice, or to sacrifice, if need be, his life to his duty. If anyone, after having publicly acknowledged these same dogmas, behaves as if he did not believe in them, then let him be put to death, for he has committed the greatest crime, that of lying before the law.

The dogmas of the civil religion must be simple and few in number, expressed precisely and without explanations or commentaries. The existence of an omnipotent, intelligent, benevolent divinity that foresees and provides; the life to come; the happiness of the just; the punishment of sinners; the sanctity of the social contract and the law—these are the positive dogmas. As for the negative dogmas, I would limit them to a single one: no intolerance. Intolerance is something which belongs to the religions we have rejected.

In my opinion, those who distinguish between civil and theological

---

① Caesar pleading for Catilina tried to establish the dogma of the mortality of the soul. Cato and Cicero, to refute it, did not waste time with philosophy; they were content to show that Caesar was speaking like a bad citizen and advancing a doctrine that was injurious to the state: And this was what the Senate had to give judgement on, not any question of theology.

却无权了解这些观点。因为主权者对于另外一个世界是无能为力的。只要臣民们今生是一个好公民，他们在来世中的命运如何便与主权者毫无关系了。

这样，就要有一个信仰的宣言，这个宣言是纯粹社会性的，决定这一宣言的条文是主权者的职能，它不像宗教教条那么严格，而只是作为社会性的感情，没有这种感情，一个人不可能成为一个好公民或者一个忠诚的臣民①。主权者并不会强迫任何一个人去信仰这些条文，它只是把不信仰这些条文的人驱逐出这个国家；驱逐一个人不是因为他的不虔诚，而是因为他是一个反社会性的人，是因为他是一个不能真诚地热爱法律和正义的人，一个在必要的时候不能为他的义务而献出生命的人。如果一个人在公开承认了这些条款之后，做起事情来却还像他并不信仰它们一样，那么就应该把他判处死刑，因为他犯了最大的罪行，即在法律面前撒了谎。

公民宗教的教条必须简单、数量较少、表达精确而且不需要解释或注释。一个全能、智慧、仁慈而且有先见之明和能深谋远虑的神明的存在；来生；公正者的幸福；对有罪的人的惩罚；社会契约和法律的神圣性——这些都是积极的教条。至于消极的教条，我把它们限制为仅有一条：不要不宽容。不宽容是属于那些我们已经抵制过的宗教的东西。

依我看来，那些把社会的不宽容和神学上的不宽容区分开来

① 恺撒在为卡提里那辩护的时候试图建立灵魂会死亡的教条。卡图和西塞罗根本不需要浪费时间从哲学上来反驳他，他们只要证明恺撒是作为一个坏公民在讲话，并且是在提出一个有害于国家的教条就足够了。元老院所要做的判断正是这一点，而不是什么神学的问题。

intolerance are mistaken. These two forms of intolerance are inseparable. It is impossible to live in peace with people one believes to be damned; to love them would be to hate the God who punishes them; it is an absolute duty either to redeem or to torture them. Wherever theological intolerance is admitted, it is bound to have some civil consequences,① and when it does so, the sovereign is no longer sovereign, even in the temporal sphere; at this stage the priests become the real masters, and kings are only their officers.

Now that there is not, and can no longer be, an exclusive national religion, all religions which themselves tolerate others must be tolerated, provided only that their dogmas contain nothing contrary to the duties of the citizen. But anyone who dares to say 'Outside the church there is no salvation' should be expelled from the state, unless the state is the church and the prince the pontiff.

---

① Marriage, for example, being a civil contract, has civil consequences without which it would be impossible for society itself to subsist. Let us suppose that in a given country the clergy reached the point of gaining the sole right of permitting marriage, a right which it is bound to usurp under any intolerant religion. Is it not then clear that in making the authority of the church supreme in this matter, it will nullify that of the prince, who will then have no subjects other than those the clergy allow him to have? Enable priests to decide whether to marry people according to their assent to this or that doctrine, their assent to this or that formula, or according to their being more or less devout, then is it not clear that if the clergy acts shrewdly and holds firm, it will in time alone dispose of inheritances, offices, the citizens and the state itself, since the latter could not endure if composed only of bastards? But, you may say, men will call upon the temporal power, issue summonses and warrants, seize church properties. What a sorry sight! If the clergy has even a little, I do not say courage, but common sense, it will allow everything to go its own way; it will quietly let the summonses, the warrants and seizures take place and still end up as master. It is no great sacrifice, I feel, to give up a part when you are sure of securing the whole.

的人都是犯了错误的。这两种形式的不宽容是不能分开的。让人们跟他们认为应该受到诅咒的人和平地生活在一起是不可能的，爱这些人就是去憎恨惩罚他们的上帝；我们绝对的义务是或者挽救他们，或者拷问他们。在任何神学上的不宽容得到承认的地方，必定会产生社会性的效果①，而且当神学上的不宽容发生了的时候，主权者就不再是主权者了，即使在世俗领域内也不是了；这时牧师成为真正的主人，国王只不过是他们的职员罢了。

既然现在没有，而且也不会再有一个唯一的国家宗教，那么所有能够宽容其他宗教的宗教都应该得到宽容，只要它们的教条中不包含违反公民义务的内容。但是如果任何一个人胆敢说“教会之外就不能得到拯救”，那么这个人就应该被逐出这个国家，除非这个国家就是教会，而国王就是教皇。这个教条只有在

---

① 比如婚姻作为一种公民的契约，就会有社会的效果，如果没有这种社会效果，社会自身就不可能存在。让我们假定在某一个给定的国家中，神职人员拿到了单独决定是否允许结婚的权利，而这种权利在任何一种不宽容的宗教下都必定是会被篡夺的。于是，为了使教会在此问题上的权力成为至高无上的，他们将会取消君主对此的权力，以便使得君主除了拥有那些神职人员允许他们拥有的臣民之外就不能再有其他的臣民，这一点不是很明显的吗？如果让牧师能够根据人们是否赞同这个或者那个教条，根据人们是否遵守这种或者那种仪式，根据人们虔诚的程度如何来决定他们能否结婚，那么我们就会很清楚地看到，如果神职人员机敏地行事并且紧紧握住这种权利，那么他们将能够独立地处理继承事务、公职事务、公民事务以及国家本身的事务。因为对国家来说，如果它仅仅是由私生子构成的话，它将不能久存啊。但是你可能会说，人们可以召回世俗的权力，可以发布传唤令和委任状，可以剥夺教会的财产啊。这是多么可怜的看法啊！神职人员只要还有一点，我还不说勇气，就只是常识，他们就会随任所有这些事情自行其是；他们会平静地让传唤、委任和剥夺发生，而最终仍然是主人。我觉得当你确定能够保全整体的时候，放弃其中的一部分就不是多么大的牺牲了。

Such a dogma is good only in a theocratic government; in any other, it is pernicious. The reason for which Henri IV is said to have embraced the Catholic religion is one which should make all honest men abandon it, above all any prince who knows how to reason.

神权政府下才是好的；而在其他所有政府中，它都是有害的。据说亨利四世信奉了罗马公教的理由，对所有诚实的人而言，恰恰应该是抛弃罗马公教的理由，更何况是对所有那些能够思考的君主而言呢。

CHAPTER 9
Conclusion

After setting out the true principles of political right, and trying to establish the state on the basis of those principles, I should complete my study by considering the foreign relations of the state, including the law of nations, commerce, the rights of war and conquest, international law, leagues, negotiations, treaties and so forth. But all this would represent a new subject too vast for my weak vision; and I would have had to keep my eyes fixed on matters within my range.

第九章　结论

在陈述了政治权利的真正原则并试图在这些原则的基础上建立国家之后，我应该通过考察国家的对外关系来完善我的研究，这包括万国公法、商业、战争和征服的权利、国际法、同盟、谈判、条约等等。但是所有这些将会呈现为一个新的课题，而这个课题对于我的微弱的观察力来讲，未免太宽阔了，所以我不得不把我的视角固定在我研究范围之内的事情上了。

译者后记

让·雅克·卢梭是18世纪法国著名的启蒙思想家，《社会契约论》是他的一部重要著作。卢梭在《社会契约论》中所阐发的民主自由思想在当时引起了强烈的反响，而使《社会契约论》成为整个资产阶级革命的纲领性著作。

卢梭在《社会契约论》中所表达出来的民主自由思想根源于18世纪法国以及当时整个世界的历史现实，反映了新兴的资产阶级的要求和愿望，其大胆而天才的设想为当时资产阶级的兴起提供了理论上的依据。不可否认，卢梭的思想对法国大革命、对美国的资产阶级民主革命的影响都是极为深远的。就现今而言，每当我们重读卢梭的《社会契约论》的时候，仍然可以感受得到这部著作的强大的启发性力量。

本书原著为法文版，译者是根据 Maurice Cranston 的英文版本译出。在翻译的过程中，参考了何兆武以及杨国政等前辈学者的翻译，前辈们的治学严谨和在翻译上的字斟句酌令译者倍感钦佩，而其在若干方面的处理都远非译者所可企及，唯有不断地努力向他们学习了。最后，由于译者本人水平所限，翻译之中的错误之处在所难免，希望各位同仁批评指正，不胜感激。

徐　强

2006年6月

《西方学术经典文库》(第一辑)

功利主义	[英]约翰·斯图亚特·穆勒
诗学·诗艺	[古希腊]亚里士多德 [古罗马]贺拉斯
经济发展理论	[美]约瑟夫·阿洛伊斯·熊彼特
经济学原理	[英]阿尔弗雷德·马歇尔
国民财富的性质与原理	[英]亚当·斯密
联邦党人文集	[美]亚历山大·汉密尔顿
就业、利息和货币通论	[英]约翰·梅纳德·凯恩斯
尼各马可伦理学	[古希腊]亚里士多德
道德情操论	[英]亚当·斯密
君主论	[意]尼科洛·马基雅弗利
新教伦理与资本主义精神	[德]马克斯·韦伯
古代法	[英]亨利·萨姆奈·梅因
第一哲学沉思集	[法]勒内·笛卡儿
查拉图斯特拉如是说	[德]弗里德里希·威廉·尼采
哲学研究	[英]路德维希·维特根斯坦
实践理性批判	[德]伊曼努尔·康德
社会契约论	[法]让·雅克·卢梭
理想国	[古希腊]柏拉图
心理学原理	[美]威廉·詹姆斯
精神现象学	[德]威廉·弗里德里希·黑格尔
神圣者的观念	[德]鲁道夫·奥托
小逻辑	[德]威廉·弗里德里希·黑格尔

论人类不平等的起源	[法]让·雅克·卢梭
道德形而上学基础	[德]伊曼努尔·康德
人性论	[英]戴维·休谟
政府论	[英]约翰·洛克
论法的精神	[法]查尔斯·路易斯·孟德斯鸠
代议制政府	[英]约翰·斯图亚特·穆勒
英国法与文艺复兴	[英]弗雷德里克·威廉·梅特兰
法律社会学基本原理	[奥]尤根·埃利希
论美国民主	[法]夏尔·阿列克西·德·托克维尔
原始社会的结构和功能	[英]A. R. 拉德克利夫-布朗
政治学	[古希腊]亚里士多德
罗马帝国编年史	[古罗马]科尔涅里乌斯·塔西佗
普通语言学教程	[瑞士]费尔迪南·德·索绪尔
货币哲学	[德]格奥尔格·西梅尔
法理学讲演录	[英]约翰·奥斯丁
思想录	[法]布莱兹·帕斯卡
利维坦	[英]托马斯·霍布斯
意识形态与乌托邦	[德]卡尔·曼海姆
忏悔录	[古罗马]圣·奥古斯丁
西太平洋上的航海者	[英]布罗尼斯拉夫·马林诺夫斯基
历史学:理论和实际	[意]贝内德托·克罗齐
逻辑哲学论	[英]路得维希·维特根斯坦